BRITAIN'S *Best*
B&Bs 2012
PERFECT PLACES TO STAY

© AA Media Limited 2012.

AA Media Limited retains the copyright in the current edition © 2012 and in all subsequent editions, reprints and amendments to editions.

© Crown copyright and database rights 2012. Ordnance Survey 100021153.

Maps prepared by the Mapping Services Department of The Automobile Association.

Maps © AA Media Limited 2012.

Advertising Sales:
advertisementsales@theAA.com

Editorial:
lifestyleguides@theAA.com

All rights reserved. No part of this publication may be reproduced, stored in a retrieval system, or transmitted in any form or by any means – electronic, photocopying, recording or otherwise – unless the written permission of the publishers has been obtained beforehand. This book may not be sold, resold, hired out or otherwise disposed of by way of trade in any form of binding or cover other than that with which it is published, without the prior consent of the Publisher.

The contents of this publication are believed correct at the time of printing. Nevertheless, the Publisher cannot be held responsible for any errors or omissions or for changes in the details given in this guide or for the consequences of any reliance on the information provided by the same.

Assessments of AA inspected establishments are based on the experience of the hotel and restaurant inspectors on the occasion of their visit(s) and therefore descriptions given in this guide necessarily dictate an element of subjective opinion which may not reflect or dictate a reader's own opinion on another occasion. We have tried to ensure accuracy in this guide but things do change and we would be grateful if readers would advise us of any inaccuracies they may encounter.

Website addresses are included in some entries and specified by the respective establishment. Such websites are not under the control of AA Media Limited and as such AA Media Limited has no control over them and will not accept any responsibility or liability in respect of any and all matters whatsoever relating to such websites including access, content, material and functionality. By including the addresses of third party websites the AA does not intend to solicit business or offer any security to any person in any country, directly or indirectly.

Every effort has been made to trace the copyright holders, and we apologise in advance for any unintentional omissions or errors. We would be pleased to apply any corrections in a following edition of this publication.

Typeset by AA Lifestyle Guides

Printed and bound by DZS Grafik, d.o.o, Slovenia

Managing editor: Fiona Griffiths

A CIP catalogue record for this book is available from the British Library

ISBN: 978-0-7495-7212-9

Published by AA Publishing, which is a trading name of AA Media Limited, whose registered office is:
Fanum House, Basing View, Basingstoke,
Hampshire RG21 4EA
Registered number 06112600

theAA.com/shop

A04799

Contents

Welcome 4
How to use the guide 6
Best quality 9
Designators 10
Awards 11
Useful information 12
International information 14
England 16
Berkshire 18
Bristol 22
Buckinghamshire 24
Cheshire 26
Co Durham 30
Cornwall 32
Cumbria 54
Derbyshire 69
Devon 79
Dorset 97
Essex 111
Gloucestershire 113
Hampshire 123
Herefordshire 131
Isle of Wight 135
Kent 141
Lancashire 151
Leicestershire 153
Lincolnshire 155
London 157
Norfolk 161

Northamptonshire 170
Northumberland 173
Oxfordshire 179
Shropshire 185
Somerset 192
Staffordshire 206
Suffolk 209
Surrey 216
Sussex, East 218
Sussex, West 235
Warwickshire 239
Wiltshire 244
Worcestershire 248
Yorkshire, East Riding of 252
Yorkshire, North 255
Yorkshire, West 271

Channel Islands 274
Scotland 276
Wales 302
Maps
Location Maps 329
County Map 345
Indexes
B&Bs Index 346
Location Index 350

Welcome

Britain's Best B&Bs is a collection of some of the finest guest houses, farmhouses, inns and restaurants-with-rooms offering bed and breakfast accommodation in England, Scotland, Wales and the Channel Islands.

A place to stay
This fully revised and updated guide makes it easy to find that special place to stay for a weekend or a longer break. There are more than 300 establishments to choose from, including smart town guest houses, contemporary city B&Bs, accessible country farmhouses and undiscovered gems in hidden-away locations.

Best quality
Establishments in this book have received either a top star or a highly commended star rating following a visit by an AA inspector. This helps ensure that you can expect a friendly welcome, comfortable surroundings, excellent food and great value for money. Further details about the AA scheme, inspections, awards and rating system can be found on pages 9–11.

Before you travel
Some places may offer special breaks and facilities not available at the time of going to press – it might be worth calling the establishment before you book.

How to use the guide

The main section of the guide is divided into four parts covering England, the Channel Islands, Scotland and Wales. The counties within each of these sections are ordered alphabetically as are the town or village locations (shown in capital letters as part of the address) within each county. The establishments are then listed alphabetically under each location name. Town names featured in the guide can also be located in the map section and in the location index at the back of the guide.

❶ Grading and awards
All entries in the guide have been inspected by the AA and, at the time of going to press, belong to the AA Guest Accommodation Scheme. For full details see page 9.

Egg cups 🥚 & **Pies** 🥧 Breakfasts and/or dinners are particularly special. For further details see page 11.

Rosettes ❀ The AA's award for food excellence. For full details see page 11.

❷ Designator
For full details see page 10.

❸ Address details

❹ Contact details
For further details see page 8.

❺ Map reference
Map page number followed by a 2-figure National Grid reference. For full details see page 8.

❻ Directions
Brief details of how to find the establishment.

❼ Rooms
Accommodation information. For full details see page 8.

Prices
These are indications only. Please check before booking. Charges shown are per night unless otherwise shown.
S (single): Bed & breakfast per person per night.
D (double): Bed & breakfast for 2 people sharing a room. In some cases twin.
T (twin) and family rooms are shown (also per night).

❽ Notes
Details relating to children, dogs, and Wi-fi. For further details see page 8.

❾ Parking
The number of parking spaces available at the property. For further details see page 8.

❿ Closed
Dates when the establishment is closed for business. For further details see page 8.

⓫ Description
Includes background information, brief history, room information, special features and description of the food if an award has been given.

⓬ Recommended in the area
Local places of interest, activities and potential day trips.

140 Isle of Wight

The Leconfield

★★★★★ ◉ 🛏 GUEST ACCOMMODATION

Address: 85 Leeson Rd, Upper Bonchurch,
VENTNOR, PO38 1PU
Tel: 01983 852196
Email: enquiries@leconfieldhotel.com
Website: www.leconfieldhotel.com
Map ref: 3 SZ57
Directions: On A3055, 3m from Old Shanklin village
Rooms: 6 en suite 5 annexe en suite (3 GF)
S £40-£180 **D** £80-£200
Notes: Wi-fi ⊗ 🚫 under 16yrs
Parking: 14
Closed: 24-26 Dec & 3-27 Jan

Paul, Cheryl and their small team welcome you to their delightful Victorian house. The Leconfield is elevated 400-feet above sea level and nestles into St Boniface Down in an Area of Outstanding Natural Beauty. There are views of the sea from nearly all the bedrooms, the sitting rooms, dining room, conservatory and garden. The Leconfield is on the island's south side and its unique micro climate is perfect for a break in the quieter winter months, while in the summer months guests can enjoy the heated outdoor swimming pool in the delightful gardens; a strictly adults-only oasis. Luxurious, individually designed bedrooms, some at ground-floor level, are equipped with en suite facilities, TVs with DVD players, hairdryers, hospitality trays, bathrobes and quality complimentary toiletries. A hearty breakfast prepared from local produce and free-range eggs is served in the Seascape Dining Room with its panoramic sea views. After a day of exploring the island's many treasures you'll be welcomed back to an AA Rosette standard evening meal with your choice from a wide selection of wines and other drinks. Your only distraction from the relaxing ambience might be the coming and going of ships on the open sea.

Recommended in the area
Ventnor Gardens; Carisbrooke Castle; Osborne House

Key to symbols

★	Black stars (see page 9)
★ (yellow)	Yellow stars (Highly commended) (see page 9)
◉	AA Rosette Award (see page 11)
🛏	Breakfast Award
🍽	Dinner Award
3 TQ28	Map reference
S	Single room
D	Double room
T	Twin room
GF	Ground floor room
⊗	No dogs allowed (assistance dogs should be allowed)
🚫	No children under age specified
Wi-fi	Wireless network connection

How to use the guide continued

Contact details
The establishment address includes a locator or place name in capitals (e.g. NORWICH). Within each county, entries are ordered alphabetically first by this place name and then by the name of the establishment.

Telephone and fax numbers, and e-mail and website addresses are given where available. The telephone and fax numbers are believed correct at the time of going to press but changes may occur. The latest establishment details are on the B&B pages at theAA.com.

Map reference
Each establishment in this guide is given a map reference for a location which can be found in the atlas section at the back of the guide. It is composed of the map page number (1–13) and two-figure map reference based on the National Grid.
For example: **Map 5, SU48**
5 refers to the page number of the map section at the back of the guide
SU is the National Grid lettered square (representing 100,000 sq metres) in which the location will be found
4 is the figure reading across the top and bottom of the map page
8 is the figure reading down each side of the map page.
Maps locating each establishment and an online route planner are available at theAA.com.

Room Information
The number of letting bedrooms with a bath or shower en suite are shown. Bedrooms that have a private bathroom adjacent may be included as en suite. Further details on private bathroom and en suite provision may also be included in the description text.
Prices: Charges shown are per night except where specified. **S** denotes bed and breakfast per person (single). **D** denotes bed and breakfast for two people sharing a room (double). In some cases prices are also given for twin (**T**), triple and family rooms, also on a per night basis. Prices are indications only, so do check before booking.

Parking
The number of parking spaces available. Other types of parking (on road or Park and Ride) may also be possible; check the descriptions for further information.

Notes
Dogs: Although some establishments allow dogs, they may be excluded from some areas of the property, and some breeds, particularly those requiring an exceptional license, may not be acceptable at all. Under the Equality Act 2010 access should be allowed for assistance dogs. Please check when making your booking.
Children: No children (🐾) means children cannot be accommodated, or a minimum age may be specified, e.g. 🐾 under 4 means no children under four years old. The main description may also provide details about facilities available for children.
Establishments with special facilities for children may provide additional equipment such as a babysitting service or baby-intercom system and facilities such as a playroom or playground, laundry facilities, drying and ironing facilities, cots, high chairs and special meals. If you have very young children, check before booking.
Other notes: Additional facilities, such as access for the disabled, or notes about other services (e.g. if credit cards are not accepted), may be listed here.

Closed
Establishments are open all year unless closing dates are shown. Please note that some places are open all year but offer a restricted service in low season.

Best quality

The AA inspects and classifies more than 3,000 guest houses, farmhouses, inns and restaurants with rooms for its Guest Accommodation Scheme. Establishments recognised by the AA pay an annual fee according to the rating and the number of bedrooms. This rating is not transferable if an establishment changes hands.

Common standards
A few years ago, the accommodation inspection organisations (The AA, VisitBritain, VisitScotland and VisitWales) undertook extensive consultation with consumers and the hospitality industry which resulted in new quality standards for rating establishments. Guests can now be confident that a star-rated B&B anywhere in the UK and Ireland will offer consistent quality and facilities.

★ Stars
AA Stars classify guest accommodation at five levels of quality, from one at the simplest, to five at the highest level of quality in the scheme. Each rating is also accompanied by a descriptive designator (further explained on page 10).

★ Highly commended
Yellow Stars indicate that an accommodation is in the top ten percent of its star rating. Yellow Stars only apply to 3, 4 or 5 star establishments.

The inspection process
Establishments applying for AA recognition are visited by a qualified AA accommodation inspector as a mystery guest. Inspectors stay overnight to make a thorough test of the accommodation, food, and hospitality. After paying the bill the following morning they identify themselves and ask to be shown around the premises. The inspector completes a full report, resulting in a recommendation for the appropriate Star rating. After this first visit, the establishment will receive an annual visit to check that standards are maintained. If it changes hands, the new owners must re-apply for a rating.

Guests can expect to find the following minimum standards at all levels:
- Pleasant and helpful welcome and service, and sound standards of housekeeping and maintenance.
- Comfortable accommodation equipped to modern standards.
- Bedding and towels changed for each new guest, and at least weekly if the room is taken for a long stay.
- Adequate storage, heating, lighting and comfortable seating.
- A sufficient hot water supply at reasonable times.
- A full cooked breakfast. (If this is not provided, the fact must be advertised and a substantial continental breakfast must be offered.)

There are additional requirements for an establishment to achieve three, four or five Stars:
- Three Stars and above – access to both sides of all beds for double occupancy.
- Three Stars and above – bathrooms/shower rooms cannot be shared by the proprietor.
- Three Stars and above – a washbasin in every guest bedroom (either in the bedroom or the en suite/private facility).
- Four Stars – half of the bedrooms must be en suite or have private facilities.
- Five Stars – all bedrooms must be en suite or have private facilities.

Designators

All guest accommodation inspected by the AA is given one of six descriptive designators to help potential guests understand the different types of accommodation available in Britain. The following are included in this guide:

B&B: B&B accommodation is provided in a private house run by the owner and with no more than six guests. There may be restricted access to the establishment, particularly in the late morning and the afternoon.

FARMHOUSE: A farmhouse usually provides good value B&B or guest house accommodation and excellent home cooking on a working farm or smallholding. Sometimes the land has been sold and only the house remains, but many are working farms and some farmers are happy to allow visitors to look around, or even to help feed the animals. However, you should always take great care and never leave children unsupervised. The farmhouses are listed under towns or villages, but do ask for precise directions when booking.

GUEST ACCOMMODATION: This general designator can be chosen by any establishment in the scheme.

GUEST HOUSE: Provides for more than six paying guests and usually offers more services than a B&B, for example dinner, served by staff as well as the owner. London prices tend to be higher than outside the capital, and normally only bed and breakfast is provided, although some establishments do provide a full meal service. Check on the service offered before booking as details may change during the currency of this guide.

INN: Traditional inns often have a cosy bar, convivial atmosphere, good beer and pub food. Those listed in the guide will provide breakfast in a suitable room, and should also serve light meals during licensing hours. The character of the properties vary according to whether they are country inns or town establishments. Check arrival times as these may be restricted to opening hours.

RESTAURANT WITH ROOMS: These restaurants offer overnight accommodation with the restaurant being the main business and open to non-residents. The restaurant usually offers a high standard of food and service.

Awards

🥚 Egg cups and 🥧 pies

Awarded only to establishments rated in the AA's Guest Accommodation Scheme.

These symbols indicate that in the AA's opinion the breakfasts and/or dinners at this establishment are really special, and have an emphasis on freshly prepared local ingredients.

theAA.com

Go to theAA.com to find more AA listed guest houses, hotels, pubs and restaurants – there are around 12,000 establishments on the site.

- The AA's easy-to-use route planner is on the home page.
- Simply enter your postcode and the establishment postcode given in this guide and click 'See your Route'. You will have a detailed route plan to take you from door-to-door.
- Use the Travel section to search, either by name or location, for Hotels, B&Bs, Restaurants and Pubs.

AA Rosette Awards

Out of the many thousands of restaurants in the UK, the AA identifies some 2,000 as the best. The following is an outline of what to expect from restaurants with AA Rosette awards. For a more detailed explanation of Rosette criteria please see **theAA.com**

❋ Excellent local restaurants serving food prepared with care, understanding and skill, using good quality ingredients.

❋❋ The best local restaurants, which aim for and achieve higher standards, better consistency and where a greater precision is apparent in the cooking. There will be obvious attention to the selection of quality ingredients.

❋❋❋ Outstanding restaurants that demand recognition well beyond their local area.

❋❋❋❋ Amongst the very best restaurants in the British Isles, where the cooking demands national recognition.

❋❋❋❋❋ The finest restaurants in the British Isles, where the cooking stands comparison with the best in the world.

Useful Information

There are so many things to remember when embarking on a short trip or weekend break. If you are unsure, always check before you book. Up-to-date information on all B&Bs can be found in the travel section at theAA.com

Booking

Advance booking is always recommended to avoid disappointment. The peak holiday periods in the UK are Easter, and from June to September; public holidays are also busy times. In some parts of Scotland the winter skiing season is a peak holiday period. Some establishments may only accept weekly bookings from Saturday, and others require a deposit on booking. Guest houses may not accept credit or debit cards. VAT (Value Added Tax) is payable in the UK and in the Isle of Man, on basic prices and additional services. VAT does not apply in the Channel Islands. Always confirm the current price before booking; the prices in this guide are indications rather than firm quotations. It is a good idea also to confirm exactly what is included in the price when booking. Remember that all details, especially prices, may change without notice during the currency of the guide.

Cancellation

Advise the proprietor immediately if you must cancel a booking. If the room cannot be re-let you may be held legally responsible for partial payment. This could include losing your deposit or being liable for compensation. You should consider taking out cancellation insurance.

Children

Restrictions for children may be mentioned in the description. Some establishments may offer free accommodation to children when they share their parents' room. Such conditions are subject to change without notice, therefore always check when booking.

Complaints

Readers who have cause to complain are urged to do so on the spot. This should provide an opportunity for the proprietor to correct matters. If the personal approach fails, readers can inform AA Hotel Services, Fanum House, Basingstoke, Hampshire, RG21 4EA.

The AA may at its sole discretion investigate any complaints received from guide users for the purpose of making any necessary amendments to the guide. The AA will not in any circumstances act as a representative or negotiator, or undertake to obtain compensation, or enter into any correspondence or deal with the matter in any other way whatsoever. The AA will not guarantee to take any specific action.

Facilities for disabled guests

The Equality Act 2010 provides legal rights for disabled people including access to goods, services and facilities, and means that service providers may have to consider making adjustments to their premises. For more information about the Act see: www.equalities.gov.uk. or www.direct.gov.uk/en/DisabledPeople/RightsAndObligations/DisabilityRights/DG_4001068

The establishments in this guide should be aware of their obligations under the Act. We recommend that you always telephone in advance to ensure that the establishment you have chosen has appropriate facilities.

Fire precautions and safety

Many of the establishments listed in the guide are subject to the requirements of the Fire Precautions Act 1971. This Act does not apply to the Channel Islands or the Isle of Man, where separate rules are exercised. All establishments should display details of how to summon assistance in the event of an emergency at night.

Licensed premises

Whereas inns hold a licence to sell alcohol, not all guest houses are licensed. Some may have a full liquor licence, or others may have a table licence and wine list. Licensed premises are not obliged to remain open throughout the permitted hours, and they may do so only when they expect reasonable trade.

Prices

The AA encourages the use of The Hotel Industry Voluntary Code of Booking Practice in appropriate establishments. The prime objective of the code is to ensure that the customer is clear about the price and the exact services and facilities being purchased, before entering into a contractually binding agreement. If the price has not been previously confirmed in writing, the guest should be handed a card at the time of registration at the establishment, stipulating the total obligatory charge.

Smoking regulations

Smoking in public places is banned in England, Scotland, Wales and the Channel Islands. If a bedroom is allocated for smokers, the establishment is obliged to clearly indicate that this is the case.

Bank and Public Holidays 2012

New Year's Day	1st January
New Year's Holiday	3rd January (Scotland)
Good Friday	6th April
Easter Monday	9th April
Early May Bank Holiday	7th May
Spring Bank Holiday	4th June
Diamond Jubilee Holiday	5th June
August Holiday	6th August (Scotland)
Summer Bank Holiday	27th August
St Andrew's Day (Scotland)	30th November
Christmas Day	25th December
Boxing Day	26th December

International information

If you're travelling from overseas, the following information will provide some useful guidance to help you enjoy your stay in Britain. The individual entries in this book will also give you information regarding travel and the best routes to take.

Money
Some establishments may not accept travellers' cheques, or credit or debit cards, so ask about payment methods when you book. Most European and American credit and debit cards allow you to withdraw cash from British ATMs.

Driving
In the UK you drive on the left and overtake on the right. Seat belts must be worn by every occupant of the car, whether they sit in the front or the rear. Speed limits are displayed in miles per hour.

Visit theAA.com for useful motoring advice, travel information and route planning.

Car rental
You will be required to present your driving licence and credit or debit card. You can also provide an International Driving Permit along with your driving licence. Further identification, such as a passport, may also be required. A minimum age limit will apply.

Trains
The UK has an extensive rail network. To find out about routes, special offers or passes, contact National Rail (www.nationalrail.co.uk, tel: 08457 484950; from overseas +44 20 7278 5240, and international rates apply) or a travel agent.

Medical treatment & health insurance
Travellers who normally take medicines or carry an appliance, such as a hypodermic syringe, should ensure that they have sufficient supply for their stay and a doctor's letter describing the condition and treatment required.

Before travelling ensure you have insurance for emergency medical and dental treatment. Many European countries have reciprocal agreements for medical treatment and require EU citizens to obtain a European Health Insurance Card (EHIC) before travel.

Telephones
Many guest houses have direct dial telephones in the rooms. Always check the call rate before dialling. Payphones usually take cash, credit or debit cards, or phonecards. Phonecards can be purchased from newsagents and post offices.

The telephone and fax numbers in this guide show the area code followed by the subscriber number. When dialling from abroad first dial the international network access code, then the country code (44 for the UK). Omit the first digit of the area code then dial the subscriber number.

For example:
From Europe   00 44 111 121212
From the US   011 44 111 121212
When dialling from the UK, dial the international network access code, then the country code.

Electrical appliances
The British electrical current is 220–240 volts and appliances have square three-pin plugs. Foreign appliances may require an adaptor for the plug, as well as an electrical voltage converter that will allow, for example, a 110-volt appliance to be powered.

Why not spend less and relax more on UK breaks?

Make AA Travel your first destination and you're on the way to a more relaxing short break or holiday.

AA Members and customers can get great deals on accommodation, from B&Bs to farmhouses, inns and hotels.

You can also save up to 10% at cottages4you, enjoy a 5% discount with Hoseasons, and up to 60% off the very best West End shows.

Thinking of going further afield?

Check out our attractive discounts on car hire, airport parking, ferry bookings, travel insurance and much more.

Then simply relax.

These are just some of our well-known partners:

Discounts apply to new bookings only, and cannot be used in conjunction with any other promotional offer or discount. The AA and its partners reserve the right to amend the discount and / or terms and conditions without prior notice. For full terms and conditions please visit theAA.com/travel. cottages4you: The discount is applied to the cottage element of the booking only and is subject to availability and cottages4you booking terms and conditions. Hoseasons: The discount is subject to availability and Hoseasons standard booking terms and conditions. Theatre Tickets: AA theatre tickets are provided by Encore Tickets Ltd. For full terms and conditions please visit http://theaa.eolts.co.uk

Visit theAA.com/travel

ENGLAND

View from Deacon Hill, Pirton, Hertfordshire

Berkshire

The Thames Path between Mapledurham and Pangbourne

The Swan Inn

★★★★ INN

Address: Craven Rd, Inkpen,
HUNGERFORD, RG17 9DX
Tel: 01488 668326
Fax: 01488 668306
Email: enquiries@theswaninn-organics.co.uk
Website: www.theswaninn-organics.co.uk
Map ref: 3 SU36
Directions: 3.5m SE of Hungerford. S on Hungerford High St past rail bridge, left to Hungerford Common, right signed Inkpen
Rooms: 10 en suite (2 fmly) **S** £70-£80 **D** £85-£105
Notes: Wi-fi ⊗ **Parking:** 50 **Closed:** 25-26 Dec

The peaceful North Wessex Downs Area of Outstanding Natural Beauty provides an idyllic setting for this 17th-century inn. Inside there are oak beams, open fires and a warm welcome from the Harris family, who are organic beef farmers, hence the excellent beef which is a permanent fixture on the menu (and is also sold in the adjoining farm shop). The menu here also features lots of fruits from the farm and other local and organic produce, and there are always fish and vegetarian options, plus smaller meals for children. The superb traditional organic ales are supplied by the nearby Butts Brewery. The beamed inn sits below Walbury Camp Iron Age hill fort at Combe Gibbet, and enjoys spectacular views. The 10 spacious en suite bedrooms provide a luxurious refuge to return to after an active day of sightseeing, walking or cycling in the beautiful Berkshire countryside. The shop is well worth a visit before leaving - here you can buy a range of traditional beef cuts and organic ready meals, as well as local beers, ciders and wines to remind you of your stay.

Recommended in the area

Combe Gibbet; Kennet and Avon Canal; Avebury Stone Circle

Berkshire

Weir View House

★★★★ GUEST ACCOMMODATION
Address: 9 Shooters Hill, PANGBOURNE, RG8 7DZ
Tel: 0118 984 2120
Fax: 0118 984 3777
Email: info@weirview.co.uk
Website: www.weirview.co.uk
Map ref: 3 SU67
Directions: A329 N from Pangbourne, after mini rdbt under rail bridge, opposite The Swan pub
Rooms: 9 en suite (6 fmly) (3 GF) **S** £90 **D** £90-£105
Notes: Wi-fi ⊗
Parking: 10

The picturesque village of Pangbourne is home to beautiful Weir View House, where you'll find a welcoming atmosphere, top-notch service and outstanding comfort. Surrounded by stunning countryside, it's hard to believe that this lovely B&B is less than an hour away from London. Soak up the beauty of the area with a stroll along the Thames Path and return to the luxury of one of the nine spacious and tastefully decorated en suite rooms - all with king- or super-king-size bed, mini-bar, TV with Freeview and DVD player, tea- and coffee-making facilities, free Wi-fi and fabulous views of Pangbourne Weir on the River Thames. A continental-style breakfast is served - laid out on a table for guests to help themselves - in the airy breakfast room. On-site parking is available, and the house also has private access to Pangbourne Station, making it an ideal stopover whether you're sightseeing in London, Oxford or Windsor, or perhaps visiting the area on business. Weir View House is also a convenient two-minute walk from Pangbourne's shops and restaurants.

Recommended in the area

Thames Path; Reading shopping; walking in the Chiltern Hills

Magna Carta

★★★★★ GUEST ACCOMMODATION
Address: Thames Side, WINDSOR, SL4 1QN
Tel: 07836 551912
Email: dominic@magna-carta.co.uk
Website: www.magna-carta.co.uk
Map ref: 3 SU97
Directions: M4 junct 5 follow signs to Datchet, then Windsor. At Windsor & Eton riverside station turn right & down to river
Rooms: 4 en suite **S** £100-£130 **D** £130-£160
Notes: Wi-fi

Magna Carta has to be Windsor's most unique accommodation. A luxuriously converted Dutch barge moored on the River Thames, it's just a few minutes walk from Windsor town centre and Windsor Castle. The boat has three luxurious double or twin cabins with super-king-size beds and one kingsize cabin. All have large en suite shower rooms with heated towel rails, air-conditioning, underfloor heating and DVD players. On the upper deck is a beautiful saloon with library, picture windows (with amazing river views) hi-fi and dining area. Outside, the split-level sun deck has teak furniture and even a hot-tub. Magna Carta is available fully crewed for cruising charters and can also be hired for dinner parties and dinner cruises, etc. Guests are made to feel at home by owner and captain Dominic Read and his crew. The award-winning breakfast is based on fresh, local ingredients, mostly organic and largely from Windsor Farm Shop. The boat is fully licensed and has a bar with an excellent variety of wines and spirits.

Recommended in the area
Windsor Castle; Eton College; Royal Ascot

Bristol

The Clifton Suspension Bridge

Westfield House

★★★★ BED AND BREAKFAST
Address: 37 Stoke Hill, Stoke Bishop,
BRISTOL, BS9 1LQ
Tel: 0117 962 6119
Fax: 0117 962 6119
Email: admin@westfieldhouse.net
Website: www.westfieldhouse.net
Map ref: 2 ST57
Directions: 1.8m NW of city centre in Stoke Bishop
Rooms: 3 en suite **S** £60-£93 **D** £75-£125
Notes: Wi-fi ⊗ under 11yrs
Parking: 5

Set in several acres of private grounds, this large white Georgian-style, family-run guest house makes an ideal retreat from Bristol's city lights. Westfield House is close to Durdham Downs - a vast expanse of open common land, which stretches from Bristol's suburbs to the cliffs of the Avon Gorge - and the Bristol University Halls of Residence. The beautifully decorated and extremely comfortable bedrooms, either single or doubles, are all en suite, and have flat-screen TVs, DVD/CD players, free Wi-fi, fridges and tea- and coffee-making facilities. The living room centres round a cosy fireplace while large bay windows lead onto a large garden terrace. Owner Ann cooks more or less to order using quality local ingredients, and a typical meal may include dishes such as salmon en croûte with puréed spinach and hollandaise sauce accompanied by potatoes dauphinoise, followed by a delicious home-made apple pie - all the better in the summer months when served on the patio overlooking the lovely rear garden. The grounds are also a haven for a variety of wildlife including owls, badgers, newts, falcons, slow worms and hedgehogs. If you still hanker for the bright lights, Westfield House is just a short walk from Bristol city centre. There is ample off-street parking for guests.

Recommended in the area

Clifton Suspension Bridge; ss Great Britain; Bristol Zoo

Buckinghamshire

View from Ivinghoe Beacon

Nags Head Inn & Restaurant

★★★★ ⦿ INN

Address: London Rd, GREAT MISSENDEN, HP16 0DG
Tel: 01494 862200 **Fax:** 01494 862685
Email: goodfood@nagsheadbucks.com
Website: www.nagsheadbucks.com
Map ref: 3 SP80
Directions: N of Amersham on A413, left at Chiltern hospital into London Rd signed Great Missenden
Rooms: 5 en suite (1 fmly) **S** £80-£120 **D** £90-£130
Notes: Wi-fi
Parking: 40

The delightful Nags Head Inn has won many awards over the years, including an AA Rosette for its restaurant. The 15th-century building has been tastefully refurbished to a high standard, whilst retaining its original country inn features, including low oak beams and a large inglenook fireplace. It has served in the past as a location for a number of TV programmes and films, and has played host to many famous names, including prime ministers and the children's author Roald Dahl - the animated film of Dahl's *Fantastic Mr Fox* actually features the inn. Located in the glorious Chiltern Hills, in the valley of the River Misbourne, the inn is within walking distance of the lovely village of Great Missenden and close to major road and rail routes. The bedrooms, all with en suite facilities, are beautifully furnished and come with flat-screen TVs and lots of thoughtful extras. In the restaurant, the menu is based on local and organic produce, and is supplemented by daily specials. There's also an award-winning wine list and a good selection of real ales.

Recommended in the area

Hughenden Manor (NT); Bekonscot Model Village; West Wycombe Park (NT)

Cheshire

Little Moreton Hall

The Pheasant Inn

★★★★★ 🍴 INN

Address: Higher Burwardsley,
BURWARDSLEY, CH3 9PF
Tel: 01829 770434
Fax: 01829 771097
Email: info@thepheasantinn.co.uk
Website: www.thepheasantinn.co.uk
Map ref: 6 SJ55 **Directions:** From A41, left to Tattenhall, right at 1st junct & left at 2nd Higher Burwardsley. At post office left, signed
Rooms: 2 en suite 10 annexe en suite (2 fmly) (5 GF)
S £75-£105 **D** £100-£155
Notes: Wi-fi **Parking:** 80

Perched high up on the Peckforton Hills, The Pheasant enjoys magnificent panoramic views of the Cheshire Plain. The beautifully restored 300-year-old Cheshire sandstone inn has to be in one of the most picturesque locations in the county. If sitting outside in the flower filled courtyard to take in the view isn't an option, you can draw up a seat by the window inside - where open fires create a cosy atmosphere in winter - and still enjoy the spectacular scene of the Cheshire countryside folding away before you, ever changing with the seasons. It's often been said that it's the little touches that can really make a place, and with seasonal menus printed daily to make best use of the local ingredients available, it's not hard to see why the place is buzzing. Good, honest, wholesome food is what you'll find here, along with four real ales on tap, and a fantastic selection of top quality wines from around the world. Housed in delightful old Cheshire sandstone buildings, the 12 en suite rooms combine both style and comfort and feature modern facilities such as complimentary Wi-fi.

Recommended in the area
Cheshire Candle Workshops; Beeston Castle; Sandstone Trail

The Bear's Paw

★★★★★ INN

Address: School Ln, WARMINGHAM, Sandbach, CW11 3QN
Tel: 01270 526317
Email: info@thebearspaw.co.uk
Website: www.thebearspaw.co.uk
Map ref: 6 SJ76
Directions: M6 junct 17, A534, A533 signed Middlewich & Northwich. Continue on A533, left into Mill Ln, left into Warmingham Ln. Right into Plant Ln, left into Green Ln
Rooms: 17 en suite (4 fmly) **S** £79-£120 **D** £99-£140
Notes: Wi-fi **Parking:** 75

Located in the heart of Cheshire, in the picturesque village of Warmingham, The Bear's Paw is a delightful 19th century character inn. The luxurious boutique-style bedrooms, beautifully designed with high quality furnishings, are sure to provide you with a wonderfully comfortable and peaceful night's sleep. All 17 rooms - including some suitable for families - are en suite and feature modern day amenities such as flat-screen TVs, complimentary Wi-fi and media hubs. The kitchen team at The Bear's Paw takes pride in offering home-cooked, wholesome food, which has been recognised with an AA Dinner Award. Only the freshest and most seasonal produce, locally sourced wherever possible, finds its way onto the menu. The bar offers six real ales from local micro breweries, along with a fantastic selection of top-quality wines from around the world. With two open fires, reclaimed antique oak flooring and more than 200 pictures adorning the oak-panelled walls, the inn retains all of its old world charm and character, yet with an injection of contemporary style.

Recommended in the area
Tatton Park; Snugburys Ice Cream; Oulton Park

Clough Brook at Wildboarclough

Co Durham

Fields above Langdon Beck

The County Restaurant with Rooms

★★★★ RESTAURANT WITH ROOMS
Address: 12 The Green, AYCLIFFE VILLAGE,
Darlington, DL5 6LX
Tel: 01325 312273
Fax: 01325 317131
Email: info@thecountyaycliffevillage.com
Website: www.thecountyaycliffevillage.com
Map ref: 7 NZ22
Directions: A1(M) junct 59, A167 towards Newton Aycliffe. In Aycliffe village turn onto village green
Rooms: 7 en suite (3 GF) **S** £49 **D** £70-£110
Notes: Wi-fi ⊗ **Parking:** 25
Closed: 25 Dec & 1 Jan

Sitting right on the pretty green in the heart of Aycliffe village, The County Restaurant with Rooms gives the impression of being miles away from anywhere, and yet it's just a short drive from the A1. Step inside the smart white and black fronted building, and you'll find a contemporary restaurant and bar done out in colourful shades, with plenty of light pouring in through large bay windows, and with a relaxed and friendly atmosphere. Only the freshest of ingredients - mostly locally sourced - go into the cooking here, with the menu offering up the likes of pan-fried haunch of venison and roast monkfish on a chorizo and spinach potato cake, alongside pub classics like homemade steak and real ale pie and cod fillet in beer batter. It's all accompanied by a wide range of real ales, including Black Sheep and The County's very own brew. The County's other big draw is its luxurious accommodation, with seven beautiful bedrooms located in a smart townhouse next door. Each room is individually designed and furnished to a very high standard. If you visit The County you'll be following in the footsteps of a couple of famous personalities: Tony Blair brought the French president Jacques Chirac here in the year 2000.

Recommended in the area

Moulton Hall (NT); Auckland Castle; Durham Coast National Nature Reserve

Cornwall

St Michael's Mount

Cotswold House

★★★★ GUEST HOUSE
Address: 49 Melvill Rd, FALMOUTH, TR11 4DF
Tel: 01326 312077
Email: info@cotswoldhousehotel.com
Website: www.cotswoldhousehotel.com
Map ref: 1 SW82
Directions: On A39 near town centre & docks
Rooms: 10 en suite (1 fmly) (1 GF)
Notes: ⊗
Parking: 10
Closed: Xmas

With Falmouth's superb sandy Gyllyngvase Beach and the busy estuary, harbour and yachting marina just a short walk away, this small family-owned and run guest house is ideal for both a holiday or a short break. The smart Victorian property is also close to the picturesque, cobbled town centre with its historic buildings and range of specialist shops. Cotswold House has been carefully refurbished to create an elegant yet entirely relaxed atmosphere, and guests are offered a genuinely warm welcome by proprietors Nicola and Martyn. All bedrooms have en suite facilities and are furnished to a high standard, with many enjoying lovely views of the sea and the River Fal. Cotswold House is open all year and offers half-board or bed and breakfast rates. If you do decide to dine in during the evenings, expect skillfully prepared traditional cuisine along with an interesting wine list and attentive, personal service. Before or after dinner you can relax with a drink in the bar or in the comfortable lounge, which has patio doors leading to a small, secluded terrace exclusively for the use of guests.

Recommended in the area

Falmouth National Maritime Museum; The Eden Project; Trebah and Glendurgan gardens

The Queens Arms

★★★ INN

Address: Breage, HELSTON, TR13 9PD
Tel: 01326 573485
Email: chris-brazier@btconnect.com
Website: www.queensarmsbreage.co.uk
Map ref: 1 SW62
Rooms: 2 en suite **D** £75-£90
Notes: Wi-fi
Parking: 15

This lively community pub can be found next to St Breaca's Church in the pretty village of Breage, about three miles from Helston. Since being taken over by Chris and Sue Brazier in 2006, the 15th-century building has been fully refurbished and now offers high quality accommodation along with a warm and friendly atmosphere, an extensive food menu and a range of drinks including six well-kept cask ales and top-notch wines. Great value lunches and dinners are served seven days a week in the cosy bar with its log fires or in the relaxing dining room, or perhaps outside in the beer garden during the summer. Dishes range from filled baguettes to Cornish fillet steak, haddock in homemade beer batter, or chicken breast served with a roasted pepper, pesto and cream sauce on saffron rice. A blackboard displays daily specials and fresh fish dishes, and there are always several interesting vegetarian options. For those with hearty appetites the homemade desserts include sticky toffee pudding with caramel sauce, and flavoured crème brulees, or you could go for the selection of Cornish cheeses with biscuits and chutney. There's live musical entertainment some Saturdays.

Recommended in the area

Mount's Bay; Eden Project; The Minack Theatre

The Crown Inn

★★★ INN

Address: LANLIVERY, Bodmin, PL30 5BT
Tel: 01208 872707
Fax: 01208 871208
Email: thecrown@wagtailinns.com
Website: www.wagtailinns.com
Map ref: 1 SX05 **Directions:** Signed from A390, 2m W of Lostwithiel. Inn 0.5m down lane into village, opposite church
Rooms: 2 en suite 7 annexe en suite (1 fmly) (7 GF)
Notes: Wi-fi **Parking:** 50

The black and white painted Crown Inn, dating from the 12th century, is one of Cornwall's oldest pubs, and is a popular stopping off point for those walking the Saint's Way. It offers relaxed, homely bed and breakfast accommodation along with top-notch traditional pub food and real ales from Cornwall's Sharp's and Skinner's breweries. There are nine comfortable bedrooms furnished in a classic style, each with en suite shower room, digital TV and tea- and coffee-making facilities. Two rooms are on the first floor of the pub, two are in a converted outbuilding, and another five are in a new building overlooking the tranquil garden. Children are welcomed at The Crown, with one room able to accommodate a family of four, while extra fold-out beds can be provided. Dogs can also be accommodated in certain rooms. Hearty Cornish breakfasts and traditional pub meals featuring lots of local produce, including plenty of seafood from the nearby harbour in Fowey, are served in the cosy bar with its low beams and open fireplaces. The pub has a lovely atmosphere and a welcome absence of piped music or fruit machines.

Recommended in the area
The Eden Project; St Austell; Fowey

Hurdon

★★★★ FARMHOUSE

Address: LAUNCESTON, PL15 9LS
Tel: 01566 772955
Map ref: 1 SX38
Directions: A30 onto A388 to Launceston, at rdbt exit for hospital, 2nd right signed Trebullett, premises 1st on right
Rooms: 6 en suite (1 fmly) (1 GF)
S £32-£38 **D** £54-£70
Notes: ⊘
Parking: 10
Closed: Nov-Apr

Hurdon is a Grade II listed Georgian farmhouse run as a bed and breakfast by Margaret Smith and family for over 40 years. Over the last four decades it has developed an excellent reputation for its high-class accommodation, fantastic food (recognised with an AA Dinner Award) and warm and friendly atmosphere - it's no wonder many guests return year after year. The house is situated in the heart of a 300-acre working farm with beef cattle, milking cows and pigs, peacefully located at the end of a tree-lined drive. The elegant 18th-century stone and granite farmhouse retains many original features, especially in the kitchen, with its open granite fireplace and original Dutch oven. Bedrooms are all en suite and individually furnished, and come with thoughtful extras such as electric blankets, hot-water bottles, bathrobes, hairdryer and even playing cards. Breakfasts and dinners make use of produce from the farm, with the home-made clotted cream a particular treat. Hurdon is situated on the outskirts of Launceston, the ancient capital of Cornwall, making it an ideal base for touring Cornwall and Devon, including both coasts, Bodmin Moor and Dartmoor.

Recommended in the area

The Eden Project; South West Coast Path; Dartmoor and Bodmin Moor

Redgate Smithy

★★★★ BED AND BREAKFAST
Address: Redgate, St Cleer, LISKEARD, PL14 6RU
Tel: 01579 321578
Email: enquiries@redgatesmithy.co.uk
Website: www.redgatesmithy.co.uk
Map ref: 1 SX26
Directions: 3m NW of Liskeard. Exit A30 at Bolventor/Jamaica Inn into St Cleer Rd for 7m, B&B just past x-rds
Rooms: 3 (2 en suite) (1 pri facs) **S** £48 **D** £75
Notes: Wi-fi ❧ under 12yrs
Parking: 3
Closed: Xmas & New Year

Redgate Smithy, situated just above Golitha Falls on the southern edge of Bodmin Moor, was built around 200 years ago and makes a great base for exploring this part of Cornwall, especially if you love walking and bird-watching. It also offers easy access to the north and south Cornish coasts and all their many fantastic sandy beaches. After a hard day of sightseeing, walking or exploring, back at Redgate Smithy guests can relax in the attractive cottage-style bedrooms, all of which have TVs with Freeview, Wi-fi, tea- and coffee-making facilities, and very comfortable beds. In the morning there's an extensive menu to choose from: tuck into the full Cornish - made from high quality local produce (including great sausages) - or perhaps try the ever popular 'Redgate Eggs Royale'. Breakfast is served in the light and airy conservatory, overlooking the patio and woodland garden, so you can watch the birds over their own breakfast while you relax and plan your day. Whatever you do during your stay, don't miss a visit to the enchanting Golitha Falls just down the lane.

Recommended in the area
Golitha Falls; The Eden Project; Bodmin Moor and The Cheesewring

Sennen Cove

Bay View Farm

★★★★ 🍽 FARMHOUSE

Address: St Martins, LOOE, PL13 1NZ
Tel: 01503 265922
Fax: 01503 265922
Email: mike@looebaycaravans.co.uk
Website: www.looedirectory.co.uk/bay-view-farm.htm
Map ref: 1 SX25
Directions: 2m NE of Looe. Off B3253 for Monkey Sanctuary, farm signed
Rooms: 3 en suite (3 GF) **S** £35-£38 **D** £65-£70
Notes: ⊗ ⅋ under 5yrs
Parking: 3

A genuine warm Cornish welcome, an air of tranquillity and great food are the hallmarks of Bay View Farm, which is home to a team of prize-winning shire horses. Mrs Elford is a delightful host and it's easy to see why her guests are drawn back to this special place again and again. The renovated and extended bungalow is situated in a truly spectacular spot with ever-changing views across Looe Bay, and is beautifully decorated and furnished throughout to give a light, spacious feel. The three en suite bedrooms each have their own very individual character - one is huge with comfy sofas and a wonderful view, the others smaller but still very inviting. Two of the rooms also have spacious private conservatories. Guests can relax at the end of the day either in the lounge or on the lovely patio and watch the sun set over Looe. Breakfasts at Bay View Farm are substantial and the evening meals feature home-made desserts accompanied by clotted cream. If you do choose to eat out there are numerous restaurants and pubs nearby. The old town of East Looe is a delight of tall buildings, narrow streets and passageways and the fishing industry brings a maritime bustle to the harbour and quayside. West Looe, the smaller settlement, has a lovely outlook across the harbour to East Looe.

Recommended in the area
Lost Gardens of Heligan; The Eden Project; Looe

Barclay House

★★★★ ◉◉ GUEST ACCOMMODATION

Address: St Martin's Rd, LOOE, PL13 1LP
Tel: 01503 262929
Fax: 01503 262632
Email: reception@barclayhouse.co.uk
Website: www.barclayhouse.co.uk
Map ref: 1 SX25
Directions: 1st house on left on entering Looe from A38
Rooms: 11 en suite 1 annexe en suite (1 fmly) (1 GF)
S £55-£117.50 **D** £110-£200
Notes: Wi-fi ⊗
Parking: 25

High on the hill overlooking the historic fishing village of Looe, but within walking distance of the town, Barclay House has striking views of the river and the ever-changing countryside beyond. The 12-bedroom Victorian villa, built in 1890 and sitting in six acres of grounds, oozes charm and offers a relaxed atmosphere. Barclay House was fully refurbished in 2010, and it shows in the smart, contemporary bedrooms and eight luxury self-catering cottages. The two AA Rosette restaurant serves a daily changing menu showcasing the very best produce Cornwall has to offer, including fresh fish landed daily at Looe. Head chef Benjamin Palmer's locally inspired dishes include Trio of Pork, steamed Fowey River Mussels, and Looe Bay Mackerel, and the excellence of the food is matched by the superb customer service. The restaurant's French doors open out to the terrace and gardens where you can enjoy a refreshing glass of local wine while watching the sun set across Looe Bay. Barclay House offers ample free parking for guests, as well as a heated outdoor swimming pool set in a natural sun-trap, and a state-of-the-art gym with sauna.

Recommended in the area

Lost Gardens of Heligan; The Eden Project; Historic fishing villages of Looe and Polperro

Bucklawren Farm

★★★★ FARMHOUSE
Address: St Martin-by-Looe, LOOE, PL13 1NZ
Tel: 01503 240738
Fax: 01503 240481
Email: bucklawren@btopenworld.com
Website: www.bucklawren.co.uk
Map ref: 1 SX25 **Directions:** 2m NE of Looe. Off B3253 to Monkey Sanctuary, 0.5m right to Bucklawren, farmhouse 0.5m on left
Rooms: 6 en suite 1 annexe (1 pri facs) (3 fmly) (1 GF) **S** £38.50-£50 **D** £64-£77
Notes: Wi-fi ⊗ ⌘ under 5yrs **Parking:** 7
Closed: Nov-Feb

Only half a mile from the coastal path, and a mile from the beach, this delightful 19th-century farmhouse sits in 400 acres in the beautiful Domesday hamlet of Bucklawren. Unsurprisingly, this part of Cornwall has been designated as an Area of Great Landscape Value, making it the perfect spot for a relaxing, peaceful holiday. The front-facing rooms at Bucklawren Farm all enjoy spectacular sea views. Breakfast is served in the dining room, with guests offered a large choice of dishes, all cooked to order using local produce wherever possible. There is a lounge and a conservatory where you can make yourself at home and enjoy the peace and quiet. The en suite bedrooms - a mixture of double, triple and family rooms - are attractively furnished and come with tea- and coffee-making facilities, mineral water, biscuits, luxury toiletries and fluffy towels. Bucklawren Farm is only a short distance away from the fishing villages of Looe and Polperro, and there are many historic houses and glorious gardens nearby, along with lovely sandy beaches and, of course, excellent walking. Head to the Granary Restaurant in an adjacent converted barn for evening meals carefully prepared from fresh local produce (March to November only).

Recommended in the area

The Eden Project; Lost Gardens of Heligan; fishing villages of Looe & Polperro

Trehaven Manor

★★★★ 🛏 🍽 **GUEST ACCOMMODATION**

Address: Station Rd, LOOE, PL13 1HN
Tel: 01503 262028
Fax: 01503 265613
Email: enquiries@trehavenhotel.co.uk
Website: www.trehavenhotel.co.uk
Map ref: 1 SX25
Directions: In East Looe between railway station & bridge. Trehaven's drive adjacent to The Globe PH
Rooms: 7 en suite (1 fmly) (1 GF)
Notes: ⊗
Parking: 7

Trehaven Manor is a family affair, run by Ella and Neil Hipkiss and their three sons, Jonathan, Matthew and James. The manor occupies an elevated position in the picturesque fishing town of Looe and offers spectacular views over the ever-changing estuary and beyond to Looe Bridge and West Looe. It is conveniently located close to the town, with Looe well positioned as a base to explore the rest of Cornwall. All rooms are en suite and tastefully furnished, with TV and tea- and coffee-making facilities, and most have lovely views over the estuary. Free Wi-fi is available and there's also a computer for guests to use. The Hipkiss family's main aim is to make sure guests feel at home during their stay, and one of Ella's homemade cream teas in the elegant lounge on arrival gets things off to a flying start. In the evenings you can unwind with a drink from the fully licensed bar after a hectic day. Fresh, local produce features at breakfast, while for all other meals there is a fantastic choice of good restaurants in Looe (Neil and Ella will happily point you in the right direction). Each room has its own guaranteed on-site parking space.

Recommended in the area

Polperro; Looe town and beach; The Eden Project; Lost Gardens of Heligan

The Old Mill House

★★★★ GUEST HOUSE

Address: PADSTOW, PL27 7QT
Tel: 01841 540388
Fax: 01841 540406
Email: enquiries@theoldmillhouse.com
Website: www.theoldmillhouse.com
Map ref: 1 SW97
Directions: 2m S of Padstow. In centre of Little Petherick on A389
Rooms: 7 en suite **S** £65-£120 **D** £80-£120
Notes: ⊗ ⚅ under 14yrs
Parking: 20
Closed: Nov-Feb

The friendly proprietors of The Old Mill House, a 16th century converted corn mill situated in an Area of Outstanding Natural Beauty, do their utmost to ensure a very comfortable stay. Just two miles from Padstow, the Grade II listed building sits next to a pretty stream that runs into the Camel Estuary - a delightful setting with a rich variety of wildlife to spot, including kingfishers. The Old Mill House has seven tastefully and individually decorated bedrooms which are all en suite and are equipped with TV, telephone/data port, hairdryer, radio/alarm clock and tea- and coffee-making facilities. Four of the rooms overlook the picturesque garden, while the remainder are at the front of the house facing the village, with a view of the stream running into the estuary. Breakfast is served in the original mill room and includes an extensive buffet with a selection of cereals and yoghurts, fresh fruit salad and home-made preserves, followed by a choice of cooked dishes. Guests are welcome to sit and unwind with a drink in the pretty gardens, as The Old Mill is fully licensed.

Recommended in the area

The Eden Project; Lost Gardens of Heligan; Camel Trail Cycle Path

Camilla House

★★★★★ GUEST HOUSE
Address: 12 Regent Ter, PENZANCE, TR18 4DW
Tel: 01736 363771
Fax: 01736 363771
Email: enquiries@camillahouse.co.uk
Website: www.camillahouse.co.uk
Map ref: 1 SW43
Directions: A30 to Penzance, at rail station follow road along harbour front onto Promenade Rd. Opposite Jubilee Bathing Pool, Regent Ter 2nd right
Rooms: 8 (7 en suite) (1 pri facs) (1 GF)
S £35-£38.50 **D** £65-£89
Notes: Wi-fi ⊗ **Parking:** 6

The friendly proprietors of this attractive Grade II listed terrace house do their utmost to ensure a comfortable stay. On arrival, guests are served with tea and coffee with 'Thunder and Lightning', a real Cornish treat. Bedrooms and bathrooms are attractively furnished, providing many added extras, such as fluffy towels and bathrobes, refreshment trays with Fairtrade products and Cornish mineral water, flat-screen Freeview TV/DVD, hairdryer, magazines and sweets. Some bedrooms and the dining room also provide delightful sea views over Mount's Bay. Wireless internet connection is available throughout, and there is also access to computers in the stylish, high-ceilinged lounge, which stocks a library of DVDs as well as Cornish Monopoly. A range of breakfast options is on offer in the dining room (home to a well-stocked residents' bar), using home-made or fresh local produce; options include Cornish cheese platters. Evening meals are available by prior arrangement. Camilla House has held the Green Tourism Business Scheme award since 2006 and is committed to operating in an environmentally responsible fashion.

Recommended in the area

Land's End; Lizard Peninsula; South West Coastal Path

Chy-an-Mor

★★★★ GUEST ACCOMMODATION
Address: 15 Regent Ter, PENZANCE, TR18 4DW
Tel: 01736 363441
Email: reception@chyanmor.co.uk
Website: www.chyanmor.co.uk
Map ref: 1 SW43
Directions: A30 to Penzance, at rail station, follow harbour front into Promenade Rd. Pass Jubilee Pool, right at Stanley Guest House
Rooms: 9 en suite **S** £40-£44 **D** £70-£92
Notes: Wi-fi ⊗ ⚑ under 14yrs
Parking: 15
Closed: 15 Nov-15 Mar

This elegant Grade II listed Regency house has an attractive sea-facing location, overlooking Mount's Bay and the promenade. Chy-an-Mor - the name is Cornish for 'house of sea' - has been refurbished to provide high standards throughout. The impressive entrance leads to spacious, high-ceilinged public rooms, and residents can linger over the changing sea views in the stylish lounge with its comfortable sofas and range of board games. Guests are also welcome to soak up the sun in the pretty south-facing garden, which features benches and a patio area, lit up by fairy lights at night. Inside, each of the en suite bedrooms is individually designed and equipped with thoughtful extras, such as flat-screen digital TVs, Fairtrade tea, coffee and hot chocolate, organic cotton wool, and shoe-polishing kits, and many of the rooms enjoy spectacular views. Satisfying breakfasts, including vegetarian options and home-made preserves and muffins, are served in the large, bright dining room on tables dressed with crisp white tablecloths and linen napkins. Ample off-street parking is available. A range of in-house beauty treatments is also a draw.

Recommended in the area

St Michael's Mount (NT); The Minnack Theatre; Land's End

Mount Royal

★★★ GUEST ACCOMMODATION

Address: Chyandour Cliff, PENZANCE, TR18 3LQ
Tel: 01736 362233
Fax: 01736 362233
Email: mountroyal@btconnect.com
Map ref: 1 SW43
Directions: Off A30 onto coast road into town
Rooms: 7 en suite (3 fmly) (1 GF)
S £60-£70 **D** £85-£95
Notes: Wi-fi ⊗
Parking: 10
Closed: Nov-Mar

Mount Royal is a stylish and elegant part-Georgian, part-Victorian house and has been a family-run business providing quality guest accommodation for over 40 years. The house overlooks the entrance of Penzance harbour, with panoramic views of St Michael's Mount and the Lizard Peninsula. The bedrooms are spacious with en suite facilities, and there are some 'premier' rooms with spectacular sea views and binoculars provided for dolphin spotting in the bay. All are tastefully furnished in keeping with the traditional style of the house, and have TVs with Freeview and free Wi-fi. The original Victorian dining room, complete with grand fireplace, wood panelling, decorative ceilings and oak parquet floors, provides an elegant backdrop for breakfast, which is served at individual tables on fine Wedgwood crockery with silver cutlery. There's an extensive menu to choose from, including fresh fruit salad, a full English and poached smoked haddock. There is free private parking within the grounds for all guests. Mount Royal offers a convenient stopover for people travelling to the Isles of Scilly. The guest house is close to the harbour, and five minutes from the town centre, coach and rail terminus.

Recommended in the area

Geevor Tin Mine Museum; Eden Project; Land's End

The Summer House

★★★★★ GUEST ACCOMMODATION

Address: Cornwall Ter, PENZANCE, TR18 4HL
Tel: 01736 363744
Fax: 01736 360959
Email: reception@summerhouse-cornwall.com
Website: www.summerhouse-cornwall.com
Map ref: 1 SW43
Directions: A30 to Penzance, at rail station follow along harbour onto Promenade, pass Jubilee Pool, right after Queens Hotel. Summer House 30yds on left
Rooms: 5 en suite **S** £105-£150 **D** £120-£150
Notes: Wi-fi ⊗ under 13yrs **Parking:** 6
Closed: Nov-Mar

The philosophy of The Summer House is to combine great food and beautiful surroundings with a happy, informal atmosphere, making it the perfect seaside retreat. Close to the seafront and harbour, this stylishly converted, stunning Grade II listed Regency house features a bold decor with polished wood, bright colours, and a curving glass-walled tower that fills the building with light. Fresh flowers are among the thoughtful extras provided in the spacious twin and double en suite bedrooms, which are light, airy and individually decorated, and enhanced by interesting family pieces and collectables. You'll find lots of home comforts to help you relax, including a TV, radio, DVD player, hairdryer, books and magazines. Fresh regional produce is simply prepared, resulting in a memorable dining experience at weekends. Dishes are distinctly Mediterranean in feel, and complemented by good wines. The restaurant opens out onto a walled garden with terracotta pots, sub-tropical planting and attractive blue tables and chairs, where in warmer weather evening drinks and dinner may be enjoyed.

Recommended in the area

St Michael's Mount (NT); Land's End; The Minack Theatre

The Droskyn Sundial on the cliffs overlooking Perran Bay

Ednovean Farm

★★★★★ FARMHOUSE

Address: PERRANUTHNOE, TR20 9LZ
Tel: 01736 711883
Email: info@ednoveanfarm.co.uk
Website: www.ednoveanfarm.co.uk
Map ref: 1 SW52
Directions: Off A394 towards Perranuthnoe at Dynasty Restaurant, farm drive on left on bend by post box
Rooms: 3 en suite (3 GF) **S** £100-£115 **D** £100-£120
Notes: Wi-fi ⊗ 🐾 under 16yrs
Parking: 4
Closed: 24-28 Dec

Ednovean Farm, an ancient farmstead overlooking the sweep of Mount's Bay, with the village of Perranuthnoe tucked in the valley below, offers the perfect combination of a peaceful retreat and easy access to Cornwall for touring. The farm is only a short drive off the A394, and yet in a tranquil setting with its acre-and-a-half of stunning landscaped gardens. Guests can leave their car at Ednovean Farm and walk across the fields to the coastal footpath, while the beach and village pub are just a few minutes' stroll away. There are three en suite bedrooms at Ednovean Farm, all with a romantic, country-chic feel - think roll-top baths, fluffy bathrobes, locally hand-made soaps, patchwork quilts, flat-screen TVs, free Wi-fi, and French doors onto private terraces. The accommodation is set within a converted 17th-century barn, surrounded by formal, landscaped terraces, and opening onto the expanse of garden with benches perfectly positioned to watch the sun set behind St Michael's Mount.

Recommended in the area

St Michael's Mount (NT); Godolphin House; Penlee House Gallery (Newlyn School paintings)

Trenake Manor Farm

★★★★ FARMHOUSE

Address: Pelynt, POLPERRO, PL13 2LT
Tel: 01503 220835
Fax: 01503 220835
Email: lorraine@cornishfarmhouse.co.uk
Website: www.cornishfarmhouse.co.uk
Map ref: 1 SX25
Directions: 3.5m N of Polperro. A390 onto B3359 for Looe, 5m left at small x-rds
Rooms: 3 en suite (1 fmly) **S** £46 **D** £72-£76
Notes: Wi-fi
Parking: 10

Situated midway between the historic fishing ports of Looe and Polperro, and just four miles from the coastal path, this welcoming 15th-century listed farmhouse was once a monastery. It has been owned by the same family for five generations and has many returning guests. The en suite bedrooms, including one family room, are spacious and boast elegant Victorian king-sized bedsteads and a number of thoughtful finishing touches. Breakfast is cooked on the Aga and served in the cosy dining room. Guests can relax in the comfortable lounge, which is full of period charm, or take tea in the lovely, well-kept garden. Trenake Manor Farm encompasses 300 acres, and guests are free to roam. There's plenty of wildlife to spot and if you wish you can watch the cows being milked. The farm aims to be as self-sufficient as possible, growing and milling all the food for the 300 milking cows and 500-strong beef herd. For keen riders, the farm also offers B&B for horses in the traditional stone-built stables.

Recommended in the area
The Eden Project; Lost Gardens of Heligan; Polperro

Hunter's Moon

★★★★ GUEST HOUSE

Address: Chapel Hill, Polgooth,
ST AUSTELL, PL26 7BU
Tel: 01726 66445
Email: enquiries@huntersmooncornwall.co.uk
Website: www.huntersmooncornwall.co.uk
Map ref: 1 SX05
Directions: 1.5m SW of town centre. Off B3273 into Polgooth, pass village shop on left, 1st right
Rooms: 4 en suite (2 fmly) **S** £55–£60 **D** £75–£80
Notes: Wi-fi ⊗ ☆ under 14yrs
Parking: 5

A warm and friendly welcome awaits you at Hunter's Moon - the perfect location for a peaceful Cornish holiday. From this central spot you can explore the whole of the county with ease, starting with the Lost Gardens of Heligan and the Eden Project which are only a few miles down the road. The en suite guest rooms are decorated and furnished to a high standard, and two rooms have super-king-size beds which can be converted into twin beds. These rooms also take a third bed to accommodate a family. There is a conservatory lounge for guests to use, and plenty of space to sit and enjoy the garden and the countryside views. At breakfast, tuck into a freshly prepared traditional English featuring locally sourced ingredients, along with juice, fruit and cereals. There's a continental style option too, and vegetarian and special diet breakfasts can be provided if advised on booking. The Polgooth Inn is just five minutes' walk away and there are many more restaurants nearby. Hunter's Moon also offers ample private parking.

Recommended in the area

The Eden Project; Lost Gardens of Heligan; Charlestown Harbour

Penarwyn House

★★★★★ GUEST ACCOMMODATION

Address: ST BLAZEY, Par, PL24 2DS
Tel: 01726 814224
Fax: 01726 814224
Email: stay@penarwyn.co.uk
Website: www.penarwyn.co.uk
Map ref: 1 SX05
Directions: A390 W through St Blazey, left before 2nd speed camera into Doubletrees School, Penarwyn straight ahead
Rooms: 4 en suite (1 fmly) **S** £60-£75 **D** £80-£160
Notes: Wi-fi ⊗ ⚹ under 10yrs
Parking: 6

This large, impressive Victorian house stands in a tranquil spot close to main routes, with the Eden Project, the Lost Gardens of Heligan, Fowey, the coastal path and National Trust properties all close by. With the Roseland Peninsula, Polperro, Looe, Padstow and Port Issac (the setting for TV series *Doc Martin*) all within 45 minutes' drive, and Land's End, the Lizard Peninsula, St Ives and Penzance less than 90 minutes' drive away, Penarwyn House really is ideally positioned for a touring holiday in Cornwall. Painstakingly restored, the spacious house offers a host of facilities, including silent refrigerators in each room. The bedrooms are particularly comfortable and well appointed, with all double rooms having luxury en suites with separate baths and showers. On arrival guests are welcomed with afternoon tea and homemade cake, and breakfast is always a highlight. Owners Jan and Mike Russell offer very welcoming hospitality and place great emphasis on first-class service. All in all, Penarwyn House offers the ideal place to unwind from the day and set yourself up for the next.

Recommended in the area

The Eden Project; Lanhydrock (NT); Lost Gardens of Heligan

Edgar's

★★★★ GUEST ACCOMMODATION

Address: Chy-an-Creet, Higher Stennack,
ST IVES, TR26 2HA
Tel: 01736 796559 **Fax:** 01736 796559
Email: stay@edgarshotel.co.uk
Website: www.edgarshotel.co.uk
Map ref: 1 SW54
Directions: 0.5m W of town centre on B3306, opposite Leach Pottery
Rooms: 7 en suite (2 fmly) (3 GF)
S £55-£85 **D** £72-£98
Notes: Wi-fi **Parking:** 7
Closed: Nov-Feb

Built in the 1920s by Edgar Skinner, a retired stockbroker who was instrumental in attracting the world-famous master potter Bernard Leach to St Ives, Edgar's is tucked away opposite the Leach Pottery and bordered by palms, trees and shrubs. With its on-site parking area for guests, Edgar's is convenient for touring beautiful West Cornwall and is a comfortable base from which to enjoy sections of the South West Coast Path or Tinners' Way. If the weather is kind, you can also enjoy arguably four of the world's best golden sandy beaches, which are just a 20-minute walk away. Edgar's has seven centrally heated, en suite guest rooms, all of which are non-smoking. Each is well-equipped, with facilities including hospitality trays and hairdryers. Resident owners David and Judith Tremelling have been welcoming returning guests to Edgar's for well over a decade. Freshly cooked-to-order breakfasts, served in the spacious breakfast room, include vegetarian options and are prepared from fine, locally sourced ingredients. A comfortable lounge where guests can unwind with a drink from the soft drinks honesty bar completes the picture.

Recommended in the area
Leach Pottery; Penlee House Gallery; Tate St Ives

Cumbria

Stockghyll Force waterfall near Ambleside

Hall Croft

★★★★ BED AND BREAKFAST

Address: Dufton, APPLEBY-IN-WESTMORLAND, CA16 6DB
Tel: 017683 52902
Email: hallcroft@phonecoop.coop
Map ref: 11 NY62
Directions: 3m N of Appleby. In Dufton by village green
Rooms: 3 (2 en suite) (1 pri facs)
S £36 **D** £62
Notes: Wi-fi **Parking:** 3
Closed: 24-26 Dec

Hall Croft is a large, detached, four-storey Victorian house in the Westmorland village of Dufton. Frei and Ray Walker have lovingly restored it, along with the substantial surrounding gardens, to offer bed and breakfast accommodation to those seeking high quality facilities in an idyllic, peaceful setting. There are three large guest rooms, two of which have en suite bathrooms, while the other has a large adjacent private bathroom. There's also a lovely guest dining room/lounge, which is full of period features. Breakfasts - which have picked up an AA Breakfast Award - are substantial, with an extensive choice, and include eggs from the resident hens. Guests are welcomed on arrival - and each afternoon - with home-made cake and tea or coffee, and packed lunches are also available. Dufton is a classic English village built around a beautiful green, right on the edge of the Pennines. Hall Croft is perfectly placed for walking the Pennine Way, and despite its quiet and seemingly remote location, it's only three miles north of Appleby and the A66, some 12 miles from the M6, and 30 minutes' from the Lake District. Hall Croft is 150 metres from the village pub, and there's a wide network of paths from Dufton for walkers to enjoy.

Recommended in the area

North Pennines (Area of Outstanding Natural Beauty); Northern Lake District; Appleby-in-Westmorland

Hazel Bank Country House

★★★★★ GUEST ACCOMMODATION

Address: Rosthwaite, BORROWDALE, Keswick, CA12 5XB
Tel: 017687 77248
Fax: 017687 77373
Email: info@hazelbankhotel.co.uk
Website: www.hazelbankcountryhouse.co.uk
Map ref: 10 NY21
Directions: From Keswick, follow B5289 towards Borrowdale, turn left after sign for Rosthwaite
Rooms: 8 en suite (2 GF) **S** £90-£96 **D** £180-£178
Notes: Wi-fi ⊗ ✗ under 10yrs
Parking: 8

From its elevated position in the picturesque Borrowdale Valley, Hazel Bank Country House boasts spectacular views across some of England's highest mountains. It's a truly stunning and peaceful setting, with four acres of beautiful grounds surrounding the house, complete with private woodland and a pretty stream. Hazel Bank was built from traditional Lakeland stone between 1840 and 1850 for Thomas Simpson and his family on their return from America, and fortunately the house has undergone very few changes since. Sir Hugh Walpole, the famous author, was a frequent visitor and used the setting in his *Rogue Herries Chronicles*. The house has eight individually designed en suite bedrooms, and a one-bedroom self-catering cottage, and is fully licensed, with a bar, lounge and restaurant. The restaurant looks out over the rear garden, where you may be lucky enough to spot red squirrels amongst the resident wildlife - it's no wonder guests come back here time after time. Plenty of walks can be started from the bottom of the garden, should you wish to go car-free during your stay.

Recommended in the area

Derwentwater boat trips; Castlerigg Stone Circle; The Cumberland Pencil Museum

The Cottage in the Wood

★★★★ ◉◉ 🍴 RESTAURANT WITH ROOMS

Address: Whinlatter Pass, BRAITHWAITE, CA12 5TW
Tel: 017687 78409
Email: relax@thecottageinthewood.co.uk
Website: www.thecottageinthewood.co.uk
Map ref: 10 NY22
Directions: M6 junct 40, A66 W. After Keswick exit for Braithwaite via Whinlatter Pass (B5292), establishment at top of pass
Rooms: 9 en suite (1 GF) **S** fr £90 **D** £110-£180
Notes: Wi-fi ⊗ 🐾 under 10yrs
Parking: 15
Closed: Jan

Located in the heart of Whinlatter, England's only mountain forest, between the bustling market towns of Keswick and Cockermouth, the Cottage in the Wood is a 17th-century coaching inn that has been lovingly restored. It offers guests a tranquil and relaxing stay and is perfectly situated for exploring the north-western fells of the Lakes. Sitting between Bassenthwaite, Derwentwater, Buttermere, Crummock Water and Loweswater, the area is ideal for walking, cycling, sailing, golf and a host of adventure activities. The Mountain View restaurant provides stunning views of the mighty Skiddaw mountain range and the forest, along with a menu rooted in seasonal, local produce, including wild foods foraged from the surrounding countryside. The result is creative and original dishes which, along with the equally high quality wines, have won the Mountain View several awards (including two AA Rosettes). The Cottage in the Wood offers a range of accommodation types: the delightful Cottage rooms are cosy and comfortable, the Mountain rooms offer breathtaking views of the surrounding countryside, Treetops, in the loft, provides a spectacular night sky, while the Garden Room is ideal for a special occasion.

Recommended in the area
Keswick; Cockermouth; walking, cycling, sailing, golf

Buttermere

Moss Grove Organic

★★★★★ GUEST ACCOMMODATION
Address: GRASMERE, Ambleside, LA22 9SW
Tel: 015394 35251
Fax: 015394 35306
Email: enquiries@mossgrove.com
Website: www.mossgrove.com
Map ref: 10 NY30
Directions: From S: M6 junct 36 onto A591 signed Keswick. From N: M6 junct 40 onto A591 signed Windermere
Rooms: 11 en suite (2 GF) **D** £114-£250
Notes: Wi-fi 🐾 under 14yrs **Parking:** 11
Closed: 24-25 Dec

Located in the centre of Grasmere, this impressive Victorian house has been refurbished using as many natural products as possible, with ongoing dedication to causing minimal environmental impact. The 11 stunning bedrooms are decorated with screen-printed wallpaper with natural inks, and natural clay paints, and feature hand-made beds and furniture constructed from reclaimed timber or other sustainable materials. All bedrooms have Bose home entertainment systems, flat-screen TVs, free Wi-fi, and spa baths and organic toiletries in the underfloor-heated en suite bathrooms. To make your stay extra special, you can pre-order some organic treats to be awaiting you in your room, including chocolates, wines, champagne and flowers. Guests are invited to enjoy the pretty and peaceful rear patio, complete with hot tub to relax in. When it comes to breakfast you certainly won't be disappointed. An extensive Mediterranean-style buffet breakfast is served in the large dining area in the residents' lounge, all made from organic ingredients, of course.

Recommended in the area
Grasmere Lake; Rydal Water; Dove Cottage & The Wordsworth Museum

The Edwardene

★★★★ GUEST ACCOMMODATION
Address: 26 Southey St, KESWICK, CA12 4EF
Tel: 017687 73586
Email: info@edwardenehotel.com
Website: www.edwardenehotel.com
Map ref: 10 NY22
Directions: M6 junct 40, A66 follow 1st sign to Keswick, right into Penrith Rd. Sharp left by war memorial into Southey St, 150mtrs on right
Rooms: 11 en suite (1 fmly) **S** fr £45 **D** £84–£92
Notes: Wi-fi ⊗
Parking: 2

A warm and friendly welcome awaits guests at The Edwardene, a beautiful Victorian Lakeland property in a peaceful location a short walk from Keswick's market place, theatre and lake. The Edwardene has 11 en suite bedrooms, all decorated to a very high standard with comfortable beds, solid-ash furniture, Sony flat-screen televisions, hairdryers and tea- and coffee-making facilities. The comfortable guest lounge is licensed, so you can sit back in front of the blazing fire and enjoy a relaxing drink after a hard day's exploring. Breakfast is a highlight of a stay here, with The Edwardene having picked up an AA Breakfast Award. If you go for the full English, expect locally smoked bacon, the finest Cumberland sausages and free-range eggs cooked to your liking.

Guests on vegetarian, vegan or coeliac diets are just as well catered for (given a little bit of advance notice). The Edwardene makes an excellent base from which to explore Keswick and the wider Lake District, with many stunning walks starting from the front door. From the gentle Castlerigg Stone Circle to the challenging summit of Skiddaw, there are walks around Keswick for all ages and abilities.

Recommended in the area

Derwentwater lake cruises; Cumberland Pencil Museum; Castlerigg Stone Circle

Ees Wyke Country House

★★★★★ ● ≘ GUEST HOUSE

Address: NEAR SAWREY, Ambleside, LA22 0JZ
Tel: 015394 36393
Email: mail@eeswyke.co.uk
Website: www.eeswyke.co.uk
Map ref: 6 SD39
Directions: On B5285 on W side of village
Rooms: 8 en suite (1 GF) **S** £56-£86 **D** £112-£138
Notes: ⊗ ⍾ under 12yrs
Parking: 12

Guests at this elegant Georgian country house, built in 1742, can enjoy the same views over Esthwaite Water and the surrounding countryside that once drew Beatrix Potter to the area. The famous children's author used Ees Wyke as a holiday home, later buying Hill Top, which is just a short walk away and is the home where she wrote many of her *Peter Rabbit* books (Hill Top is now owned by the National Trust and is well worth a visit). Ees Wyke Country House, perched on high ground near Sawrey, has stunning views from many of its bedrooms, the lounge and restaurant across the lake and the fells beyond, from Coniston Old Man to the Langdale Pikes, and the extensive woodland of Grizedale Forest. The thoughtfully equipped en suite bedrooms are supremely comfortable and all have been furnished to a high standard. The lavish Lakeland breakfasts are a real draw, as is the daily five-course dinner menu featuring plenty of local produce. There are excellent walks nearby to suit all abilities, from easy and relaxing strolls to more challenging fell walks.

Recommended in the area

Grizedale Forest; Coniston Old Man; Langdale Pikes; Hill Top (NT)

Brandelhow

★★★★ 🛏 GUEST HOUSE

Address: 1 Portland Place, PENRITH, CA11 7QN
Tel: 01768 864470
Email: enquiries@brandelhowguesthouse.co.uk
Website: www.brandelhowguesthouse.co.uk
Map ref: 11 NY53
Directions: In town centre on one-way system, left at town hall
Rooms: 5 (4 en suite) (1 pri facs) (2 fmly)
S £37.50 **D** £75
Notes: Wi-fi ⊗
Closed: 31 Dec & 1 Jan

Brandelhow Guest House is situated in the fine historic market town of Penrith, at the heart of the unspoilt Eden Valley on the north-eastern fringes of the Lake District. Surrounded by mountains, lakes, castles and a wealth of history, and located right on the Sea to Sea (C2C) cycling route, this luxurious bed and breakfast makes the ideal base for a holiday. Whether you're cycling, walking or touring by car, at Brandelhow you can be assured of a warm welcome, with hot drinks and home-made cakes offered upon arrival. The en suite bedrooms are traditionally furnished, spotlessly clean and comfortable. Breakfasts, served in the Cumbria-themed dining room overlooking the courtyard garden, are based on ingredients from some of the best Lakeland producers, and include a traditional full English as well as a range of alternatives; it's no wonder Brandelhow has picked up an AA Breakfast Award. Cream and high teas are available by prior arrangement, as are packed lunches. Brandelhow Guest House is conveniently located for exploring the Lakes, Hadrian's Wall and the Borders.

Recommended in the area

Hadrian's Wall; Aira Force (NT); Langwathby Ostrich Farm; Ullswater steamers

The Queen's Head

★★★★ INN

Address: Townhead, TROUTBECK,
Windermere, LA23 1PW
Tel: 015394 32174
Fax: 015394 31938
Email: reservations@queensheadtroutbeck.co.uk
Website: www.queensheadtroutbeck.co.uk
Map ref: 6 NY40 **Directions:** M6 junct 36 onto A591, past Windermere towards Ambleside. At mini-rdbt, right onto A592 for Ullswater, 3m on left
Rooms: 10 en suite 5 annexe en suite (1 fmly) (2 GF)
S £75-£90 **D** £120-£150
Notes: Wi-fi **Parking:** 65

Tucked away in the Troutbeck Valley near Windermere, this warm and welcoming place has everything you'll need to make the most of a relaxing break in the beautiful Lake District. The individually designed bedrooms - some with four-poster beds - have lots of character features along with a contemporary decor. All are sumptuously furnished, with rich fabrics and splashes of bright, bold colour, and each comes with a flat-screen TV, hot drinks facilities and a luxurious bathroom. The rooms are split between the original coaching inn and a wonderful old converted barn, and most have lovely views across the Troutbeck Valley and beyond. The first-class accommodation is by no means the only draw here: the food at the Queen's Head is worth checking in for alone. The extensive menu is founded upon locally sourced and home-made produce - think local duck eggs, home-made sausage of the day, and The Queen's Head's renowned pork scratchings and battered green bean chips. There's also a great selection of real ales to try.

Recommended in the area

Bowness on Windermere; Ullswater; Grasmere

Haverigg lighthouse, Millom

Applegarth Villa & JR's Restaurant

★★★★★ GUEST ACCOMMODATION
Address: College Rd, WINDERMERE, LA23 1BU
Tel: 015394 43206
Fax: 015394 46636
Email: info@lakesapplegarth.co.uk
Website: www.lakesapplegarth.co.uk
Map ref: 6 SD49
Directions: M6 junct 36, A591 towards Windermere. On entering town left after NatWest Bank into Elleray Rd. 1st right into College Rd, Applegarth on right
Rooms: 15 en suite **S** £62-£67 **D** £120-£206
Notes: Wi-fi ⊗ under 18yrs
Parking: 16

Applegarth Villa is a true gem - a magnificent five-star bed and breakfast along with an award-winning restaurant in Windermere, at the very heart of the Lake District. The accommodation is individually designed to the highest standard, with sumptuous fabrics and top quality furnishings all carefully chosen to complement each other and make your stay as comfortable and as memorable as possible. Wall mounted flat-screen TVs, radio alarms, i-Pod docks, Wi-fi, refreshment trays, bottled Lakeland water, bathrobes and power showers all come as standard, plus there are spa facilities nearby that Applegarth Villa guests can use at no extra charge. Only the best locally sourced produce is served in the restaurant, while the oak-panelled bar is a cosy place to relax and unwind in front of a roaring fire after enjoying a day out and about exploring the Lakes. Here you'll find one of the finest whisky selections in the area, along with a vast wine list and award-winning real ales. Equally, the summer terrace is the perfect outdoor space to dine in warmer weather whilst watching the sun set over the distant fells.

Recommended in the area

Blackwell (Arts & Crafts house); Windermere lake steamers; Wordsworth House (NT)

Cumbria

Fairfield House and Gardens

★★★★ GUEST HOUSE

Address: Brantfell Rd,
BOWNESS-ON-WINDERMERE LA23 3AE
Tel: 015394 46565 **Fax:** 015394 46564
Email: tonyandliz@the-fairfield.co.uk
Website: www.the-fairfield.co.uk
Map ref: 6 SD49
Directions: Into Bowness town centre, turn opposite St Martin's Church & sharp left by Spinnery restaurant, house 200yds on right
Rooms: 10 en suite (2 fmly) (3 GF)
S £60-£70 **D** £88-£160
Notes: Wi-fi under 10yrs **Parking:** 10

Situated close to Bowness Bay, this establishment is the perfect place to take a tranquil break. Owners Tony and Liz Blaney offer genuine hospitality and high standards of personal service at their 200-year-old home, which is set in half an acre of its own beautifully landscaped gardens. All rooms are en suite and there are twin as well as double rooms; the deluxe rooms feature spa baths. There are four-poster rooms too, one with a wet room and power shower. A roof-space penthouse (featured on TV), has a glass shower and spa bath as well as two TVs, DVD player and MP3 with surround-sound. Options are available for guests to have champagne or Belgian chocolates in their room on arrival and, for special occasions, to have rose petals scattered on the bed. Special facilities are available for visitors with restricted mobility. Breakfasts come in hearty or healthy versions, each made with the finest ingredients. There is free internet access via a public terminal, and Wi-fi is available.

Recommended in the area

Blackwell (The Arts & Crafts House); Windermere lake steamers; Wordsworth House (NT)

The Coppice

★★★★ 🛏 🍴 GUEST HOUSE

Address: Brook Rd, WINDERMERE, LA23 2ED
Tel: 015394 88501
Fax: 015394 42148
Email: chris@thecoppice.co.uk
Website: www.thecoppice.co.uk
Map ref: 6 SD49
Directions: 0.25m S of village centre on A5074
Rooms: 9 en suite (2 fmly) (1 GF)
Notes: Wi-fi
Parking: 10

This traditional Lakeland vicarage, built in local stone, retains all its character and charm. It sits in an elevated position between the villages of Windermere and Bowness, close to the lake, and is perfectly placed for touring, walking or sailing. Hosts Chris and Barbara promise a memorable experience and can provide extras like flowers, chilled champagne and handmade chocolates for your arrival. The bedrooms are all individually designed and have their own charm and character. Some come with spa baths, others with showers, while all have TVs with Freeview and DVD player, Wi-fi access, a mini decanter of sherry and refreshments tray. Excellent Lakeland breakfasts and dinners (available five evenings a week) are served in the light and airy dining room, while pre-dinner drinks can be taken in the comfortable lounge by the coal fire. Menus feature plenty of local and seasonal ingredients, such as local championship sausages, fell-bred beef, pork and lamb, and fish from Fleetwood. In the mornings expect homemade breads, marmalades and jams, award-winning local sausages and fine cured bacon. Vegetarians are catered for, while most special diets can be accommodated with prior notice. Guests can enjoy complimentary access to a nearby health club.

Recommended in the area

Hill Top (Beatrix Potter's home) (NT); Wordsworth's homes - Rydal Mount and Dove Cottage

The Willowsmere

★★★★ 🛏 GUEST HOUSE

Address: Ambleside Rd, WINDERMERE, LA23 1ES
Tel: 015394 43575
Fax: 015394 44962
Email: info@thewillowsmere.com
Website: www.thewillowsmere.com
Map ref: 6 SD49
Directions: On A591, 500yds on left after Windermere station, towards Ambleside
Rooms: 12 en suite (1 GF) **S** £40-£45 **D** £68-£90
Notes: Wi-fi ⊗ 🐾 under 12yrs
Parking: 15

Wonderful views of Lake Windermere are available only a few minutes' stroll from this luxuriously renovated gentleman's residence dating from 1850. The town centre and the railway station, too, are just an eight-minute walk away, and ample off-road parking is provided on site. Willowsmere is an imposing property, built from Lakeland stone, set in large, landscaped gardens which have won the titles 'Windermere in Bloom 2010, Best Hotel Garden', and 'Cumbria in Bloom 2010, Best Guest House Garden'. Guests can relax in the secluded gardens during fine weather or in either of the two lounges. The large, comfortable bedrooms are all en suite and include single, twin, double and four-poster rooms. Luxury pocket sprung beds and Egyptian cotton duvets ensure a sound night's sleep. A double ground floor room has wheelchair access and a bathroom with facilities for the disabled. No family rooms are available so only children of 12 years or older can be accommodated. English breakfasts, home cooked to order, are served at individual tables in the stylish dining room.

Recommended in the area

Brockhole Lake District Visitor Centre; Townend; The World of Beatrix Potter

Derbyshire

Ladybower Reservoir in the Peak District National Park

Yorkshire Bridge Inn

★★★★ INN

Address: Ashopton Rd, BAMFORD,
Hope Valley, S33 0AZ
Tel: 01433 651361 **Fax:** 01433 651361
Email: info@yorkshire-bridge.co.uk
Website: www.yorkshire-bridge.co.uk
Map ref: 7 SK28 **Directions:** From A57 between Sheffield & Glossop take A6013 to Bamford. Or from Sheffield take A625, then A6187, through Hathersage, right onto A6013 to Bamford
Rooms: 14 en suite (3 fmly) (4 GF)
S £60-£65 **D** £76-£120
Notes: Wi-fi **Parking:** 50

This popular inn in the village of Bamford gets its name from a 17th-century stone bridge on the ancient trade route from Derbyshire's Hope Valley across the moors to Yorkshire. These days the bridge and the inn sit within the confines of the Peak District National Park - Britain's oldest national park - close to the shores of the Ladybower Reservoir. Keen walkers can take their pick from a multitude of routes and trails right on the inn's doorstep, while the Yorkshire Bridge Inn is also ideally placed for visiting Chatsworth House, Castleton, Bakewell, Dovedale and many more places of interest in and around the Hope Valley and beyond. Under the stewardship of the Illingworth family for the last 15 years, the inn is renowned for its quality accommodation - with 14 comfortable, well-presented en suite rooms, including a four-poster - along with excellent home-cooked food using plenty of local produce, and welcoming hospitality. The Yorkshire Bridge Inn is the perfect place to enjoy a few days away from it all.

Recommended in the area

Ladybower Reservoir; Castleton Caves; Chatsworth House

Chevin Green Farm

★★★★ GUEST ACCOMMODATION
Address: Chevin Rd, BELPER, DE56 2UN
Tel: 01773 822328
Fax: 01773 822328
Email: davidrmarley@btinternet.com
Website: www.chevingreenfarm.org.uk
Map ref: 7 SK34
Directions: Exit A6 opposite Strutt Arms at Milford into Chevin Rd, 1.5m on left
Rooms: 5 en suite (1 fmly) (1 GF)
S £45-£70 **D** £70-£90
Notes: ⊗ ⚲ under 16yrs **Parking:** 5
Closed: Xmas & New Year

Nestling in beautiful Derbyshire countryside, yet highly accessible just a short drive from Belper, this peaceful B&B is a great place to relax and unwind. Chevin Green Farm, built around 200 years ago from traditional Derbyshire stone, has been lovingly restored and appointed to a high standard, whilst retaining its original features. The bedrooms - available as singles, twins, doubles and a family room - are individually styled and feature high quality furnishings, lots of thoughtful extra touches, and excellent bathrooms. Each room comes with tea- and coffee-making facilities and flat-screen digital TVs with Freeview. After a restful night's sleep, guests can take a seat at their own private dining table to enjoy a breakfast featuring ingredients sourced from some of Derbyshire's finest producers. Guests are also welcome to relax during their stay in the comfortable lounge or in the wonderful gardens, where the views across the Derwent Valley and beyond are simply stunning.

Recommended in the area

Peak District National Park; Alton Towers; Chatsworth

Derbyshire

Dannah Farm Country House

★★★★★ 🛏 GUEST ACCOMMODATION
Address: Bowmans Ln, Shottle, BELPER, DE56 2DR
Tel: 01773 550273 & 550630
Fax: 01773 550590
Email: slack@dannah.co.uk
Website: www.dannah.co.uk
Map ref: 7 SK34 **Directions:** A517 from Belper towards Ashbourne, 1.5m right into Shottle after Hanging Gate pub on right, over x-rds & right
Rooms: 8 en suite (1 fmly) (2 GF)
S £79-£95 **D** £150-£275
Notes: Wi-fi ⊗ **Parking:** 20
Closed: 24-26 Dec

Dannah, a Georgian farmhouse on a working farm on the Chatsworth Estate, is home to Joan and Martin Slack and their collection of pigs, hens, cats and a trio of good-natured English setters, who will be delighted to take you for a walk! Each bedroom and suite has its own individual character and is filled with a wealth of thoughtful extras. The rooms all look out onto green fields and rolling countryside, and some have private sitting rooms, four-poster beds and stunning bathrooms with spa baths big enough for two. The Studio and Granary suites even have private terraces with outdoor hot tubs. The Spa Cabin is a unique facility available to book by the day for exclusive use, complete with a huge outdoor hot tub, Finnish sauna and double steam shower. Breakfast at Dannah Farm is a true delight, served in relaxed and elegant surroundings. For all other meals, there are some excellent pubs and restaurants within easy reach. Situated in the heart of the Derbyshire Dales, there are endless wonderful things to see and do right on the doorstep. Footpaths criss-cross the surrounding countryside, making Dannah Farm an ideal base for walking enthusiasts.

Recommended in the area
Chatsworth; Dovedale; Alton Towers

Derbyshire 73

Buxton's Victorian Guest House

★★★★★ GUEST HOUSE
Address: 3A Broad Walk, BUXTON, SK17 6JE
Tel: 01298 78759
Fax: 01298 74732
Email: buxtonvictorian@btconnect.com
Website: www.buxtonvictorian.co.uk
Map ref: 6 SK07 **Directions:** Signs to Opera House, proceed to Old Hall Hotel, right onto Hartington Rd, car park 100yds on right
Rooms: 7 en suite (2 fmly) (1 GF)
S £50-£70 **D** £78-£100
Notes: Wi-fi ⊗ ⚹ under 4yrs **Parking:** 9
Closed: 22 Dec-12 Jan

Standing in a prime position on the pedestrianised Broad Walk overlooking the magnificent Pavilion Gardens, this delightfully furnished Grade II listed house was built in 1860 for the Duke of Devonshire. It has been extensively refurbished in recent years and offers high quality accommodation, along with its own private car park. The seven en suite bedrooms have individual themes and are well-equipped with flat-screen TVs, hairdryers, hospitality trays and luxury toiletries. Complimentary Wi-fi is available. The breakfasts - which have been recognised with an AA Breakfast Award - are prepared using locally sourced produce wherever possible, and all dietary requirements are catered for. The guest drawing room is spacious and well stocked with maps and guide books of the area to help you plan your days out. Buxton's Victorian Guest House is conveniently located in the heart of the historic spa town of Buxton, with the Opera House Theatre and a wide variety of restaurants and shops only a few minutes' walk away. Many of the Peak District's main attractions are also within a short drive.

Recommended in the area

Buxton Opera House; Poole's Cavern; Chatsworth House

Crich Tramway Museum

Roseleigh

★★★★ GUEST HOUSE

Address: 19 Broad Walk BUXTON SK17 6JR
Tel: 01298 24904
Fax: 01298 24904
Email: enquiries@roseleighhotel.co.uk
Website: www.roseleighhotel.co.uk
Map ref: 6 SK07 **Directions:** A6 to Morrisons rdbt, into Dale Rd, right at lights, 100yds left by Swan pub, down hill, right into Hartington Rd
Rooms: 14 (12 en suite) (2 pri facs) (1 GF)
S £40-£92 **D** £78-£92
Notes: Wi-fi ⊗ ⛔ under 6yrs **Parking:** 9
Closed: 16 Dec-16 Jan

Roseleigh is a comfortable and elegant Victorian property that benefits from a prime location overlooking Buxton's 23-acre Pavilion Gardens - the land on which it stands was once owned by the Duke of Devonshire. Built in 1871 and situated on the pedestrianised Broad Walk, it is just a five-minute walk from the heart of the town and benefits from its own car park. The quality furnishings and decor throughout highlight the house's many original features. Most of the sympathetically furnished bedrooms in this family-run establishment have smart en suite shower rooms; all have TV and tea- and coffee-making facilities, and several have good views over the Pavilion Gardens. The comfortable guest lounge, which overlooks the lake, is the place simply to relax, or you can plan the next day's itinerary by poring over the many books on the Peak District provided by your hosts, Gerard and Maggi. They are knowledgeable about the local area and are happy to advise on suitable pubs, restaurants and activities. The elegant dining room offers a range of breakfast choices, including vegetarian options, from a menu that makes use of local produce where possible. Free Wi-fi access.

Recommended in the area

Buxton Opera House; Chatsworth; Peak District National Park

Underleigh House

★★★★★ ≣ GUEST ACCOMMODATION

Address: Lose Hill Ln, HOPE, Hope Valley, S33 6AF
Tel: 01433 621372
Fax: 01433 621324
Email: info@underleighhouse.co.uk
Website: www.underleighhouse.co.uk
Map ref: 6 SK18
Directions: From village church on A6187 into Edale Rd, 1m left into Lose Hill Ln
Rooms: 5 en suite (2 GF) **S** £65-£85 **D** £85-£105
Notes: Wi-fi ⊁ under 12yrs
Parking: 6
Closed: Xmas, New Year & Jan

In the heart of the Peak District and surrounded by glorious scenery, Underleigh House is an award-winning barn and cottage conversion dating from 1873. Its Hope Valley location, at the foot of Lose Hill and overlooking the Noe Valley, is as tranquil as it is stunning and appeals particularly to walkers. For those more interested in Derbyshire's many stately homes and attractive towns and villages, it's only a short journey from here to Chatsworth, Haddon Hall, Lyme Hall and Hardwick Hall, not forgetting the charms of Castleton, Hathersage, Eyam, Tideswell, Bakewell and Buxton. The genuine hospitality, delightful en suite bedrooms - two with their own lounges - and memorable breakfasts (which have been awarded an AA Breakfast Award) all add to the Underleigh experience. The stone-flagged breakfast room, with its original beams and cosy atmosphere, is where home-made bread, porridge cooked on the Aga, muesli, compôtes and preserves, together with hot dishes made from locally sourced produce, are served at a communal table. Proprietor Vivienne Taylor, who runs Underleigh House with husband Philip, was a finalist in the AA's 'Friendliest Landlady' awards in 2009.

Recommended in the area

Castleton caverns; Chatsworth; Eyam

The Pines

★★★★ BED AND BREAKFAST

Address: 12 Eversleigh Rd, Darley Bridge,
MATLOCK, DE4 2JW
Tel: 01629 732646
Email: info@thepinesbandb.co.uk
Website: www.thepinesbandb.co.uk
Map ref: 7 SK35
Directions: From Bakewell or Matlock take A6 to Darley Dale. Turn at Whitworth Hotel onto B5057, pass Square & Compass pub & The 3 Stags Heads, The Pines on right
Rooms: 3 en suite **S** £40-£60 **D** £70-£80
Notes: Wi-fi **Parking:** 5

The Pines is situated on the edge of the Peak District National Park in the small village of Darley Bridge on the River Derwent. The house dates back to 1825 and is full of original features such as open fires and exposed beams. In recent years it has been fully refurbished to the highest standards, and offers three tastefully decorated en suite bedrooms with every modern comfort, including hot drinks facilities, complimentary bottled water, radio, TV, heated towel rail, hairdryer and free Wi-fi. Breakfast, featuring local and homemade produce, is served in the delightful breakfast hall or on the patio during the summer, and is the highlight of any stay. The Pines has a lovely front garden with a giant sequoia tree and walled drive, while behind the house wild deer can often be seen crossing to the woods. At The Pines everyone can expect an extremely warm welcome - and that extends to well-behaved dogs. The Pines has plenty of private parking and is ideally located for walking, fishing, cycling and touring the splendid Derbyshire countryside.

Recommended in the area

Chatsworth House; Haddon Hall; Peak District National Park; Bakewell; Buxton

Derbyshire

The Smithy

★★★★★ GUEST ACCOMMODATION
Address: NEWHAVEN, Biggin, SK17 0DT
Tel: 01298 84548
Email: lynnandgary@thesmithybedand
breakfast.co.uk
Website: www.thesmithybedandbreakfast.co.uk
Map ref: 6 SK16
Directions: 0.5m S of Newhaven on A515. Adjacent to Biggin Ln, private driveway opposite Ivy House
Rooms: 4 en suite (2 GF) **S** £40-£50 **D** £70-£90
Notes: Wi-fi ⊗ ⚞
Parking: 8

Lynn and Gary Jinks have restored this former 17th-century drovers' inn and blacksmith's shop to a high standard and today it offers top-quality accommodation with all modern comforts and a very personal service. The Smithy sits in four acres of land, with lovely views from the guest bedrooms in the converted barn - just across the cobbled courtyard - of the surrounding hills and fields. The four en suite rooms are well-decorated and a good size, and are equipped with TV, DVD player and refreshments. The old blacksmith's shop, complete with original forge, bellows, anvil and tools, is the atmospheric setting for breakfast. Take your pick from the selection of cereals, yoghurts, fresh and dried fruit on the buffet table, before tucking into a full English served with tea or coffee and toast and home-made preserves. Vegetarian and other dietary needs can be catered for. The comfortable lounge, with its beamed ceiling and mullioned windows overlooking the gardens and dew pond, is a lovely place to sit and relax with a pot of coffee or tea, particularly in winter when the log fire blazes. On warmer days the terrace and garden are there for guests to enjoy.

Recommended in the area
Chatsworth; Tissington and High Peak trails (within walking distance); Peak District National Park

Devon

Cliffs at the Valley of Rocks, Exmoor National Park

Greencott

★★★★ GUEST HOUSE

Address: Landscove, ASHBURTON, TQ13 7LZ
Tel: 01803 762649
Map ref: 2 SX76
Directions: 3m SE of Ashburton. Exit A38 at Peartree junct, Landscove signed on slip road, village green 2m on right, opposite village hall
Rooms: 2 en suite **S** £25 **D** £50
Notes: ⊗
Parking: 3
Closed: 25-26 Dec

A warm welcome awaits friends old and new at Greencott, a lovely house in the pretty village of Landscove near Ashburton. Greencott stands in a delightful garden with panoramic views across open countryside. Those same views can be enjoyed from the en suite bedrooms, which are attractively furnished and well equipped with tea- and coffee-making facilities. The house is centrally heated throughout. A TV, books, maps and information about the area are provided in the comfortable guests' sitting room, and a traditional English breakfast, including home-made bread, is served around the oak dining table. Landscove is a charming village, complete with a lovely church, a pub serving excellent food and a garden centre specialising in out-of-the-ordinary plants. There's plenty to do in the area, including a good selection of golf courses, riding, fishing, walking and sailing. There are also some excellent leisure and craft centres nearby, while Totnes, Dartington, Ashburton, Buckfast Abbey and the South Devon Steam Railway are just a 10-minute drive away. Exeter, Plymouth and the coast are only 40 minutes' drive from Greencott.

Recommended in the area

Dartington; Buckfast Abbey; riding, fishing and golf nearby

West Down

★★★★ FARMHOUSE

Address: Little Eastacombe, ATHERINGTON, Umberleigh, EX37 9HP
Tel: 01769 560551
Fax: 01769 560551
Email: info@westdown.co.uk
Website: www.westdown.co.uk
Map ref: 1 SS52
Directions: 0.5m from Atherington on B3227 to Torrington, turn right, 100yds on left
Rooms: 2 en suite 2 annexe en suite (2 GF)
S £43-£45 **D** £68-£76
Notes: Wi-fi ⊗ **Parking:** 8

A small, friendly farm guest house combining the utmost comfort with excellent service, West Down is a lovely place to stay. The house sits in 25 tranquil acres of gardens and grounds right on the edge of Exmoor, making it ideally situated for touring this beautiful part of North Devon. West Down is spacious and elegant, yet it still has a homely feel - the owners certainly do their best to put across the message to guests that nothing is too much trouble. There's a choice of rooms to relax in, including a spacious lounge with a large wood burner, which is always a favourite spot to curl up in with a good book when the weather isn't kind. The en suite bedrooms - some of which are on the ground floor - are large and well-equipped. West Down has won an AA Dinner Award every year since 1997, so you can be assured that the home-cooked four-course evening meals, using plenty of local produce, are worth staying in for, and that breakfast will be a real treat.

Recommended in the area

RHS Rosemoor Garden; Arlington Court; Clovelly; Lundy Island; Hartland Point

The Bark House

★★★★ GUEST ACCOMMODATION

Address: Oakfordbridge, BAMPTON, EX16 9HZ
Tel: 01398 351236
Website: www.thebarkhouse.co.uk
Map ref: 2 SS92
Directions: A361 to rdbt at Tiverton onto A396 for Dulverton, then onto Oakfordbridge. House on right
Rooms: 6 (5 en suite) (1 pri facs) (1 fmly)
S £54 **D** £80–£98
Parking: 6

The Bark House is set in the tree lined valley of the River Exe, a beautiful rural location within easy reach of Exmoor and the North Devon coast. The cottage has six bedrooms of different sizes, all well-equipped and tastefully decorated in a traditional style. There's also a comfortable and cosy lounge with an open fire on cooler days, plenty of books to borrow and information on the area. In the licensed restaurant proprietors Melanie and Martin use local suppliers wherever possible, with meat, milk and eggs coming from farms in the Bampton area. Menus are changed daily and everything is home-made, including the bread at dinner and the fruitcake served with tea in the afternoons. Bookings are essential in the evenings and for Sunday lunch. Melanie and Martin pride themselves on offering a warm welcome and are more than happy to suggest ideas for things to see and do in the area. The Bark House has ample parking (and always assistance with baggage), an orchard and a lovely garden for hot, sunny afternoons, part of which can be used to exercise pets.

Recommended in the area

Knightshayes Court; Exmoor National Park; North Devon coast

Pines at Eastleigh

★★★★ GUEST ACCOMMODATION

Address: The Pines, Eastleigh,
BIDEFORD, EX39 4PA
Tel: 01271 860561
Fax: 01271 861689
Email: pirrie@thepinesateastleigh.co.uk
Website: www.thepinesateastleigh.co.uk
Map ref: 1 SS42 **Directions:** A39 onto A386 signed East-the-Water. 1st left signed Eastleigh, 500yds next left, 1.5m to village, house on right
Rooms: 6 en suite (1 fmly) (4 GF)
S £55-£69 **D** £79-£89
Notes: Wi-fi under 9yrs **Parking:** 20

With a magnificent hilltop position overlooking the Torridge Estuary and Lundy Island, this Georgian country house, standing in seven acres, is perfect for a relaxing break. King-size beds, breakfasts by a log fire, a garden room bar with library and maps, and a warm welcome await guests. Breakfast is served in the drawing room where a log fire burns on cold and frosty mornings, and the view from the window stretches from Hartland Point to Lundy Island over the little white town of Bideford. Food is freshly prepared using home-produced and locally sourced ingredients: fruit from the garden, home-made yoghurt and prize-winning local meats. Special diets can be catered for on request. Ground floor rooms are available in the converted stables, with direct access to the gardens. There are also two lovely cottage suites, each with its own sitting room, fully-equipped galley kitchen, dining area and daily maid service. The Pines is a non-smoking establishment. Pets are welcome by arrangement.

Recommended in the area

Instow & Clovelly; cycling and walking the Tarka Trail; Hartland Heritage Coast

Hansard House

★★★★ GUEST ACCOMMODATION

Address: 3 Northview Rd,
BUDLEIGH SALTERTON, EX9 6BY
Tel: 01395 442773
Fax: 01395 442475
Email: enquiries@hansardhousehotel.co.uk
Website: www.hansardhousehotel.co.uk
Map ref: 2 SY08
Directions: 500yds W of town centre
Rooms: 12 en suite (1 fmly) (3 GF)
S £52-£57 **D** £89-£98
Notes: Wi-fi
Parking: 11

Hansard House is ideally situated in a quiet area of Budleigh Salterton, only five minutes' walk from the Jurassic Coast and the beautiful sandy beach. The en suite rooms are tastefully decorated and well-equipped with a TV, hospitality tray, hairdryer and free Wi-fi. Most rooms have views across the rooftops of the town to the hills beyond, while others look out over the surrounding tree lined gardens. The rooms on the first floor can be accessed by lift. Breakfasts are hearty and healthy, including a selection of stewed and fresh fruit, cereal, juices, toast, tea or coffee, as well as a traditional full English. Nearby is the renowned East Devon Golf Club, while also within easy reach are the coastal path, Woodbury Common and the River Otter with its bird sanctuary and hides. The area has something for everyone, from museums to botanical gardens and great walking, along with sporting activities such as horse-riding, croquet, bowls, tennis, cricket and soccer. Hansard House is only a few minutes' stroll from the town centre, which has several good restaurants. Budleigh Salterton also hosts annual music and literary festivals, which attract many well-known names.

Recommended in the area

Otter Estuary Bird Sanctuary; Bicton Park Botanical Gardens

Tor Cottage

★★★★★ GUEST ACCOMMODATION
Address: CHILLATON, PL16 0JE
Tel: 01822 860248
Fax: 01822 860126
Email: info@torcottage.co.uk
Website: www.torcottage.co.uk
Map ref: 1 SX48 **Directions:** A30 Lewdown exit through Chillaton towards Tavistock, 300yds after Post Office right signed 'Bridlepath No Public Vehicular Access' to end
Rooms: 1 en suite 3 annexe en suite (3 GF)
S £98 **D** £150-£155 **Notes:** Wi-fi ⊗ ✢ under 14yrs
Parking: 8 **Closed:** mid Dec-beg Feb

This romantic cottage offers tranquillity and seclusion in 28 acres of grounds. Nothing is too much trouble for Maureen Rowlatt, who has equipped the en suite rooms with everything you could wish for. Each one is individually designed, from the warmth and style of the Art Deco Room to the blue and cream elegance of The Craftsman's Room - both converted from an original craftsman's workshop. One room is in the cottage wing and the others are in converted barns - each has a private terrace/garden and a log fire. Laughing Waters, the garden suite, is nestled in its own private valley. Breakfast is an imaginative range of dishes, and can be taken in the conservatory-style dining room or on the terrace in fine weather. The gardens are a feature in their own right with many private corners, a stream and, in summer, a heated swimming pool. Woodlands cloaking the hillside behind the cottage are home to a variety of wildlife including badgers, pheasants and deer that enjoy the cover of the gorse, while buzzards and the occasional heron can be seen overhead. Special-priced autumn and spring breaks are available.

Recommended in the area
Dartmoor; The Eden Project; National Trust houses and gardens

Angélique Rooms

★★★★ ◎◎ RESTAURANT WITH ROOMS

Address: 51 Victoria Rd, DARTMOUTH, TQ6 9RT
Tel: 01803 839425
Fax: 01803 839505
Email: info@angeliquedartmouth.co.uk
Website: www.angeliquedartmouth.co.uk
Map ref: 2 SX85
Directions: In Dartmouth take one-way system, 1st left at NatWest Bank
Rooms: 6 en suite (2 fmly) **S** £85–£105 **D** £95–£125
Notes: Wi-fi ⊗
Closed: Jan

The Angélique Rooms offer stylish accommodation in the heart of Dartmouth's pretty town centre. The rooms, all individual in design, are beautifully furnished and offer the perfect, relaxing haven for you to retreat to after a day of exploring the beautiful South Hams region. All rooms are equipped with a plasma-screen TV, tea- and coffee-making facilities, Wi-fi and a mini-bar stocked with complimentary bottled water. Room sizes range from doubles and twins to the newly refurbished Britannia Suite, a fully equipped, ground-floor apartment, allowing guests the freedom of a self-contained flat without missing out on the comforts and service of a hotel, including a daily maid service. The Britannia Suite is particularly suitable for families looking for flexible accommodation, with parking, in the centre of Dartmouth. It's just a short stroll from the Angélique Rooms to the picturesque waterfront and the establishment's celebrated Angélique Restaurant, where breakfast, lunch and dinner are served. The restaurant, run by renowned chef Alan Murchison, boasts an open kitchen and stunning views over the Dart Estuary.

Recommended in the area

Dartmoor National Park; Dartmouth Castle; Bayards Cove Fort

Nonsuch House

★★★★★ 🛏 🍽 GUEST ACCOMMODATION

Address: Church Hill, Kingswear,
DARTMOUTH, TQ6 0BX
Tel: 01803 752829
Fax: 01803 752357
Email: enquiries@nonsuch-house.co.uk
Website: www.nonsuch-house.co.uk
Map ref: 2 SX85 **Directions:** A3022 onto A379 2m before Brixham. Fork left onto B3205. Left up Higher Contour Rd, down Ridley Hill, house on bend on left at top of Church Hill
Rooms: 4 en suite (2 GF) **S** £85-£125 **D** £110-£170
Notes: Wi-fi ⊗ 🐾 under 12yrs **Parking:** 4

Nonsuch sits on a south-facing hill in Kingswear with incomparable views over to Dartmouth and out to sea - making it a very special place to stay. Bedrooms are stylish and extremely comfortable, and the conservatory and terrace are great places to while away time watching the activity on the river whilst enjoying a cup of tea or coffee, or sipping a glass of chilled white wine. Breakfasts here - which have been recognised with an AA Breakfast Award - are a highlight, while dinner is of the same very high quality, with proprietor Kit Noble buying from local producers wherever possible, and some of the vegetables coming from Nonsuch House's own kitchen garden. There are endless possibilities for things you can do in the area, such as walking (the South West Coast Path is on the doorstep), boating, shopping, sailing, canoeing, fine dining, visiting National Trust properties, taking a train or ferry trip, wine tasting, or perhaps just sitting on the lovely sun terrace and doing nothing all day but reading a good book and admiring the view.

Recommended in the area
Dartmouth; Brixham; South West Coast Path

Widecombe in the Moor in Dartmoor National Park

Collingdale Guest House

★★★★ GUEST HOUSE
Address: 13 Larkstone Ter, ILFRACOMBE, EX34 9NU
Tel: 01271 863770
Email: stay@thecollingdale.co.uk
Website: www.thecollingdale.co.uk
Map ref: 1 SS54
Directions: Take A399 E through Ilfracombe, on left past B3230 turning
Rooms: 9 (8 en suite) (1 pri facs) (3 fmly)
S £44-£55 **D** £65-£85
Notes: Wi-fi ⊗ 🐾 under 8yrs
Closed: Nov-Feb

The Collingdale is an award-winning guest house in an attractive Victorian building in an enviable location directly on the South West Coastal Path at Ilfracombe. Splendid views across the harbour and magnificent cliff top scenery of Hillsborough Nature Reserve come as standard, and it's just a few minutes' walk to the historic harbour with its wide selection of restaurants, shops, cafés and galleries, and the ferry to Lundy Island. The nine bedrooms are well presented, with comfortable beds, flat-screen TVs and many thoughtful little extras. Six rooms boast fabulous sea views. There is a cosy well-stocked bar, while the guest lounge provides a pleasant and relaxed atmosphere to sit and read, play a board game or simply take in the splendid scenery. Freshly cooked breakfasts are served in the elegant dining room. There's a fantastic sun terrace where you can relax and enjoy a morning coffee or an aperitif whilst taking in the views across the harbour and the Welsh coast beyond.

Recommended in the area

Lundy Island; Tunnels Beaches; Chambercombe Manor; Exmoor National Park

Moor View House

★★★★★ ● GUEST ACCOMMODATION

Address: Vale Down, LYDFORD, EX20 4BB
Tel: 01822 820220
Fax: 01822 820220
Website: www.moorview.org.uk
Map ref: 1 SX58
Directions: 4m from Sourton A30/A386, signed Tavistock, NE of Lydford
Rooms: 4 en suite **S** £45-£50 **D** £70-£85
Notes: ⊗ ⚹ under 12yrs
Parking: 15
Closed: 23 Dec-2 Jan

Moor View House, which dates back to the 1860s, is so named because of its location on the lower western slopes of Dartmoor, just outside the National Trust village of Lydford. The house has been run as a B&B by David and Wendy Sharples for over two decades, and has been upgraded extensively over the years to provide accommodation of the highest order. The four en suite bedrooms come with tea- and coffee-making facilities, flat-screen TVs with Freeview, bathrobes and lots of other little extras. Evening meals are served in the large dining room, and have been recognised for their quality and emphasis on freshly prepared local ingredients with an AA Dinner Award. Guests have a choice of two sitting rooms, one of which leads to a large conservatory overlooking the garden. On colder days log fires blaze, while during the warmer weather the garden is a lovely spot to sit and enjoy a drink (the house is licensed). There's plenty to see and do within a short distance, including visiting the gorge and castle at Lydford, several National Trust properties, and walking on the moor. Moor View is also well placed for touring the Devon coasts and across into Cornwall.

Recommended in the area
Lydford Gorge: The Eden Project; Tavistock

Rock House

★★★★ GUEST ACCOMMODATION
Address: Manor Grounds, LYNMOUTH, EX35 6EN
Tel: 01598 753508
Fax: 0800 7566964
Email: enquiries@rock-house.co.uk
Website: www.rock-house.co.uk
Map ref: 2 SS74 **Directions:** From A39, at foot of Countisbury Hill right into drive, pass Manor Green (play area) to Rock House
Rooms: 8 en suite (1 GF)
S £45 **D** £99-£119
Notes: Wi-fi **Parking:** 8
Closed: 24-25 Dec

The location of 18th-century Rock House is quite magical, standing alone at the entrance to the harbour in the pretty town of Lynmouth. As you might expect, the views from here - of the comings and goings of boats in the harbour and further out to sea - are simply stunning. The bedrooms, some with four-poster beds, are well appointed and furnished to a high standard, all with en suite facilities, TV/DVD, Wi-fi, hairdryers, alarm clocks, and tea- and coffee-making facilities. They all boast superb views of the Lyn Valley, the river or the sea. As its name suggests, The Harbourside Restaurant overlooks Lynmouth Harbour, providing fabulous views whilst you dine. A choice of menus is also offered for lunches and evening meals in the spacious Garden Restaurant adjoining the fully licensed bar. The large, beautifully maintained gardens are a popular spot for cream teas throughout the year. Rock House offers easy access to Exmoor National Park and the South West Coast Path. Whether you're touring on foot or by car, or a bit of both, it's the perfect base for exploring the beautiful coast of North Devon.

Recommended in the area

Combe Martin Wildlife & Dinosaur Park; Lyn & Exmoor Museum; Arlington Court

Victoria Lodge

★★★★★ GUEST ACCOMMODATION

Address: 30-31 Lee Rd, LYNTON, EX35 6BS
Tel: 01598 753203
Email: info@victorialodge.co.uk
Website: www.victorialodge.co.uk
Map ref: 2 SS74
Directions: Off A39 in village centre opposite Post Office
Rooms: 8 en suite **S** £60-£119 **D** £70-£140
Notes: Wi-fi ⊗ ⚑ under 11yrs
Parking: 6
Closed: Nov-23 Mar

Victoria Lodge is a large, elegant villa, built in the 1880s and conveniently located in the heart of the village of Lynton, a short stroll from a good range of restaurants. Full of character and original features, the house offers luxurious accommodation with quality furnishings and thoughtful extras. The bedrooms are named after Queen Victoria's daughters and daughters-in-law, and reflect the style of the period. Each is individually decorated in rich colours and features coronets, half-testers and four-poster beds. Guests can relax in the gardens, sitting out on the colourful front patio or the pleasant south-facing terrace at the rear of the house. Inside, there are two guest lounges with bay windows, comfortable sofas, and plenty of books, magazines and board games to play. Free Wi-fi is available throughout. An exceptional choice is offered at breakfast, which is served by friendly staff in the sumptuously decorated dining room with its period fireplace and over-mantle. Start with toast and homemade preserves, before moving on to pancakes with maple syrup, eggs Benedict, or 'the full Exmoor works' with egg, sausage, bacon, tomato, mushrooms, hash brown and the Devon delicacy of hog's pudding. Vegetarian and gluten-free options are also offered.

Recommended in the area

Exmoor National Park; Valley of the Rocks; the Tarka Trail

Merritt House B&B

★★★★ GUEST ACCOMMODATION

Address: 7 Queens Rd, PAIGNTON, TQ4 6AT
Tel: 01803 528959
Email: bookings@merritthouse.co.uk
Website: http://merritthouse.co.uk
Map ref: 2 SX86
Directions: From Paignton seafront, turn right onto Torbay Rd, then 1st left onto Queens Rd, house on right
Rooms: 7 en suite (3 GF) **S** £27-£34 **D** £54-£72
Notes: Wi-fi ✗ under 14yrs
Parking: 4
Closed: 20 Dec-7 Jan

Just a five-minute stroll from the seafront and town centre, this elegant Victorian townhouse is ideally situated to make the most of the traditional seaside resort of Paignton and neighbouring Torquay. Merritt House offers a warm and friendly welcome, along with first-class accommodation and superb breakfasts, which have been recognised for their high quality and extensive choice with the AA Breakfast Award. The en suite bedrooms - including one with a king-size four-poster bed and two with super-king-size beds - are split between the ground and first floors, and are light, airy and well appointed. Each room is individually designed and furnished in a period style in keeping with the age of the house, which was built in the 1880s. Free Wi-fi is available in the rooms, and there's also a computer for guests to use on the ground floor. Merritt House is in a quiet residential area, only five minutes' level walk to Paignton town centre - where you'll find many good restaurants and pubs - as well as the seafront, and the bus and rail stations.

Recommended in the area

Paignton Zoo and Living Coasts; Paignton and Dartmouth Steam Railway; Oldway Mansion

Devon

Strete Barton House

★★★★ GUEST HOUSE

Address: Totnes Rd, STRETE, Dartmouth, TQ6 0RK
Tel: 01803 770364
Fax: 01803 771182
Email: info@stretebarton.co.uk
Website: www.stretebarton.co.uk
Map ref: 2 SX84
Directions: Off A379 coastal road into village, just below church
Rooms: 5 (4 en suite) (1 pri facs) 1 annexe en suite
D £100-£150
Notes: Wi-fi ♥ under 8yrs
Parking: 4

Strete Barton House is a 16th century manor house in extensive grounds in the picturesque village of Strete, near Dartmouth in the South Hams area of Devon. The house enjoys panoramic sea views across Start Bay from Start Point lighthouse to the mouth of the River Dart, and is just 200 yards from the South West Coast Path. Blackpool Sands and Slapton Sands are only a mile away. The contemporary interior offers spacious double bedrooms with king-size beds (one with a super-king, four poster) and twin-bedded rooms. All bedrooms feature luxurious pocket-sprung mattresses, Egyptian cotton sheets and feather down pillows, fluffy towels, wall mounted flat-screen TV with DVD/CD player, Wi-fi access, extensive beverage tray, mineral water and luxury toiletries. There's also a luxurious cottage suite which has its own living room with an inglenook fireplace and log-burning stove. Breakfast is served in the dining room overlooking the garden and includes seasonal fruit, fresh homemade fruit salad, poached fruit and local farm yoghurts as well as a full English using local ingredients. On arrival guests are offered homemade cake and tea or coffee, either in the drawing room with its comfortable sofas and open fireplace, or on the terrace overlooking the sea.

Recommended in the area

Greenway (NT); Blackpool Sands; South West Coast Path

Thomas Luny House

★★★★★ GUEST ACCOMMODATION

Address: Teign St, TEIGNMOUTH, TQ14 8EG
Tel: 01626 772976
Email: alisonandjohn@thomas-luny-house.co.uk
Website: www.thomas-luny-house.co.uk
Map ref: 2 SX97
Directions: A381 to Teignmouth, at 3rd lights right to quay, 50yds left into Teign St, after 60yds right through white archway
Rooms: 4 en suite **S** £64-£75 **D** £80-£102
Notes: Wi-fi ⊗ ⛔ under 12yrs
Parking: 8
Closed: open all year

In Teignmouth's heyday, when the town was highly fashionable and favoured by several of Nelson's admirals and captains, Thomas Luny, the renowned marine artist, built his house here. The house is now a delightful bed and breakfast run by Alison and John Allan (who have actually lived here for over 23 years). Sitting within walled gardens, it is a haven of tranquillity yet within easy walking distance of the seafront, the river, beach and several excellent restaurants. The four en suite bedrooms are elegantly furnished, and two have views of the River Teign. In the morning you can look forward to a superb, freshly cooked full English breakfast, including homemade bread and conserves. Afternoon tea with homemade cake can be taken in the garden during the summer months, or in the drawing room in front of a blazing log fire in winter. For those who need to keep in touch, free Wi-fi is available, and there is ample secure parking for residents. Arrangements can be made to pick up guests arriving by train at Teignmouth Station.

Recommended in the area

Tuckers Maltings; Powderham Castle; Cockington Village

The Cary Arms

★★★★★ INN

Address: Babbacombe Beach, TORQUAY, TQ1 3LX
Tel: 01803 327110
Fax: 01803 323221
Email: enquiries@caryarms.co.uk
Website: www.caryarms.co.uk
Map ref: 2 SX96 **Directions:** A380 at Ashcombe Cross onto B3192 to Teignmouth. Right at lights to Torquay on A379, left at lights to Babbacombe. Left into Babbacombe Downs Rd, left into Beach Rd
Rooms: 8 en suite (1 fmly) (3 GF)
S £105-£210 **D** £155-£260
Notes: Wi-fi **Parking:** 15

Known as 'the inn on the beach', The Cary Arms exudes charm, fun and good English pub values along with all the style, comfort and luxury of a top-class boutique hotel. The kitchen serves up the very best of gastropub food (complemented by a great selection of real ales), so you can indulge during your stay in hearty breakfasts, long lunches and lazy suppers. Sheltering in its own unsung part of the south Devon coast, The Cary Arms is a place for all seasons: whether it's blustery and wild, or sunny and warm, a stay at The Cary Arms is romantic, surprising, and full of simple pleasures and seaside fun. It's also a place for all ages and all-comers: the young are welcomed with their very own fishing net and there are plenty of activities to keep them occupied, the adults are invited to relax with sundowners on the terraces, while dogs get their own beds and bowls in the rooms. Created by the de Savary family, The Cary Arms is the perfect luxury inn to enjoy a slice of chic beach-side living.

Recommended in the area

Babbacombe beaches; South West Coast Path; Living Coasts

Dorset

Dorset

Druid House

★★★★★ GUEST ACCOMMODATION
Address: 26 Sopers Ln, CHRISTCHURCH, BH23 1JE
Tel: 01202 485615
Fax: 01202 473484
Email: reservations@druid-house.co.uk
Website: www.druid-house.co.uk
Map ref: 3 SZ19
Directions: From A35 exit at Christchurch main rdbt into Sopers Ln, establishment on left
Rooms: 8 en suite (3 fmly) (4 GF)
S £35-£60 **D** £70-£96
Notes: ⊗
Parking: 8

Overlooking a tranquil park, this lovely family-run guest accommodation is just a short stroll from the high street with its many excellent restaurants, as well as just a stone's throw away from Christchurch Priory and the quay. Bedrooms are stylish and elegantly furnished with comfortable beds, crisp cotton sheets, thick, sumptuous bathrobes and luxury toiletries. You will also find tea- and coffee-making facilities, flat-screen TV with Freeview, DVD player, iPod docking station, direct-dial telephone and free Wi-fi. Some rooms have balconies while others on the ground floor have a private patio, and larger rooms have their own lounge area. There is a welcoming garden with tables and chairs for warmer days, a conservatory to relax in, and a licensed bar and lounge where you can enjoy a drink before going out for a meal or to the theatre. An excellent breakfast is freshly prepared to order from a wide selection of locally sourced produce, and served in a relaxed and restful atmosphere. Private family events can be catered for.

Recommended in the area

Christchurch Priory; New Forest National Park; Bournemouth beaches

Grosvenor Lodge

★★★★ GUEST HOUSE
Address: 53 Stour Rd, CHRISTCHURCH, BH23 1LN
Tel: 01202 499008
Fax: 01202 486041
Email: bookings@grosvenorlodge.co.uk
Website: www.grosvenorlodge.co.uk
Map ref: 3 SZ19
Directions: A35 from Christchurch to Bournemouth, at 1st lights left into Stour Rd. Lodge on right
Rooms: 8 en suite (4 fmly) (1 GF)
S fr £30 **D** fr £50
Notes: Wi-fi ⊗ **Parking:** 10

Grosvenor Lodge Guest House is a warm and welcoming place where guests are encouraged to relax and be themselves. Close to the station, airport and beaches, and open throughout the year, it makes a great base for those wanting a relaxing break or on business in Christchurch or Bournemouth. Owner Yas and her team do their utmost to offer the highest standards of hospitality. Big, hearty breakfasts are served early or late to suit you, and can be brought to your room if required; packed lunches are crammed with goodies; the decor is soothing; and the eight recently upgraded rooms are spotlessly clean and come with en suite shower-rooms, flat-screen TVs and free Wi-fi. There are ground floor and air-conditioned rooms available. Grosvenor Lodge is a short distance away from the River Stour and River Avon, as well as Christchurch Harbour and the open sea, making it the ideal place to stay for surfers and anglers. The guest house has a safe storage facility for wet watersports gear, angling equipment and bikes.

Recommended in the area

Christchurch Priory; Mudeford; New Forest National Park

The Acorn Inn

★★★★ ⚜ INN

Address: EVERSHOT, DT2 0JW
Tel: 01935 83228
Fax: 01935 83707
Email: stay@acorn-inn.co.uk
Website: www.acorn-inn.co.uk
Map ref: 2 ST50
Directions: From A37 between Yeovil & Dorchester, follow Evershot & Holywell signs, 0.5m to inn
Rooms: 10 en suite (2 fmly) **S** £79-£149 **D** £99-£194
Notes: Wi-fi
Parking: 40

This 16th-century coaching inn was immortalised as the Sow and Acorn in Thomas Hardy's *Tess of the D'Urbervilles*. It stands at the heart of the village of Evershot, in an Area of Outstanding Natural Beauty, with walking, fishing, shooting and riding all nearby. Inside are two oak-panelled bars - one flagstoned, one tiled - with logs blazing in carved hamstone fireplaces, and a cosy restaurant. There's also a skittle alley in what was once the stables, and it's rumoured that the residents' sitting room was once used by Hanging Judge Jeffreys as a court room. The en suite bedrooms are all individually styled, and each named after a character from Hardy's novel - several feature interesting four-poster beds. All of the rooms, including two family rooms, have a TV, free Wi-fi, a beverage tray and hairdryers. Irons are available on request. Fresh, local produce features on the varied and interesting menu, with most of the food sourced from within a 15-mile radius, including local fish and game, and bolstered by blackboard specials. Bar snacks and lighter meals are also available, accompanied by a selection of real ales and a comprehensive wine list. Plenty of parking spaces are available.

Recommended in the area

Evershot village; Forde Abbey; Lyme Regis

Farnham Farmhouse

★★★★ GUEST ACCOMMODATION
Address: FARNHAM, Blandford Forum, DT11 8DG
Tel: 01725 516254
Fax: 01725 516306
Email: info@farnhamfarmhouse.co.uk
Website: www.farnhamfarmhouse.co.uk
Map ref: 2 ST91
Directions: Off A354 Thickthorn x-rds into Farnham, continue NW from village centre T-junct, 1m bear right at sign
Rooms: 3 en suite **S** £70-£80 **D** £90-£100
Notes: ⊗ **Parking:** 7
Closed: 25-26 Dec

Farnham Farmhouse, deep within Thomas Hardy country and with magnificent rural views, dates back to the 1880s. It retains many of its period features, such as flagstone floors and open fires, and has three comfortable and traditionally furnished en suite bedrooms, all with flat-screen TVs and extensive views of the countryside. There's a lovely one-acre garden where you'll find the added luxuries of a heated outdoor pool and the Sarpenela Natural Therapy Centre with its range of therapeutic treatments. Farnham Farmhouse sits in a tranquil spot, right in the heart of the rolling slopes of the Cranborne Chase - an Area of Outstanding Natural Beauty. Guests are welcome to explore the 350-acre working farm, part of a private estate owned by the descendants of General Pitt-Rivers, a prominent landowner and archaeologist in the 1800s. With so many lovely walks to do right on the doorstep, you'll need a hearty breakfast to set you up for the day, and that's what you'll get - lashings of hot tea and coffee, a choice of starters from the buffet in the attractive dining room, followed by a traditional English or vegetarian breakfast served hot from the Aga, and featuring lots of local produce.

Recommended in the area

Cranborne Chase; Kingston Lacey (NT); Larmer tree Gardens

Longpuddle

★★★★ BED AND BREAKFAST

Address: 4 High St, PIDDLEHINTON, DT2 7TD
Tel: 01300 348532
Email: ann@longpuddle.co.uk
Website: www.longpuddle.co.uk
Map ref: 2 SY79
Directions: From Dorchester (A35) take B3143, after entering village 1st thatched house on left after village cross
Rooms: 2 annexe en suite (2 fmly)
S £50-£60 **D** £80-£90
Notes: Wi-fi
Parking: 3

Set in the Piddle Valley, midway between the abbey town of Sherborne and the county town of Dorchester, Longpuddle is well placed for exploring Thomas Hardy's Dorset and the Jurassic Coast. The 400-year-old thatched cottage, originally a farmhouse, overlooks the embryo river Piddle which runs through the garden and paddocks. There are two spacious, tastefully decorated rooms - one double and one twin - ideal for an extended stay. Both are en suite and come with TV, radio and hairdryer. A third bed can be made available. Breakfasts are cooked freshly to order by the proprietor using quality local produce. Guests are invited to relax in the large, comfortable lounge, complete with TV, log fire in winter, and views over the garden and paddocks. The name 'Longpuddle' comes from Thomas Hardy, who used it to refer collectively to the villages of the Piddle Valley. There are several excellent pubs in the valley where you can enjoy good food prepared from local produce, and there's plenty to see and do. The many bridleways offer a chance to spot local wildlife, and organised badger watching is available. The delightful village of Cerne Abbas, with its famous Giant carved into the hillside, is just a short drive away.

Recommended in the area

Cerne Abbas Giant; Maiden Castle near Dorchester; Sherborne

The Piddle Inn

★★★★ INN

Address: PIDDLETRENTHIDE, Dorchester, DT2 7QF
Tel: 01300 348468
Fax: 01300 348102
Email: piddleinn@aol.com
Website: www.piddleinn.co.uk
Map ref: 2 SY79
Directions: 7m N of Dorchester on B3143 in middle of Piddletrenthide
Rooms: 3 en suite (1 fmly)
S fr £55 **D** fr £75
Notes: Wi-fi
Parking: 15

The Piddle Inn is a traditional village free-house in the heart of Thomas Hardy walking country. Surrounded by rolling Dorset downland in the unspoilt Piddle Valley, and only half-an-hour drive from the Jurassic Coast, it's a delightful place to stay. The inn, which is family-owned and run, dates from the 1760s and takes its name from the river flowing through the beer garden (right past the sunny patio). The Piddle Inn offers three en suite rooms with lovely views over the river and surrounding countryside. The rooms are fully-equipped with flat-screen TVs and DVD players, tea- and coffee-making facilities, direct-dial telephones, clock-radios, electric safes and free Wi-fi, all combining to make your stay as enjoyable as possible. The team at The Piddle Inn pride themselves on using the freshest locally sourced and seasonal produce they can get their hands on, which is evidenced by the quarterly change to the menu. Meals - including breakfast - are served in the bright, open-plan bar, which is popular with the locals and has a friendly, homely atmosphere.

Recommended in the area

Dorchester; Jurassic Coast; Salisbury Cathedral

Cliff lift, Bournemouth

Offley Bed & Breakfast

★★★★ GUEST ACCOMMODATION
Address: Looke Ln, PUNCKNOWLE,
Dorchester, DT2 9BD
Tel: 01308 897044 & 07792 624977
Map ref: 2 SY58
Directions: Off B3157 into village centre, left after Crown Inn into Looke Ln, 2nd house on right
Rooms: 3 (2 en suite) (1 pri facs) **S** £45 **T** £60 **D** £70
Parking: 3

Magnificent valley views are one of the many highlights of a stay at this delightful bed and breakfast. The house is furnished with many period pieces, giving it a warm and homely feel which is completed by roaring log fires in winter and homemade cake and tea served on arrival by your friendly host, Sue Collier. The bedrooms are well equipped with TVs, hairdryers and tea- and coffee-making facilities, along with fresh fruit and flowers, and there's a garden and patio for guests to use in the warmer months. Breakfast is a real treat, featuring lots of homemade and local produce. Offley Bed and Breakfast is in the heart of some great walking country, as well as being within easy reach of the historic towns of Dorchester and Bridport, with its weekly street markets and brass band. Also a short drive away are the swannery at Abbotsbury and the magnificent Jurassic Coast with its many attractions, including Chesil Beach and Lyme Bay. You won't be short of good eating places during your stay, with local favourites including the renowned Hive Beach Cafe at Burton Bradstock and - a bit closer to home - The Crown Inn in Puncknowle and the White Horse Inn just a stone's throw away across the fields in Litton Cheney.

Recommended in the area

South West Coast Path; Horse riding and golf; Abbotsbury Swannery

Avalon Townhouse

★★★★ BED AND BREAKFAST
Address: South St, SHERBORNE, DT9 3LZ
Tel: 01935 814748
Email: enquiries@avalontownhouse.co.uk
Website: www.avalontownhouse.co.uk
Map ref: 2 ST61
Directions: A30 from Shaftesbury, towards Sherborne town centre, left into South St
Rooms: 3 en suite
S £70-£80 **D** £80-£90
Notes: Wi-fi ⊗ ⚹ under 18yrs

Avalon is an elegant Edwardian townhouse at the centre of the historic monastic town of Sherborne. The building, recently refurbished to a high standard, retains many original features, such as the open fire in the lounge, while the small garden has been redesigned to create a feeling of space. There are three double guest bedrooms, all en suite, which are spacious, attractively furnished and supremely comfortable. Each room comes with flat-screen TV with Freeview, free Wi-fi, tea- and coffee-making facilities, power shower and luxury toiletries. Breakfast is cooked to order, with ingredients sourced from selected local suppliers, and served around a magnificent oak table in the spacious farmhouse-style kitchen. Avalon is only a few minutes' walk away from the train station, which is on the London to Exeter line, and while some limited private parking is available, a public car park can be found just around the corner. Avalon is open throughout the Christmas and New Year period.

Recommended in the area
Sherborne Abbey; Sherborne Castle; Jerram Gallery

The Kings Arms

★★★★★ 🍴 INN

Address: Charlton Horethorne,
SHERBORNE, DT9 4NL
Tel: 01963 220281
Fax: 01963 220496
Email: admin@thekingsarms.co.uk
Website: www.thekingsarms.co.uk
Map ref: 2 ST61
Directions: From A303 follow signs for Templecombe & Sherborne onto B3145 to Charlton Horethorne
Rooms: 10 en suite (1 fmly) **D** £110-£125
Notes: Wi-fi **Parking:** 30

Situated in the heart of the pretty village of Charlton Horethorne, the Kings Arms has benefited from a total refurbishment, resulting in impressive standards throughout. Behind the imposing Edwardian façade, the atmosphere remains that of a traditional English country pub, but with all modern facilities and conveniences. Indeed, the experienced owners have created something for everyone with a convivial bar, snug and choice of dining environments, including the garden terrace with lovely countryside views. There's also a croquet lawn beside the terrace. All of the bedrooms possess individuality, quality and style, with marble bathrooms, robes and powerful showers, as well as Wi-fi and flat-screen TVs and DVD players. Some of the rooms are in the newly-built part of the pub, while others are found in the older part of the building. Three have lift as well as stair access, and one room is specially adapted for wheelchair users. The food, which has won an AA Dinner Award, is taken seriously here, with assured cooking from a menu majoring on quality local produce. Much is cooked and prepared on the premises - from the fresh-baked bread to the home-made ice cream and pasta.

Recommended in the area

Fleet Air Arm Museum; Sherborne Old Castle; Haynes International Motor Museum; Stourhead (NT)

Munden House

★★★★★ GUEST ACCOMMODATION

Address: Munden Ln, Alweston,
SHERBORNE, DT9 5HU
Tel: 01963 23150
Email: stay@mundenhouse.co.uk
Website: www.mundenhouse.co.uk
Map ref: 2 ST61
Directions: A352 from Sherborne, left onto A3030 to Alweston, pass village shop on right, 250yds on left at Oxfords Bakery sign
Rooms: 4 en suite 3 annexe en suite (3 fmly) (4 GF)
S £70-£95 **D** £80-£130
Notes: Wi-fi **Parking:** 14

Munden House was originally a collection of old farm cottages dating back more than 300 years. With its many period features restored and maintained, it is these days a beautiful, peaceful and well-equipped haven less than three miles from the historic market town of Sherborne. There are four delightful en suite bedrooms, all individually furnished with comfortable king-size beds and crisp Egyptian cotton linen. The three self-contained cottages offer more flexible and spacious accommodation with fully-equipped kitchenettes. There's no need to stray beyond the front door to enjoy some excellent cuisine. Home-cooked breakfasts and dinners are served in the light, airy dining room with outstanding views over the large garden to the Blackmore Vale. The guest sitting room with its lofty beamed ceiling, original limestone walls and enormous old fireplace is the perfect place to unwind over a glass of wine. In the heart of Thomas Hardy country, Munden House is the ideal base from which to explore Dorset, or to rest overnight on journeys to or from the West Country. Being so close to Sherborne, Munden House is also well situated for those on business in the area or visiting Sherborne's schools and its many attractions.

Recommended in the area
Sherborne; Dorset heritage coastline; Thomas Hardy country

A Great Escape Guest House

★★★★ GUEST ACCOMMODATION
Address: 6 Argyle Rd, SWANAGE, BH19 1HZ
Tel: 01929 475853 & 07867 508724
Email: stay@agreatescapeguesthouse.co.uk
Website: www.agreatescapeguesthouse.co.uk
Map ref: 3 SZ07
Rooms: 5 (4 en suite) (1 pri facs) (1 fmly) (1 GF)
S £65-£85 **D** £80-£98
Notes: Wi-fi ⊗ ⚙ under 3yrs

The aptly named A Great Escape Guest House is set in a 19th century townhouse in the heart of Swanage, and offers a warm, friendly welcome and high quality bed and breakfast accommodation. The guest house is just a short walk from the beach and pier and the famous Swanage Steam Railway, as well as conveniently placed for all the sights of the Isle of Purbeck. There are five bedrooms to choose from - including family rooms, super-kings, doubles and twins - with en suite bathrooms, flat-screen televisions with Freeview, free Wi-fi, totally silent fridges stocked with fresh milk and filtered water, hairdryers, safes, iPhone/iPod docks, clock radios and tea- and coffee-making facilities. Some rooms have stunning views across to the Purbeck Hills. After a restful night's sleep, head to the lovely breakfast room for a full English prepared from locally sourced produce. Your friendly hosts, Sue and Eric Searle, will happily cater for special diets on request.

Recommended in the area
Swanage Steam Railway; Corfe Castle (NT); Monkey World

Les Bouviers Restaurant with Rooms

★★★★★ ◎◎ ☒ RESTAURANT WITH ROOMS
Address: Arrowsmith Rd, Canford Magna,
WIMBORNE MINSTER, BH21 3BD
Tel: 01202 889555 **Fax:** 01202 639428
Email: info@lesbouviers.co.uk or info@lb-bistro.co.uk
Website: www.lesbouviers.co.uk or www.lb-bistro.co.uk
Map ref: 2 SZ09 **Directions:** A31 onto A349. In 0.6m turn left. In approx 1m right into Arrowsmith Rd. Establishment approx 100yds on right
Rooms: 6 en suite (4 fmly) **S** £88-£183 **D** £94-£215
Notes: Wi-fi **Parking:** 50

Chef-patron James Coward and his wife Kate have converted this large detached house into a family-run restaurant with rooms. Ideally located in over five acres of peaceful, landscaped grounds, Les Bouviers gives the feeling of being deep in the country, yet it's close to Wimborne, Poole and Bournemouth. Every room overlooks the landscaped grounds, and each bedroom has been individually designed with many luxuries and home comforts provided, such as Vi-Spring beds, air baths and steam showers in some rooms, coffee machines and Wi-fi. James has won many awards for his culinary skills, and the fine cuisine here, accompanied by wines from an extensive cellar, is a highlight of any stay. The award-winning breakfasts are equally memorable, and service is friendly and attentive. There are two function rooms available (one seating 40 and the other 120), which are perfect for weddings (Les Bouviers holds a civil ceremony licence), christenings, funeral wakes and corporate events.

Recommended in the area
Wimborne Model Town; Purbeck Hills; Poole Harbour

Essex

Epping Forest

The Bull at Great Totham

★★★★ ◎◎ RESTAURANT WITH ROOMS

Address: 2 Maldon Rd, GREAT TOTHAM, CM9 8NH
Tel: 01621 893385 & 894020
Fax: 01621 894029
Email: reservations@thebullatgreattotham.co.uk
Website: www.thebullatgreattotham.co.uk
Map ref: 4 TL81
Directions: Exit A12 at Witham junct to Great Totham
Rooms: 4 en suite (2 GF) **S** £59-£79 **D** £69-£85
Notes: Wi-fi ⊗
Parking: 80

This 16th century coaching inn, opposite the cricket pitch in the village of Great Totham, has been fully restored and transformed in recent years to cater for the 21st century guest's every need. Step through the doors of the listed building and you'll find a fine-dining restaurant, a gastropub and a little snug where you can enjoy a pint, perhaps while watching the big match. You'll also find a delightful cottage in the grounds which has been tastefully renovated to provide four beautifully appointed double en suite bedrooms. The rooms are individually decorated in a contemporary style with luxurious bedding and carefully chosen matching accessories. Each room offers a comfortable double bed, flat-screen television with Freeview, tea- and coffee-making facilities and Wi-fi. An extensive breakfast menu is served in The Bull's gastropub, adjacent to the cottage. There's no need to stray beyond The Bull for dinner, as you can take your pick between the hearty, robust dishes on the gastropub menu, and the more creative cuisine of The Willow Room Restaurant, which holds two AA Rosettes. Whichever setting you choose, you can be assured that everything on your plate will be as fresh, seasonal and locally sourced as possible.

Recommended in the area
Tiptree; Maldon; Colchester

Gloucestershire

Gloucester Cathedral

The Old Passage Inn

★★★★ ◎◎ RESTAURANT WITH ROOMS

Address: Passage Rd, ARLINGHAM, GL2 7JR
Tel: 01452 740547
Fax: 01452 741871
Email: oldpassage@btconnect.com
Website: www.theoldpassage.com
Map ref: 2 SO71 **Directions:** A38 onto B4071 through Arlingham. Through village to river
Rooms: 3 en suite **S** £60-£130 **D** £80-£130
Notes: Wi-fi
Parking: 30
Closed: 25 & 26 Dec

This restaurant with rooms is delightfully located right on a horse-shoe bend of the River Severn, making it a wonderfully quiet rural retreat. The en suite bedrooms look out across the river and beyond to the picturesque village of Newnham on Severn and the Forest of Dean. The vista changes constantly with the changing weather, and on fine days the sunsets here are quite spectacular. Each bedroom is light and airy with a contemporary feel, and comes with welcoming extras such as air-conditioning, mini-bar and tea- and coffee-making equipment. There are some wonderful walks (including many circular routes) along and around the River Severn starting right from the doorstep, so you should easily be able to work up a hearty appetite for dinner in the lovely restaurant. The Old Passage is predominantly a seafood restaurant, but there are options for meat-eaters and a vegetarian dish can be prepared on request. Oysters and lobsters are available from the kitchen's seawater tanks. The restaurant is light and airy with doors leading onto the terrace, where you can enjoy some alfresco drinking and dining during the warmer months.

Recommended in the area

Dean Heritage Centre; Lydney Park Gardens; Edward Jenner Museum

Beaumont House

★★★★★ GUEST ACCOMMODATION
Address: 56 Shurdington Rd,
CHELTENHAM, GL53 0JE
Tel: 01242 223311
Fax: 01242 520044
Email: reservations@bhhotel.co.uk
Website: www.bhhotel.co.uk
Map ref: 2 SO92
Directions: S side of town on A46 to Stroud
Rooms: 16 en suite (3 fmly) **S** £69-£249 **D** £90-£249
Notes: Wi-fi ⊗
Parking: 16
Closed: 24-26 Dec

Built in the 1850s, Beaumont House has been sympathetically renovated and converted into a very special five-star guest house set in a pleasant and spacious garden, with lovely rooms and free parking. The house is within walking distance of Cheltenham town centre and the fashionable Montpellier quarter, with plenty of shops, restaurants and pubs just a five-minute stroll away. Bedrooms are beautifully designed and have free Wi-fi access, flat-screen televisions with Sky Sports, as well as many other home comforts. There are several luxury and themed rooms, some en suite with whirlpool baths. Room service evening meals are available from Monday to Thursday until 8pm (excluding public holidays). The hearty breakfasts, freshly cooked to order, are a real treat, and you can expect friendly and efficient service. There's a lovely lounge for guests to relax in, complete with an honesty bar, and a comfortable conservatory where you can help yourself to complimentary teas, coffees (even cappuccinos if you fancy) and biscuits.

Recommended in the area

The Cotswolds; Sudeley and Berkeley castles; Gloucester Cathedral; Slimbridge Wildfowl & Wetland Trust

Lypiatt House

★★★★ GUEST ACCOMMODATION
Address: Lypiatt Rd, CHELTENHAM, GL50 2QW
Tel: 01242 224994
Fax: 01242 224996
Email: stay@lypiatt.co.uk
Website: www.lypiatt.co.uk
Map ref: 2 SO92
Directions: M5 junct 11 to town centre. At Texaco petrol station mini-rdbt take exit signed Stroud. Fork right, pass shops, turn sharp left onto Lypiatt Rd
Rooms: 10 en suite (2 GF) **S** £78-£95 **D** £95-£130
Notes: Wi-fi ⊗ ⚘ under 10yrs
Parking: 10

Close to Cheltenham's exclusive and fashionable Montpellier area, Lypiatt House is within walking distance of the main shopping centre, restaurants and theatres, as well as being well located for the many festivals that take place in the town. A very fine house, built in typical Victorian style, it is set in its own grounds and provides ample residents' parking. Inside, the atmosphere is intimate and tranquil, with contemporary decor enhancing the building's traditional features. Guests are welcome to relax in the spacious and elegant drawing room or in the conservatory, with the latter featuring an honesty bar. The bedrooms and bathrooms, all en suite, come in a range of shapes and sizes, but all of the rooms are decorated and maintained to a high standard and include a range of welcome extras, such as TVs, beverage trays, direct-dial telephones and free Wi-fi; two of the rooms are on the ground floor. Full English breakfasts are served, and a laundry service is available. All in all, this makes a relaxing base for a stay in Cheltenham, whether travelling on business or for pleasure.

Recommended in the area
Pittville Pump Room; Gloucester Cathedral; Gloucestershire Warwickshire Steam Railway

Seagrave Arms

★★★★ ⊚ INN

Address: Friday St, Weston-sub-Edge, CHIPPING CAMPDEN, GL55 6QH **Tel:** 01386 840192
Email: info@seagravearms.co.uk
Website: www.seagravearms.co.uk
Map ref: 3 SP13 **Directions:** From Moreton-in-Marsh take A44 towards Evesham. Approx 7m right onto B4081 signed Chipping Campden. Becomes Sheep St. At junct with High Street, left into Dyers Ln. 0.5m over Dovers Hill, into Weston-sub-Edge, becomes Church St. Pub on left
Rooms: 5 en suite 1 annexe en suite (1 GF)
D £95-£115 **Notes:** Wi-fi **Parking:** 15

The Seagrave Arms is a charming country inn and restaurant, set midway between Broadway and Chipping Campden in the glorious Cotswolds. The restored Georgian Cotswold stone house is just 20 minutes' drive from Stratford-upon-Avon in one direction, and Cheltenham in the other. There are six en suite bedrooms, all individually designed, with king-size beds, luxury Egyptian cotton sheets and flat-screen TVs. The house retains many period features, including original fireplaces where log fires blaze in the winter months. The kitchen sources all of its ingredients from the local area, including partridge and pheasant from local shoots during the game season. You can dine in the restaurant where a full a la carte menu is served, or in the comfortable and cosy bar where the extensive bar snacks menu offers the likes of sharing boards of local cheeses and home cured chorizo. On Sundays, in addition to the main menu, there's always a traditional roast, such as sirloin of Hereford beef, or roast leg of Gloucester Old Spot pork. The bar stocks real ales from local breweries Hook Norton, Goffs and Purity, local cider from Hogan's, and lager from the award-winning Cotswold Brewing Company.

Recommended in the area

Hidcote House & Gardens (NT); Stratford-upon-Avon; Cheltenham; Broadway

Bibury

The Wharf House

★★★★ RESTAURANT WITH ROOMS
Address: Over, GLOUCESTER, GL2 8DB
Tel: 01452 332900
Fax: 01452 332901
Email: thewharfhouse@yahoo.co.uk
Website: www.thewharfhouse.co.uk
Map ref: 2 SO81
Directions: Off A40 between Gloucester & Highnam at Over
Rooms: 6 en suite (1 fmly) (1 GF) **D** £85-£135
Notes: Wi-fi
Parking: 37
Closed: 24 Dec-4 Jan

The Wharf House restaurant with rooms is a delightful place to stay, conveniently located just outside the historic city of Gloucester, close to Cheltenham and midway between the Cotswolds, the Forest of Dean and the Wye Valley. You can enjoy a relaxed, fine-dining experience in the AA Rosette-awarded restaurant, where the superb contemporary European food is matched by first-class service. After a memorable meal, return to one of the six beautiful guest rooms overlooking the canal or the River Severn, all of which come with free Wi-fi and widescreen television. Some have the added luxury of a relaxing whirlpool bath. The high standard of cooking extends to breakfast, with a varied menu served in the restaurant. The Wharf House is owned by the Herefordshire and Gloucestershire Canal Trust, which in 2010 installed 94 solar panels on the roof to generate electricity for the building. All profits made by the Wharf House go towards the restoration of the Herefordshire and Gloucestershire canals, and you can learn all about the canal basin and river at the on-site visitor centre (which also has a shop selling locally produced food, crafts and artwork).

Recommended in the area
Gloucester; Cheltenham; Cotswold Wildlife Park

The Feathered Nest Inn

★★★★★ ◉◉ INN

Address: NETHER WESTCOTE,
Chipping Norton, OX7 6SD
Tel: 01993 833030
Fax: 01993 833031
Email: info@thefeatherednestinn.co.uk
Website: www.thefeatherednestinn.co.uk
Map ref: 3 SP22
Directions: A424 between Burford & Stow-on-the-Wold, follow signs
Rooms: 4 en suite (1 fmly) **D** £130-£180
Notes: Wi-fi ⊗ **Parking:** 45 **Closed:** 25 Dec

Originally an old malthouse, the updated and thoughtfully refurbished Feathered Nest Inn offers a cosy, warm and welcoming atmosphere - it's hardly surprising it was named AA Pub of the Year for England 2011-2012. The quality of the food is at the heart of The Feathered Nest, with the talented kitchen team offering a daily-changing menu of modern British cuisine based on locally sourced, seasonal ingredients, including herbs and vegetables from the kitchen garden. You can dine in the cosy bar in front of the log fire, or out in the garden on the terrace, which is naturally shaded by the sycamore tree, during the warmer months. The menu is complemented by an eclectic wine list of over 200 bins (25 of which are available by the glass), combining the classics with carefully selected alternative wines from both the Old and New Worlds. For traditional beer fans there's a good choice of local cask-conditioned ales. There are four individually decorated, stylish bedrooms at The Feathered Nest, each beautifully furnished with antiques and comfortable beds. A wholesome home-cooked breakfast of your choice is served in the lovely Garden Room, along with optional browsing of the daily papers.

Recommended in the area
Burford; Bourton-on-the-Water; Cheltenham shopping

Aston House

★★★★ BED AND BREAKFAST

Address: Broadwell, STOW-ON-THE-WOLD, GL56 0TJ
Tel: 01451 830475
Email: fja@astonhouse.net
Website: www.astonhouse.net
Map ref: 3 SP12
Directions: A429 from Stow-on-the-Wold towards Moreton-in-Marsh, right at Broadwell/Donnington x-rds to Broadwell, Aston House 0.5m on left
Rooms: 3 (2 en suite) (1 pri facs) (1 GF) **D** £75-£85
Notes: Wi-fi ⊗ 🐾 under 10yrs
Parking: 3
Closed: Nov-Feb

Aston House is in the quiet village of Broadwell, with its ford and village green. It's ideally situated for touring the beautiful Cotswolds, with Stow-on-the-Wold just a mile-and-a-half away, and Bourton-on-the-Water, Broadway, the Slaughters, Cotswold Farm Park, Hidcote Manor Gardens and Snowshill Manor all within easy driving distance. Stratford-upon-Avon, Warwick Castle, Blenheim Palace, Gloucester and Oxford are all within 28 miles. Aston House's enthusiastic owner has thought of everything when it comes to comfort, with armchairs in all the rooms, electric blankets and fans, tea- and coffee-making facilities, bedtime drinks and biscuits, Freeview TV, radios, hairdryers and quality toiletries in the en suite bathrooms. Although the rooms are not suitable for wheelchair users, there is a stairlift for those with limited mobility, plus help with luggage. A full English breakfast is served and there is a good pub within walking distance, although it's advisable to bring a torch for the return journey.

Recommended in the area

Cotswolds villages; Blenheim Palace; Hidcote Manor Gardens; Warwick Castle

No.1 Woodchester Lodge

★★★★ BED AND BREAKFAST

Address: Southfield Rd, North Woodchester,
STROUD, GL5 5PA
Tel: 01453 872586
Email: anne@woodchesterlodge.co.uk
Website: www.woodchesterlodge.co.uk
Map ref: 2 SO80
Directions: A46 into Selsley Rd, 2nd left, house 200yds on left
Rooms: 3 (1 en suite) (2 pri facs) (1 fmly)
S £50-£55 **D** £75-£80
Notes: Wi-fi ⊗ **Parking:** 4
Closed: Xmas & Etr

A former timber merchant's property built in Victorian times, No. 1 Woodchester Lodge occupies a peaceful village setting in the heart of the beautiful Cotswolds. The house is constructed of mellow Cotswold stone and is surrounded by a lovely garden where guests are welcome to relax when the weather is kind - perhaps with a cup of tea and a homemade cake. The house is brimming with original features, including high ceilings, bay windows, carved woodwork, stained glass and cast-iron fireplaces. The bedrooms are large, light and airy, furnished in a traditional style and recently redecorated to a high standard. All have views over the gardens and towards the hills beyond, and are equipped with TV, alarm clock, hairdryer and tea tray with homemade cookies. There is a large guest living/dining room overlooking the garden, where a log fire blazes in the colder months, and breakfast, evening meals and afternoon tea with homemade cakes are served. All meals are prepared by a qualified chef, with many of the ingredients harvested from No. 1 Woodchester Lodge's own garden, along with eggs supplied by the resident chickens.

Recommended in the area
Cotswold villages; Cheltenham; Bath; Woodchester Mansion; Slimbridge; Westonbirt Aboretum

The Cottage Lodge

★★★★★ GUEST ACCOMMODATION
Address: Sway Rd, BROCKENHURST, SO42 7SH
Tel: 01590 622296
Fax: 01590 623014
Email: enquiries@cottagelodge.co.uk
Website: www.cottagelodge.co.uk
Map ref: 3 SU30 **Directions:** Exit A337 opposite Careys Manor Hotel into Grigg Ln, 0.25km over x-rds, cottage next to war memorial
Rooms: 11 en suite 4 annexe en suite (7 GF)
S £50-£120 **D** £60-£160
Notes: Wi-fi under 10yrs **Parking:** 15
Closed: Xmas

This charming, award-winning B&B is right in the heart of the popular New Forest village of Brockenhurst. The lovely beamed building, at one time a hotel, is run with love and care by Christina Simons, who welcomes guests with tea or coffee and cakes, served in front of a roaring fire during the winter months. There are 15 individually designed en suite bedrooms, all with flat-screen TVs with Freeview, DVD players, coffee and tea trays (fresh milk is available in the Snug Bar), safes and hairdryers. Cottage Lodge has, not surprisingly, picked up an AA Breakfast Award for its use of top-notch New Forest produce. For evening meals you'll be spoilt for choice with three pubs and seven restaurants within a few minutes' walk. Cottage Lodge is ideally situated for enjoying all that the New Forest National Park has to offer, including cycling (bike rental is available just a stone's throw away), horse-riding and walking (you can be in the open forest within minutes). The railway station is just around the corner, while those guests travelling by car can take advantage of free parking at the front of the building. For those who need to stay in touch, there's free Wi-fi in the Snug Bar.

Recommended in the area

National Motor Museum, Beaulieu; Exbury Gardens; walking, cycling and horse riding

Ravensdale

★★★★ BED AND BREAKFAST

Address: 19 St Catherines Rd,
HAYLING ISLAND, PO11 0HF
Tel: 023 9246 3203 & 07802 188259
Email: phil.taylor@tayloredprint.co.uk
Website: www.ravensdale-hayling.co.uk
Map ref: 3 SU70 **Directions:** A27 onto A3023 at Langstone, cross Hayling Bridge, 3m to mini rdbt, right into Manor Rd, 1m. Right by Barley Mow into Station Rd, 3rd left into St Catherines Rd
Rooms: 3 (2 en suite) (1 pri facs) **S** £42-£44 **D** fr £68
Notes: Wi-fi ⊗ ⛔ under 8yrs **Parking:** 4
Closed: last 2wks Dec

A warm welcome awaits at Ravensdale, where Phil and Jane will make you feel at home in a relaxed and friendly environment. Situated in a quiet, tree-lined road close to the beach and golf course, the house offers tastefully decorated, comfortable accommodation with numerous thoughtful extras. There are three guest rooms - two with double beds and en suite bathrooms, and another with three single beds and a private bathroom - and each comes with TV, tea- and coffee-making facilities, fresh flowers and chocolates. Home cooking can be enjoyed at breakfast (and in the evenings by prior arrangement) in the triple aspect dining room, where there is also a lounge area. On the island, sailing, windsurfing and kitesurfing are popular sports. There are many enjoyable walks on and off the island, including around Emsworth, Bosham and Old Portsmouth, as well as the Farlington Marshes, a popular area for bird-watching. Your hosts will be happy to provide a packed lunch on request. Other sights to be enjoyed nearby include Chichester Cathedral, Portsmouth Historic Dockyard with the ships Victory, Warrior and the Mary Rose, and also the spectacular Spinnaker Tower with panoramic views over the Solent to the Isle of Wight.

Recommended in the area

Chichester Cathedral; Portsmouth Historic Dockyard; walking on the South Downs

Temple Lodge

★★★★ GUEST ACCOMMODATION

Address: 2 Queens Rd, LYNDHURST, SO43 7BR
Tel: 023 8028 2392
Fax: 023 8000 0091
Email: templelodge@btinternet.com
Website: www.templelodge-guesthouse.com
Map ref: 3 SU30
Directions: M27 junct 2/3 onto A35 to Ashurst & Lyndhurst. Temple Lodge on 2nd corner on right, opposite forest
Rooms: 6 en suite (2 fmly) **D** £60-£120
Notes: Wi-fi ⊗ ⚑ under 12yrs
Parking: 6

Temple Lodge is a beautiful Victorian residence which has been lovingly restored by its present owners and retains many original features. There are six beautifully decorated, spacious and well appointed en suite bedrooms, all with generous hospitality trays, TVs and DVD players, and mini fridges. The attractive guest lounge has a good selection of books and magazines and comfortable leather sofas. The award-winning breakfasts are freshly prepared using local ingredients wherever possible, and served in the elegant dining room which overlooks the pretty, well stocked gardens. Temple Lodge caters for holiday-makers as well as business travellers. It is located only a few minutes' walk from the village of Lyndhurst with its traditional pubs and good quality restaurants. Directly opposite the entrance to the New Forest National Park, it is a superb base for walking, cycling, horse riding and exploring the surrounding countryside. The coast is only a short drive away, as is the Motor Museum at Beaulieu and Exbury Gardens. Secure cycle storage and free Wi-fi are available.

Recommended in the area

Buckler's Hard; Lymington; Christchurch & Bournemouth

King John's Hunting Lodge at Wilk's Water, Odiham

The Woolpack Inn

★★★★ ◉◉ INN

Address: Totford, NORTHINGTON, Alresford, SO24 9TJ **Tel:** 01962 734184 & 0845 293 8066
Email: info@thewoolpackinn.co.uk
Website: www.thewoolpackinn.co.uk
Map ref: 3 SU53 **Directions:** From Basingstoke take A339 towards Alton. Under motorway, turn right (across dual carriageway) onto B3036 signed Candovers & Alresford. Pub between Brown Candover & Northington
Rooms: 7 en suite (1 fmly) (4 GF)
S £85-£105 **D** £85-£145
Notes: Wi-fi **Parking:** 20 **Closed:** 25 Dec eve

The Woolpack Inn, in a delightful rural setting yet just a short drive from Winchester, is looking dapper after undergoing an extensive refurbishment. The whole of the Grade II listed building has been lovingly made over by owners Brian and Jarina Ahearn, including the seven en suite bedrooms. All are attractively furnished and come with every home comfort, including king-size or twin beds, plasma screen TV, DVD player, Wi-fi, mini-bar, hairdryer, iron and ironing board, tea- and coffee-making facilities, and toiletries by The White Company. There's no need to stray beyond the front door for some excellent dining, with a wide choice of pub classics and more refined dishes on offer on The Woolpack's seasonally changing menus.

Everything is based on high quality local produce, and traditional roasts with all the trimmings are a big draw on Sundays. Food is served in the cosy bar, the 50-cover dining room or the heated outside area, and there's also a beer garden with children's play area for the warmer months. As you might imagine from this AA two Rosette inn, breakfast - and brunch on Saturdays and Sundays - is a real treat.

Recommended in the area

Alresford; Winchester Cathedral; Southampton and Basingstoke shopping

Moortown Lodge

★★★★ GUEST ACCOMMODATION

Address: 244 Christchurch Rd,
RINGWOOD, BH24 3AS
Tel: 01425 471404
Fax: 01425 476527
Email: enquiries@moortownlodge.co.uk
Website: www.moortownlodge.co.uk
Map ref: 3 SU10
Directions: 1m S of Ringwood. Exit A31 at Ringwood onto B3347, follow signs to Sopley. Lodge adjacent to David Lloyd Leisure Club
Rooms: 7 en suite (3 fmly) (2 GF) **D** £86-£96
Notes: Wi-fi **Parking:** 9

Moortown Lodge is a charming, family-run Georgian property in the attractive market town of Ringwood, the western gateway to the New Forest, where there is a wide range of unusual shops, traditional pubs and lovely restaurants. It offers guests a warm welcome and luxury B&B accommodation with many of the features found in a good class hotel. The seven elegantly furnished en suite rooms include one with a romantic four-poster bed and two easy access ground-floor rooms. All suites have digital TV and DVD, free broadband connection and free national direct-dial phones. Generous traditional breakfasts are cooked to order with lighter and vegetarian breakfast options available. Wherever possible fresh New Forest produce is used in the cooking. The peace and tranquillity of the open forest as well as the unspoilt water meadows of the River Avon are only minutes away. Moortown Lodge is the ideal stopover for business people as well as an excellent base for touring and leisure visitors. There are special arrangements for guests wishing to use the bar, restaurant and outstanding recreational facilities at the adjacent private David Lloyd leisure club.

Recommended in the area

Bournemouth; New Forest National Park; Stonehenge

Giffard House

★★★★ GUEST HOUSE
Address: 50 Christchurch Rd,
WINCHESTER, SO23 9SU
Tel: 01962 852628
Fax: 01962 856722
Email: giffardhotel@aol.com
Website: www.giffardhotel.co.uk
Map ref: 3 SU42
Directions: M3 junct 11, at rdbt 3rd exit onto A333 St Cross road for 1m. Pass BP garage on right, take next left then 2nd right. 150mtrs on left
Rooms: 13 en suite (1 fmly) (4 GF) **S** £73 **D** £95
Notes: Wi-fi ⊗ **Parking:** 13 **Closed:** 24 Dec-2 Jan

Visitors to this stunning 19th-century Victorian house, located a 10-minute walk from Winchester town centre, with its many amenities and points of interest, will find the recently refurbished establishment maintained to a high standard. Conference facilities are available, making it a good choice for business as well as leisure travellers. Inside, it combines elegance with comfort, and the well-equipped en suite bedrooms come with crisp white bed linen, luxurious bathrooms, beverage trays, direct-dial telephones and TV and radio facilities as standard. A family room and ground-floor rooms are available - one room is large enough for wheelchair users and grab rails can be provided - and for special occasions there is a suite. Guests are welcome to make use of Giffard House's garden, as well as the fully licensed bar, which is set in the elegant conservatory. Traditional breakfasts are served in the dining room and a self-service continental option is also on offer. Special diets can be catered for by arrangement. Wi-fi access is available, and there is ample free parking in the car park.

Recommended in the area

Winchester Cathedral; St Cross Hospital; Winchester City Mill (NT)

Herefordshire

Edward Elgar and his Sunbeam bike, near the Cathedral in Hereford

Somerville House

★★★★★ GUEST ACCOMMODATION

Address: 12 Bodenham Rd, HEREFORD, HR1 2TS
Tel: 01432 273991
Fax: 01432 268719
Email: enquiries@somervillehouse.net
Website: www.somervillehouse.net
Map ref: 2 SO53
Directions: A465, at Aylestone Hill rdbt towards city centre, left at Southbank Rd, leading to Bodenham Rd
Rooms: 12 en suite (2 fmly) (1 GF) **S** £60 **D** £77-£112
Notes: Wi-fi ⊗
Parking: 10

An imposing Victorian villa set in a quiet tree-lined road, Somerville House is run by Bill and Rosie, who provide modern boutique-style accommodation. The house is just a short walk from the railway station, bus station and Hereford city centre shops, restaurants and main attractions, and parking is available within the grounds. To relax after a busy day, guests can sit with a drink on the terrace or in the lovely lounge with its open fire and later, perhaps, take a stroll around the garden. A mixture of large, luxury and smaller character bedrooms all have high quality en suite bathrooms, Wi-fi access, flat-screen Freeview televisions, ironing equipment, hairdryers, hospitality trays and mini-bars. Luxury rooms are more spacious and have large beds, CD and DVD players. Flavours of Herefordshire are supported in-house, so enjoy locally produced drinks and snacks, such as Lulham Court wine and Tyrrell's crisps. The dining room has contemporary appeal, and here the full English breakfast is a speciality, using quality, locally sourced, organic produce with vegetarian options. There are also delicious local organic yoghurts, fruit juices, cereals, muesli and fresh fruit. Continental breakfast and healthy options are also offered. Special breaks are available.

Recommended in the area

Hereford Cathedral, Mappa Mundi & Chained Library; Hereford Museum; beautiful country walks

Wall Hills House

★★★★ GUEST ACCOMMODATION

Address: Hereford Rd, LEDBURY, HR8 2PR
Tel: 01531 632833
Email: wallhills@btinternet.com
Website: www.wallhills.com
Map ref: 2 SO73
Directions: Leave Ledbury on A438, entrance to drive within 200yds on left after rdbt
Rooms: 3 (2 en suite) (1 pri facs) **D** £84–£90
Notes: Wi-fi ⊗
Parking: 6
Closed: Xmas & New Year

A true cut above your typical bed and breakfast, Wall Hills House offers the added bonus of a residents-only restaurant where guests can enjoy a three-course meal complemented by their choice of wine from an extensive list. Dinners are freshly prepared to order by chef-proprietor David, using locally sourced meat and game, top-quality fish, and vegetables mostly picked from the garden. Wall Hills House, which stands on the hill slopes overlooking the old market town of Ledbury, dates back to Georgian times, so you can expect spacious and elegant rooms full of period character. All three bedrooms come with excellent beds, fluffy white towels, wonderful views and a relaxing atmosphere. There's a large Victorian walled garden which guests are welcome to enjoy, while for those business travellers who have to work, free Wi-fi is provided. Keen bird watchers are advised to bring their binoculars, as the fields below and woods behind the house attract a wide variety of species. Wall Hills House is the perfect place to recharge your batteries and enjoy the many charms of Ledbury with its independent shops, historic cobbled lanes and alleyways, and its old-fashioned friendliness.

Recommended in the area

Historic Ledbury; Hampton Court Castle & Gardens; Eastnor Castle

Portland House Guest House

★★★★ ⌂ GUEST ACCOMMODATION
Address: WHITCHURCH, Ross-on-Wye, HR9 6DB
Tel: 01600 890757
Email: info@portlandguesthouse.co.uk
Website: www.portlandguesthouse.co.uk
Map ref: 2 SO51
Directions: Exit A40 between Monmouth & Ross-on-Wye. Follow signs for Whitchurch & Symonds Yat West
Rooms: 6 en suite (2 fmly) (1 GF)
S £55-£70 **D** £70-£95
Notes: Wi-fi **Parking:** 6
Closed: 25-26 Dec

This elegant, Grade II listed Georgian house offers first-class guest accommodation and a very warm welcome just five minutes away from the River Wye in an Area of Outstanding Natural Beauty. Portland House sits right next to the Forest of Dean and just a stone's throw from the Symonds Yat rock and gorge. The house, which has a fascinating history (ask owners Jenny and John Jarvis to fill you in), is tastefully furnished throughout. There's a lovely lounge where you can relax and read or play chess, while the spacious en suite bedrooms all have divinely comfortable beds, TV, hospitality tray and seating areas. The Lloyd Suite overlooks the award-winning garden and is the only room available for those travelling with (well-behaved) dogs; the Ross Suite, with views across countryside, has two bedrooms and a doll's house and games table, and can accommodate a family of five or six; and the Monmouth Suite, with its four-poster bed and Victorian bathroom with ornate black chandelier, makes the perfect choice for a romantic break. The superb three-course breakfasts, cooked in the Aga and served in the elegant dining room, have justly earned the AA Breakfast Award.

Recommended in the area
Symonds Yat Rock & Gorge; Canoeing on the River Wye; Forest of Dean

Isle of Wight

The Needles

Isle of Wight

Enchanted Manor

★★★★★ GUEST ACCOMMODATION
Address: Sandrock Rd, NITON, PO38 2NG
Tel: 01983 730215
Email: info@enchantedmanor.co.uk
Website: www.enchantedmanor.co.uk
Map ref: 3 SZ57
Rooms: 7 en suite (2 GF)
D £160-£200
Notes: Wi-fi
Parking: 15

If you're a bit of a telly addict, The Enchanted Manor may well seem familiar. This rather unique retreat, with its fairytale theme, has featured in many a TV show, including ITV's *This Morning* and *Three in a Bed*. The Enchanted Manor is tucked away in a secluded wooded spot just a stone's throw from the rugged coastline around St Catherine's Bay. It's popular for romantic breaks (check out the special packages), as well as for intimate fairytale weddings and vow renewals, which can be conducted in the elegant wedding room or outside under the gold and white pagodas. There are seven luxurious suites, most with four-poster beds, and all well-equipped and furnished to the highest standard, with lots of thoughtful extra touches. The manor has a relaxed, informal atmosphere, and owners Ric and Maggie pride themselves in doing everything possible to make your stay special. Pampering health and beauty treatments are available in the Zodiac Salon, or you may prefer to de-stress in the garden hot tub. Also available are champagne high teas, evening badger watching from the garden follies, barbecues in the woodland grill hut, gourmet picnics and cheese and wine evenings.

Recommended in the area
Coastal walks; Ventnor Botanic Gardens; Osborne House

The Lawns

★★★★ GUEST ACCOMMODATION
Address: 72 Broadway, SANDOWN, PO36 9AA
Tel: 01983 402549
Email: lawnshotel@aol.com
Website: www.lawnshotelisleofwight.co.uk
Map ref: 3 SZ58
Directions: On A3055 N of town centre
Rooms: 13 en suite (2 fmly) (2 GF)
S £40-£50 **D** £72-£88
Notes: Wi-fi ⊗
Parking: 13
Closed: Nov-Feb

A warm welcome always awaits you at The Lawns, which has been lovingly upgraded by owners Nick and Stella to provide every home comfort. The Lawns was built in 1865 and stands in its own southwest-facing gardens offering ample parking. Situated in the pleasing area of Sandown, it is just a short walk away from a blue-flag beach, public transport and the town centre, with its restaurants and shops, and is an ideal base from which to explore the rest of the island. Other local attractions on offer include the pier, go-karting, crazy golf and the Tiger and Big Cat Sanctuary, as well as many opportunities to take part in water sports. The Lawns has a comfortable lounge, with Freeview TV and a selection of games available, as well as a bar. Evening meals are available by arrangement. Service is friendly and attentive, and the bedrooms, two of which are on the ground floor, include three superior rooms. All are comfortably equipped with flat-screen TVs and hospitality trays. All bathrooms are of a very high standard and include wall-mounted hairdryers.

Recommended in the area
Isle of Wight Zoo; Dinosaur Isle; Sandown Pier

Chair lift, Alum Bay

The Boat House

★★★★ INN

Address: Springvale Rd, SEAVIEW, PO34 5AW
Tel: 01983 810616
Email: info@theboathouseiow.co.uk
Website: www.theboathouseiow.co.uk
Map ref: 3 SZ69
Rooms: 4 en suite (1 fmly)
S fr £55 **D** fr £100
Notes: Wi-fi
Parking: 20

The Boat House sits in an enviable location right on the seafront in the appropriately named village of Seaview. The pub has been recently refurbished and offers top-class accommodation, with its four en suite rooms beautifully furnished in a modern nautical style. There is one twin room and three superior doubles, all with comfortable beds, crisp white linen, i-Pod docks and luxurious bathrooms, and a truly homely feel. While the high quality accommodation is one good reason to book a stay at The Boat House, the food is another. The experienced head chef endeavours to source as much local produce as possible, which is put to good use in a menu of classic dishes with a modern twist. With plenty of fresh fish dishes, a daily specials board, vegetarian options, a smaller appetites menu, traditional pub favourites and mouthwatering desserts, there's something to suit all tastes. There's also an extensive wine selection and lots of superb real ales, and you can enjoy your favourite drink either in the spruced up bar area or out on the patio overlooking The Solent.

Recommended in the area

Osborne House; Isle of Wight Zoo; The Garlic Farm

The Leconfield

★★★★★ ◉ GUEST ACCOMMODATION
Address: 85 Leeson Rd, Upper Bonchurch,
VENTNOR, PO38 1PU
Tel: 01983 852196
Email: enquiries@leconfieldhotel.com
Website: www.leconfieldhotel.com
Map ref: 3 SZ57
Directions: On A3055, 3m from Old Shanklin village
Rooms: 6 en suite 5 annexe en suite (3 GF)
S £40-£180 **D** £80-£200
Notes: Wi-fi ⊗ under 16yrs
Parking: 14
Closed: 24-26 Dec & 3-27 Jan

Paul, Cheryl and their small team welcome you to their delightful Victorian house. The Leconfield is elevated 400-feet above sea level and nestles into St Boniface Down in an Area of Outstanding Natural Beauty. There are views of the sea from nearly all the bedrooms, the sitting rooms, dining room, conservatory and garden. The Leconfield is on the island's south side and its unique micro climate is perfect for a break in the quieter winter months, while in the summer months guests can enjoy the heated outdoor swimming pool in the delightful gardens: a strictly adults-only oasis. Luxurious, individually designed bedrooms, some at ground-floor level, are equipped with en suite facilities, TVs with DVD players, hairdryers, hospitality trays, bathrobes and quality complimentary toiletries. A hearty breakfast prepared from local produce and free-range eggs is served in the Seascape Dining Room with its panoramic sea views. After a day of exploring the island's many treasures you'll be welcomed back to an AA Rosette standard evening meal with your choice from a wide selection of wines and other drinks. Your only distraction from the relaxing ambience might be the coming and going of ships on the open sea.

Recommended in the area

Ventnor Gardens; Carisbrooke Castle; Osborne House

Kent

Cliffs near Dover

Chislet Court Farm

★★★★ FARMHOUSE
Address: Chislet, CANTERBURY, CT3 4DU
Tel: 01227 860309 & 07980 841890
Fax: 01227 860444
Email: kathy@chisletcourtfarm.com
Website: www.chisletcourtfarm.com
Map ref: 4 TR15
Directions: Off A28 in Upstreet, farm on right 100yds past church
Rooms: 2 en suite **S** £50 **D** £80
Notes: Wi-fi ⊗ ⊮ under 12yrs
Parking: 4
Closed: Xmas

Chislet Court is a quintessentially English Grade II listed Queen Anne house, surrounded by 800 acres on a working arable farm. It's tucked away in the small, peaceful village of Chislet, yet is only six miles from the city of Canterbury with all its many attractions, making it an ideal base for exploring Kent. The house is set in large mature gardens, which overlook the ancient village church, a three-kiln oast house and the surrounding countryside. The friendly owners, Mike and Kathy Wilkinson, invite guests to wander around the garden or relax in the comfortable conservatory with its far-reaching views. The accommodation consists of two spacious en suite rooms with bath and shower, both south-facing and overlooking the garden and church. Each room has a king-size bed, flat-screen TV, DVD player, tea- and coffee-making facilities and free Wi-fi. Breakfast is served in the conservatory, while for evening meals, there's a wide range of excellent pubs and restaurants in the area.

Recommended in the area
Canterbury Cathedral; Whitstable; Wildwood Wild Animal Park

House of Agnes

★★★★ GUEST ACCOMMODATION
Address: 71 Saint Dunstans St,
CANTERBURY, CT2 8BN
Tel: 01227 472185
Fax: 01227 470478
Email: info@houseofagnes.co.uk
Website: www.houseofagnes.co.uk
Map ref: 4 TR15 **Directions:** On A290 between London Rd & Orchard St, 300mtrs from West Gate
Rooms: 8 en suite 8 annexe en suite (2 fmly) (8 GF)
S £60-£130 **D** £70-£130
Notes: Wi-fi ⊗ ⛔ under 5yrs **Parking:** 13
Closed: 24-26 Dec

The House of Agnes is Grade II* listed and dates back to the 15th century; it was even referred to by name in Charles Dickens' novel *David Copperfield*. Centrally located, it boasts the largest walled garden in Canterbury, along with plenty of free parking, and is close to Canterbury West railway station and a short walk from the cathedral. There are eight boutique-style bedrooms in the main house and a further eight newly created rooms in the converted 15th-century stables. All are stylishly furnished and with amenities including flat-screen TV, DVD player (with DVD library), free Wi-fi, MP3 docking station, hairdryer and well stocked beverage tray. The House of Agnes has a welcoming and relaxed atmosphere, with guests invited to pour themselves a drink from the honesty bar and unwind in the comfortable lounge with its eclectic decor and quirky furnishings. Breakfast, set out in the wood-panelled Quadrant Room, is a particular highlight, with a continental-style buffet to choose from, followed by a freshly cooked Kentish breakfast using local farm produce.

Recommended in the area
Canterbury Cathedral; Whitstable; Herne Bay

Magnolia House

★★★★★ GUEST ACCOMMODATION
Address: 36 St Dunstan's Ter,
CANTERBURY, CT2 8AX
Tel: 01227 765121 & 07776 236459
Fax: 01227 765121
Email: info@magnoliahousecanterbury.co.uk
Website: www.magnoliahousecanterbury.co.uk
Map ref: 4 TR15 **Directions:** A2 E onto A2050 for city centre, left at 1st rdbt signed University of Kent. St Dunstan's Terrace 3rd right
Rooms: 7 en suite (1 GF) **S** £55 **D** £95-£125
Notes: Wi-fi ⊗ ⚲ under 12yrs
Parking: 5

A warm welcome, personal service and attention to detail are what set this B&B in a lovely Georgian home apart from the rest. It's just a short walk from the city centre, so perfect for exploring Canterbury's many sights or for those visiting on business, as well as having easy access to the beautiful Kent countryside and coast. Each bedroom is professionally designed and equipped with digital TV, fridge and Wi-fi. You can relax in the guest sitting room, which is well-stocked with books, magazines and board games, or sit in the lovely secluded garden after a busy day of sightseeing or shopping. The excellent breakfasts, cooked freshly to order from local produce, are a feature of any stay. Enjoy a range of fresh fruit, cereals, yoghurts and dried fruit before taking your pick from a traditional English, a fish dish or a continental breakfast, served along with copious amounts of fresh ground coffee or speciality teas in the dining room overlooking the garden.

Recommended in the area

Wingham Wildlife Park; Herne Bay; Canterbury Castle

Yorke Lodge

★★★★ GUEST ACCOMMODATION
Address: 50 London Rd, CANTERBURY, CT2 8LF
Tel: 01227 451243
Fax: 01227 462006
Email: info@yorkelodge.com
Website: www.yorkelodge.com
Map ref: 4 TR15
Directions: M2 junct 7, A2, exit left signed Canterbury onto A2050. At 1st rdbt left into London Rd
Rooms: 8 en suite (1 fmly) **S** £58-£70 **D** £90-£130
Notes: Wi-fi 🐾 under 5yrs
Parking: 5

Easy to spot with its colourful window boxes and canopies, this attractively presented B&B is just a 10-minute stroll from the city centre and cathedral. Yorke Lodge was established as a bed and breakfast nearly 40 years ago, and has been run by the same family for eight years. It still retains all the charm and character of a Victorian villa, with many original features inside, along with contemporary furniture and coordinated fabrics, resulting in a stylish, elegant look. The eight en suite bedrooms are individually decorated, with all mod-cons, and offer a comfortable home-from-home feel. Superior rooms come with king-size four-poster beds. A traditional English breakfast, cooked in the Aga, is served in the spacious dining room or in the light and airy conservatory that opens out onto the sun terrace. Free private parking and Wi-fi is available. Yorke Lodge is just a short distance away from the University of Kent and Canterbury's boarding schools. The Kent coast and the county's many famous castles and stately homes are all within half-an-hour's drive.

Recommended in the area
Canterbury Cathedral; Whitstable; Leeds Castle

Dover Castle

Sondes Lodge

★★★ GUEST ACCOMMODATION

Address: 14 Sondes Rd, DEAL, CT14 7BW
Tel: 01304 368741 & 07817 178186
Email: info@sondeslodge.co.uk
Website: www.sondeslodge.co.uk
Map ref: 4 TR35
Directions: From Dover take A258 to Deal, pass Deal Castle, towards town centre. 4th right into Sondes Rd. Lodge on right
Rooms: 3 en suite (1 fmly) (1 GF) **S** £40-£60 **D** fr £60
Notes: Wi-fi

Sondes Lodge is a great-value B&B in the very heart of the seaside town of Deal, just a few steps from the beach, shops, bus and train station, restaurants and pubs. It makes a perfect base from which to explore Kent, or a good alternative to Dover (which is just 20 minutes' drive away). Sondes Lodge, which dates back to Victorian times, has three very comfortable en suite bedrooms - including a family room. It is furnished to a high standard and rooms come with Freeview TV, radio-alarm, complimentary toiletries, fresh flowers and tea- and coffee-making facilities. At breakfast you can go continental or enjoy a freshly cooked full English or a vegetarian version. Early breakfasts can be provided for those who are catching a ferry (or heading out to play golf on one of the many international-standard courses nearby). Deal is a relaxing alternative to bustling Dover with a lovely seaside atmosphere, and offers plenty to see and do, including walking, fishing and bird-watching. There's also Deal Castle, the Maritime Museum and the Timeball Tower.

Recommended in the area

Deal Castle; Dover Castle; Canterbury

The Relish

★★★★★ GUEST ACCOMMODATION
Address: 4 Augusta Gardens,
FOLKESTONE, CT20 2RR
Tel: 01303 850952
Fax: 01303 850958
Email: reservations@hotelrelish.co.uk
Website: www.hotelrelish.co.uk
Map ref: 4 TR23
Directions: Off A2033 (Sandgate Rd)
Rooms: 10 en suite (2 fmly) **S** fr £69 **D** £95-£145
Notes: Wi-fi ⊗
Closed: 23 Dec-2 Jan

"Check-in, chill-out, relax" is The Relish's motto, and it's not a hard one to follow when your stay begins with a complimentary glass of wine or beer on arrival. In fact, you can enjoy a glass of wine or beer, as well as unlimited fresh coffee and tea with homemade cakes, every day of your stay - all at no extra charge. What's more, the 10 bedrooms at The Relish - a 150-year-old townhouse - are furnished to the highest standard with sumptuous beds (by Hypnos), stunning en suite facilities, and luxury touches like crisp white linen and huge bath towels. Free Wi-fi is available, there are plenty of magazines to borrow and each room comes with a DVD player so you can relax and watch your favourite movie if the weather isn't playing ball. The Relish is centrally located in the fashionable West End, within 500 yards of some of the best restaurants in town. The Coastal Park and The Leas are just 200 yards away. Whether you're just staying one night or for a longer break, The Relish offers the perfect escape from the pressures of everyday life.

Recommended in the area

Dover Castle; Romney, Hythe and Dymchurch Railway; Canterbury

Merzie Meadows

★★★★★ BED AND BREAKFAST

Address: Hunton Rd, MARDEN, TN12 9SL
Tel: 01622 820500 & 07762 713077
Fax: 01622 820500
Email: pamela@merziemeadows.co.uk
Website: www.merziemeadows.co.uk
Map ref: 4 TQ74
Directions: A229 onto B2079 for Marden, 1st right into Underlyn Ln, 2.5m at large Chainhurst sign, right onto drive
Rooms: 2 en suite (1 fmly) (2 GF) **D** £98-£110
Notes: Wi-fi ⊗ ⛔ under 15yrs **Parking:** 4
Closed: mid Dec-mid Feb

Uniquely designed Merzie Meadows is set in peaceful, idyllic, mature grounds that have been created with conservation in mind. The house has been built to be in touch with its environment, with the surrounding three-acre garden a haven for birds and wildlife. It is situated near many of the South East's famous historic houses and glorious gardens, including Scotney Castle, Sissinghurst and Leeds Castle, and is surrounded by beautiful Kentish countryside. The superb en suite accommodation is in separate wings of the house, providing space, comfort and privacy. Each room has a king-size bed, digital TV and Wi-fi, along with lovely views across the garden and grounds. One room is a suite with its own terrace. At breakfast - served in the light and airy breakfast room with superb garden views - there's an extensive menu to choose from. Merzie Meadows is ideal for longer holidays touring the beautiful Kent countryside, as well as being within easy reach of London.

Recommended in the area

Sissinghurst Castle Garden (NT); Leeds Castle; Bedgebury National Pinetum & Forest; Pashley Manor Gardens

Danehurst House

★★★★★ 🛏 BED AND BREAKFAST

Address: 41 Lower Green Rd, Rusthall,
ROYAL TUNBRIDGE WELLS, TN4 8TW
Tel: 01892 527739
Fax: 01892 514804
Email: info@danehurst.net
Website: www.danehurst.net
Map ref: 4 TQ53
Directions: 1.5m W of Tunbridge Wells in Rusthall.
Exit A264 into Coach Rd & Lower Green Rd
Rooms: 4 en suite (1 fmly)
Notes: ⊗ 🐾 under 8yrs **Parking:** 6
Closed: Xmas

Angela and Michael Godbold's spacious Victorian home stands just west of the historic spa town of Tunbridge Wells. The couple offer a warm welcome and personal attention to all guests, and the house has a lovely, relaxed feel. The superb home cooking is a highlight of any stay, with a full English breakfast - or alternatively fish, cold meats, cheese or a continental breakfast - served in the pretty Victorian-style conservatory overlooking the lovely garden. In the summer months guests are invited to enjoy the sunny front terrace, whilst at all other times of year the guest sitting room - complete with games, maps, books, a baby grand piano and television - provides a comfortable place to relax after an active day. Danehurst House doesn't offer evening meals, but the Godbolds will happily recommend local pubs and restaurants, some of which are within walking distance. The four cosy en suite bedrooms are tastefully furnished to an extremely high standard, and come with supremely comfortable beds with handmade mattresses, flat-screen TV, radio/alarm clock, cafetière coffee and other hot drinks facilities, and luxury toiletries.

Recommended in the area

Groombridge Place; Hever Castle; Chartwell (NT)

Lancashire

View along the River Hodder, Forest of Bowland

Bona Vista

★★★★ GUEST ACCOMMODATION

Address: 104-106 Queens Promenade,
BLACKPOOL, FY2 9NX
Tel: 01253 351396
Fax: 01253 594985
Email: enquiries@bonavistahotel.com
Website: www.bonavistahotel.com
Map ref: 6 SD33
Directions: 0.25m N of Uncle Toms Cabin & Castle Casino
Rooms: 19 (17 en suite) (4 fmly)
S £25-£34 **D** £50-£68
Notes: Wi-fi **Parking:** 16

The Bona Vista has a seafront location on Queens Promenade north of the town centre. It's a peaceful spot only minutes away from the attractions of the town, which can easily be reached by tram thanks to a new tram stop right opposite the guest house. You can expect all the usual facilities at The Bona Vista, along with a delightful sun lounge running the full width of the building which is ideal for viewing the Illuminations. Meals are available in the modern and airy dining room, with menus changing daily and personal dietary requirements catered for. If you prefer a lighter meal, snacks are served in the cosy bar. A major benefit of staying at The Bona Vista, particularly during Illuminations time, is the on-site, off-street parking. The owners strive to create a relaxed and friendly environment for all guests - from single people and couples through to families - but do not welcome hen and stag parties, which are more associated with the town centre.

Recommended in the area

Blackpool Tower; North Pier; Blackpool Pleasure Beach

Leicestershire

Old John Tower folly at Bradgate Country Park

The Manners Arms

★★★★ ● RESTAURANT WITH ROOMS

Address: Croxton Rd, KNIPTON,
Grantham, NG32 1RH
Tel: 01476 879222
Fax: 01476 879228
Email: info@mannersarms.com
Website: www.mannersarms.com
Map ref: 7 SK83
Directions: Off A607 into Knipton
Rooms: 10 en suite (1 fmly)
Notes: Wi-fi
Parking: 60

The Manners Arms is a delightful country restaurant with rooms, nestling in the village of Knipton in the picturesque Vale of Belvoir. It was originally built for the 6th Duke of Rutland as a hunting lodge in the 1880s, and remained in the Duke's family until the 1950s when it was converted into a hotel and restaurant. The 10 en suite bedrooms have been recently refurbished and each has its own individual style. The restaurant is charming, relaxed and welcoming - the sort of place where you immediately feel at home. You can sit back on one of the comfortable chairs in the bar to enjoy a pint of local ale or a glass of wine in front of a blazing open fire, or in summer make the most of the long nights in the beautiful garden or the conservatory.

A variety of menus are available throughout the day in the bar and restaurant. On Sundays a traditional roast lunch is served, while Sunday evening steak nights are proving popular. The kitchen team use only the freshest, best quality local produce, with much of the seasonal game coming from the nearby Belvoir Estate.

Recommended in the area

Belvoir Castle; countryside walks; Barnsdale Gardens

Lincolnshire

Beach and dunes at Saltfleet Haven

The Brownlow Arms

★★★★★ ◉ INN

Address: High Rd, HOUGH-ON-THE-HILL, Grantham, NG32 2AZ
Tel: 01400 250234
Fax: 01400 271193
Email: armsinn@yahoo.co.uk
Website: www.thebrownlowarms.com
Map ref: 7 SK94
Rooms: 4 en suite 1 annexe en suite (1 GF)
S £65-£70 **D** £98-£110
Notes: Wi-fi ⊗ ⚄ under 12yrs
Parking: 20
Closed: 25-27 Dec & 31 Dec-1 Jan

This 17th-century stone-built country inn enjoys a tranquil location in the heart of a picturesque village. Once owned by Lord Brownlow, today it offers exceptional modern comforts along with good, old-fashioned country hospitality, in a peaceful and relaxing setting. Enjoy a meal in the award-winning restaurant, which has the look and feel of an intimate country house. Chef Oliver Snell only works with premium produce to offer menus that are traditional but with modern influences, supported by an interesting wine list. The accommodation at The Brownlow Arms is of the highest order. There are four double en suite rooms, all tastefully furnished to provide every comfort and facility for the business traveller or tourist, including LCD flat-screen TV, DVD player (and movies), power-shower and free Wi-fi. The friendly bar serves prize-winning real ales from the hand pump. Food and drinks can be enjoyed here in front of the open fire during the winter, or out on the lovely landscape terrace during the warmer months.

Recommended in the area

Belton House; Belvoir Castle; Lincoln Cathedral

County Hall and the London Eye from Westminster Bridge

The Cottage

★★★★ GUEST ACCOMMODATION
Address: 150-152 High St, Cranford,
HEATHROW AIRPORT, TW5 9WB
Tel: 020 8897 1815
Email: info@the-cottage.eu
Website: www.the-cottage.eu
Map ref: 3 TQ17
Directions: M4 junct 3, A312 towards Feltham, left at lights, left after 1st pub on left
Rooms: 14 en suite 6 annexe en suite (4 fmly) (12 GF) **S** £95 **D** £120-£160
Notes: Wi-fi ⊗ **Parking:** 16
Closed: 24-26 Dec & 31 Dec-1 Jan

This lovely 19th-century family-run property is just a few minutes' drive from Heathrow Airport, yet it benefits from a peaceful location. Guests here can rely on a friendly atmosphere combined with spacious and comfortable accommodation. The en suite bedrooms are tastefully decorated in a country style, using neutral colours and wooden furniture, and all come with a range of home comforts such as hospitality tray, TV, free Wi-Fi, alarm clock and hairdryer. Some of the rooms in the main house, which include family rooms, are on the ground floor. There are now six newer bedrooms located at the rear of the landscaped garden, where guests will find fruit trees, shrubs and flowerbeds. These rooms are connected to the main building by a covered walkway overlooking the stunning courtyard, and all have beamed ceilings, fridges, ironing facilities and luxury bathrooms with power showers. Breakfast, cooked or continental, is served in the stylish dining room, which opens on to a conservatory overlooking the garden. Fully secure CCTV-covered parking is free for those in residence. Be sure to mention the AA when booking at The Cottage for a good discount.

Recommended in the area
Hampton Court Palace; Legoland; Kew Gardens; Windsor Castle, Twickenham rugby; Thorpe Park

The Gallery

★★★★ GUEST ACCOMMODATION
Address: 8-10 Queensberry Place,
South Kensington, LONDON, SW7 2EA
Tel: 020 7915 0000
Fax: 020 7970 1805
Email: reservations@eeh.co.uk
Website: www.eeh.co.uk
Map ref: 4 TQ38
Directions: Off A4 (Cromwell Rd) opposite Natural History Museum, near South Kensington tube station
Rooms: 34 en suite **S** £105-£325 **D** £130-£325
Notes: Wi-fi ⊗

This stylish property, close to Kensington and Knightsbridge and opposite the Natural History Museum, offers friendly hospitality, attentive service and sumptuously furnished accommodation. The 34 guest rooms are all en suite and decorated in a traditional Victorian style with elaborately patterned fabrics and antiques. Each room comes with satellite TV, broadband internet connection, hairdryer, electronic safe, desk, and tea- and coffee-making facilities. There are two master suites each with the extra luxuries of a private roof terrace, jacuzzi bath and CD/DVD player. Public areas include a mahogany panelled lobby decorated with oriental porcelain, a choice of lounges including one with original artworks, an imposing Jacobean Revival chimney piece and plump sofas (along with internet access), and an elegant bar. Guests can choose from a full English or continental breakfast, and 24-hour room service is available. The Gallery is in a prime location a short walk from South Kensington tube station, with Hyde Park, the fashionable shops of Knightsbridge and a wide selection of restaurants and bars right on the doorstep.

Recommended in the area

Natural History Museum; Victoria & Albert Museum; Harrods

San Domenico House

★★★★★ GUEST ACCOMMODATION

Address: 29-31 Draycott Place,
LONDON, SW3 2SH
Tel: 020 7581 5757
Fax: 020 7584 1348
Email: info@sandomenicohouse.com
Website: www.sandomenicohouse.com
Map ref 4 TQ38
Rooms: 16 en suite (9 smoking) **S** £230 **D** fr £255 (ex VAT)
Notes: ⊗

This newly extended and redesigned townhouse property, located in the heart of fashionable Chelsea, just a short walk from Sloane Square underground, offers luxurious boutique-style accommodation and an intimate atmosphere. With easy access to the City and West End, it's ideally suited to business executives and leisure travellers alike. Behind its Victorian façade, San Domenico House offers all the luxuries of a large palace, whilst offering friendly, personalised service and plenty of charm and character in its 16 guest rooms. The individually styled bedrooms and suites, all with antique and period pieces and rich soft furnishings, are air-conditioned, have a mini-bar, flat-screen TV, free Wi-fi, and stylish en suite facilities with Molton Brown toiletries, hairdryers and fluffy bathrobes. An extensive room service menu is also available. There is a beautiful drawing room - decorated with interesting artworks - where guests can relax and indulge in a traditional afternoon tea. A full English breakfast, or a lighter continental option chosen from the a la carte menu, is served in the elegant dining room, or in your bedroom if you prefer. A rooftop terrace with far-reaching views provides a magnificent setting for alfresco meals and drinks.

Recommended in the area

Shopping in Sloane Street; King's Road; Royal Hospital Chelsea

Norfolk

A field of lavender in West Newton

Shrublands Farm

★★★★ FARMHOUSE

Address: Church St, Northrepps, CROMER, NR27 0AA
Tel: 01263 579297
Email: youngman@farming.co.uk
Website: www.shrublandsfarm.com
Map ref: 8 TG24
Directions: Off A149 to Northrepps, through village, past Foundry Arms, cream house 50yds on left
Rooms: 2 (1 en suite) (1 pri facs)
S £44-£47.50 **D** £68-£75
Notes: ⊗ ✖ under 12yrs
Parking: 5

Shrublands is a working 300-acre arable farm in the small village of Northrepps in an Area of Outstanding Natural Beauty. The 18th-century farmhouse is surrounded by mature gardens and makes an ideal base for exploring the coast and countryside of north Norfolk, whether by car, bicycle or on foot. There are two comfortable bedrooms with TVs, radio-alarms and tea- and coffee-making facilities, plus a cosy lounge for guests to use with a log fire, books and a TV. The highlight of any stay here is the excellent breakfast using home-grown and fresh local produce, served at a large table in the dining room. The coastline of high cliffs and safe sandy beaches is right on the doorstep, with the nearest beach just one mile away, and to the west of nearby Sheringham are salt marshes and bird sanctuaries. A short walk from the front door will bring you to the village pub, which serves good quality food. The fine city of Norwich, with its splendid cathedral and Norman castle, is just a 30-minute drive away.

Recommended in the area

Blickling Hall and Felbrigg Hall (NT); sandy beaches at Cromer and Overstrand; Blakeney Point

Orchard Cottage

★★★★ BED AND BREAKFAST

Address: The Drift, Gressenhall,
DEREHAM, NR20 4EH
Tel: 01362 860265
Email: ann@walkers-norfolk.co.uk
Website: www.walkers-norfolk.co.uk
Map ref: 8 TF91
Directions: 2m NE of Dereham. Exit B1146 in Beetley to Gressenhall, right at x-rds into Bittering St, right at x-rds, 2nd right
Rooms: 2 en suite (2 GF) **S** £48-£54 **D** £64-£70
Notes: Wi-fi ⊗
Parking: 2

Orchard Cottage is an attractive, newly-built Norfolk flint house in the historic rural village of Gressenhall, just four miles from the market town of Dereham. It makes the ideal base for active holidays, with plenty of lovely walking and cycling country right on the doorstep (and secure cycle storage on-site), as well as for quiet breaks and weekends away. It's also the perfect stopover for business people visiting the area. The comfortable, country-style en suite bedrooms - available as a double or twin - are smartly decorated and situated on the ground floor. The rooms are bright and furnished to a high standard, complete with underfloor heating, solid oak floors, tea- and coffee-making facilities, radio-alarm clock, room thermostat, TV with Freeview and Wi-fi. Public rooms include a lounge and a study, along with a lovely dining room overlooking the garden. It's here that excellent breakfasts - a choice of continental or a full English cooked in the Aga - are served. Local produce is used as much as possible, and all the bread is homemade. Evening meals are available by prior arrangement. Orchard Cottage is suitable for wheelchair users and children are welcomed.

Recommended in the area

Gressenhall Farm and Workhouse; Pensthorpe Nature Reserve & Gardens; Dinosaur Adventure Park

Edmar Lodge

★★★ GUEST ACCOMMODATION

Address: 64 Earlham Rd, NORWICH, NR2 3DF
Tel: 01603 615599
Fax: 01603 495599
Email: mail@edmarlodge.co.uk
Website: www.edmarlodge.co.uk
Map ref: 4 TG20
Directions: Exit A47 (S bypass) onto B1108 (Earlham Rd), follow university & hospital signs
Rooms: 5 en suite (1 fmly) **S** £38-£45 **D** £48-£55
Notes: Wi-fi
Parking: 6

Just 10 minutes' walk from the historic centre of Norwich, this friendly, family-run guest house boasts a convenient location and ample private parking. The five individually decorated en suite bedrooms, including one family room, all have double- or triple-glazed windows and are smartly appointed. Each room has a flat-screen digital TV, DVD player (with a selection of films for guests to borrow), tea- and coffee-making facilities, hairdryer, trouser press, radio/alarm clock and Wi-fi. At breakfast in the cosy dining room there's plenty to choose from, including a hearty - or not so hearty if you have a smaller appetite - full English cooked to order. Various diets can be catered for and there's a good selection of herbal and specialist teas. Edmar Lodge doesn't offer evening meals but owners Ray and Sue are happy to recommend local restaurants, while a microwave and fridge along with plates and utensils are provided for guests to use. There's a pretty garden in which to relax on warmer days.

Recommended in the area

Norwich Cathedral; Norfolk Broads; Norwich Castle

Gothic House Bed & Breakfast

★★★★ GUEST ACCOMMODATION
Address: King's Head Yard, Magdalen St, NORWICH, NR3 1JE
Tel: 01603 631879 **Email:** charvey649@aol.com
Website: www.gothic-house-norwich.com
Map ref: 4 TG20 **Directions:** Follow signs for A147, exit at rdbt past flyover into Whitefriars. Right into Fishergate, at end, right into Magdalen St
Rooms: 2 (2 pri facs) **S** £65 **D** £95
Notes: Wi-fi ⊗ ⚹ under 18yrs
Parking: 2 Closed: Feb

Set in a quiet courtyard (with parking) in the heart of the most historic part of Norwich, Gothic House is a Grade II listed building barely five minutes' walk from the cathedral. The area has a wealth of elegant Georgian and earlier architecture to admire, while Elm Hill with its many antique shops is a short stroll away. Gothic House has been lovingly restored and retains much of its original Regency character. It was reputedly built in the early 1800s as a residence for a lord mayor of the city. There are two spacious and stylish guest rooms: one double with a king-size bed, and a twin room with two 4ft beds. Due to the listed status of the house, neither room can be altered to create an en suite, but each has a dedicated private bathroom close by (stocked with Molton Brown toiletries). Each bedroom is traditionally and comfortably furnished and comes with luxurious bathrobes, slippers, TV and tea- and coffee-making facilities. The house is no-smoking throughout and free Wi-fi is provided. Breakfast - with the options including a traditional English, kippers or smoked haddock Florentine - is served in the elegant dining room.

Recommended in the area
Norwich Castle; Norwich Aviation Museum; Norwich Gallery

Horsey Mere, Norfolk Broads National Park

Old Thorn Barn

★★★★ GUEST ACCOMMODATION

Address: Corporation Farm, Wymondham Rd,
Hethel, NORWICH, NR14 8EU
Tel: 01953 607785 & 07894 203208
Fax: 01953 601909
Email: enquiries@oldthornbarn.co.uk
Website: www.oldthornbarn.co.uk
Map ref: 4 TG20
Directions: 6m SW of Norwich. Follow signs for Lotus Cars from A11 or B1113, on Wymondham Rd
Rooms: 5 en suite 2 annexe en suite (7 GF)
S £36-£40 **D** £64-£68
Notes: Wi-fi ⊗ **Parking:** 14

Old Thorn Barn is a collection of sympathetically restored and renovated barns, dating back to the 17th century, surrounded by open countryside where deer can sometimes be spotted. The barn is part of an old farming complex which used to supply food for The Great Hospital at Bishopgate in Norwich, which was founded in the 13th century for the poor and destitute of the city. The many oak beams and flagstone floors inside the barn testify to its age. The guest lounge/dining area benefits from the comfort of a traditional wood burner in the colder months, along with comfortable sofas and a large flat-screen TV. All bedrooms are en suite, individually decorated and beautifully furnished, and have their own flat-screen TVs, hairdryers and tea- and coffee-making facilities. The breakfast menu is wide ranging, and includes porridge, kippers or smoked haddock, vegetarian options and a full traditional English, all served in the spacious Long Barn. The lovely landscaped gardens include a large sun-deck, which overlooks the water gardens, providing a great place to relax.

Recommended in the area

North Norfolk coast; Thursford Museum; Walsingham

Holly Lodge

★★★★ 🍴 BED AND BREAKFAST

Address: The Street, THURSFORD, NR21 0AS
Tel: 01328 878465
Fax: 01328 878465
Email: info@hollylodgeguesthouse.co.uk
Website: www.hollylodgeguesthouse.co.uk
Map ref: 8 TF93
Directions: Off A148 into Thursford, village green on left. 2nd driveway on left past green
Rooms: 3 en suite (3 GF) **S** £70-£100 **D** £90-£120
Notes: Wi-fi ⊗ ✿ under 14yrs
Parking: 6

This 18th-century house is beautifully situated in the quiet north Norfolk village of Thursford, famous for the Thursford Show and the Thursford Collection of steam engines and organs, and just seven miles away from the superb beaches and salt marshes of the coast. Holly Lodge is also close to the many historic houses of north Norfolk including Sandringham, Holkham Hall and Blickling Hall, and the lovely Georgian town of Holt. The house and the former stable block have been transformed into a splendid guest house with stylish ground-floor bedrooms that are individually decorated and superbly furnished. Guests are greeted with lots of thoughtful extras in their rooms, including a complimentary bottle of wine, homemade cake, fruit and chocolates. All rooms have a TV with Freesat, as well as Wi-fi. The house is surrounded by an acre of lovely landscaped grounds, including an orchard and a large sundeck where guests can relax whilst looking out over the water gardens. The attractive public areas are full of character, with flagstone floors, oak beams and open fireplaces. Breakfasts and evening meals are served in the magnificent conservatory overlooking the grounds.

Recommended in the area

North Norfolk coast; Thursford Museum; Walsingham

Red House Farm Bed & Breakfast

★★★★ BED AND BREAKFAST
Address: Station Rd, TIVETSHALL ST MARGARET, Norwich, NR15 2DJ
Tel: 01379 676566
Email: office@redhousefarm.info
Website: www.redhousefarm.info
Map ref: 4 TM18
Directions: 500mtrs from A140
Rooms: 2 en suite **S** £37.50 **D** £70-£75
Notes: Wi-fi **Parking:** 4

Red House Farm is a small working farm with a very warm welcome. High quality B&B accommodation is provided in a 17th-century converted barn, which successfully combines old world charm with modern day style, comfort and technology. Situated just off the A140, Red House Farm is conveniently situated for Diss, Norwich and Ipswich, making it ideal for business visitors to the area. For leisure guests wishing to explore, the Norfolk Broads and the Waveney Valley, with its beautiful walks along the Boudicca Way, are within easy reach. The luxurious bedrooms provide double or twin accommodation, and are equipped with en suite shower rooms, TV and tea- and coffee-making facilities. Breakfast is served fresh from the Aga in the friendly atmosphere of the kitchen, and is made with local bacon and sausages, and home-produced eggs. Free wireless broadband is available.

Recommended in the area
Banham Zoo; Bewilderwood; Go Ape

Northamptonshire

Canons Ashby House

The Exeter Arms

★★★★ ⍟ INN

Address: 21 Stamford Rd,
EASTON-ON-THE-HILL, PE9 3NS
Tel: 01780 756321
Fax: 01780 753171
Email: reservations@theexeterarms.net
Website: www.theexeterarms.net
Map ref: 3 TF00 **Directions:** A1 Nbound take exit signed Easton-on-the-Hill; A1 Sbound take exit signed A47/A43 Corby/Kettering, on left entering village
Rooms: 5 en suite 1 annexe en suite (2 fmly)
S £60-£150 **D** £65-£150
Notes: Wi-fi **Parking:** 40

The Exeter Arms is located on the edge of the historical village of Easton on the Hill, just two miles outside the picturesque town of Stamford. Michael Thurlby and his sister Sue, who grew up on the family farm at nearby Tallington, have restored The Exeter Arms back to its former glory since taking over the pub in 2010. The building has been extended to include a beautifully light and airy orangery (where breakfast is served), plus a snug and extensive patio areas. The pub has six individually designed en suite bedrooms, three of which can be twin-bedded and two of which can interconnect, making them ideal for families. A deluxe double room has a day bed, enabling it to sleep up to four people. Dining at The Exeter Arms is a real treat, with head chef Simon Pollendine offering a range of menus based on seasonal and local produce, including meats and vegetables from the farm at Tallington. The restaurant even has a proper pizza oven, so you can choose anything from a thin-based pizza to one of Simon's signature dishes or a comforting pub classic. The Exeter Arms is perfectly situated for business travellers and holiday-makers alike.

Recommended in the area
Stamford shopping; Stamford Priory; Burghley House

The Queens Head Inn

★★★★ ⚜ INN

Address: 54 Station Rd, NASSINGTON, PE8 6QB
Tel: 01780 784006
Fax: 01780 781539
Email: info@queensheadnassington.co.uk
Website: www.queensheadnassington.co.uk
Map ref: 3 TL09
Directions: A1 Nbound exit junct 17, follow signs for Yarwell, then Nassington. Queens Head on left on entering the village
Rooms: 9 en suite (2 fmly) (9 GF)
S £50-£120 **D** £50-£120
Notes: Wi-fi ⊗ **Parking:** 45

A warm welcome and traditional hospitality lie in store for visitors to the Queens Head Inn, which sits on the banks of the River Nene in the picturesque village of Nassington near Peterborough. The nine comfortable and spacious en suite bedrooms are arranged around a courtyard on the ground floor and are all chalet-style, with LCD TV with Freeview, complimentary Wi-fi, desk, tea- and coffee-making facilities and complimentary mineral water. All rooms are non-smoking and there are two bedrooms suitable for families. The restaurant, which has been awarded one AA Rosette, offers classic and contemporary dishes freshly prepared using local and seasonal produce, and served by friendly staff. In the winter the lounge bar is a warm and welcoming spot with open fires to snuggle up in front of, while in the summer months you can choose to dine alfresco on the patio or enjoy a snack and drinks on the grassy banks of the river. Situated a short drive away from the A1 Great North Road, The Queens Head is ideally situated for visiting Peterborough, Oundle and Stamford.

Recommended in the area
Nassington; Peterborough; Oundle

Northumberland

Northumberland National Park

The Old Manse

★★★★★ GUEST ACCOMMODATION

Address: New Rd, CHATTON, Wooler, NE66 5PU
Tel: 01668 215243 & 07811 411808
Email: chattonbb@aol.com
Website: www.oldmansechatton.co.uk
Map ref: 11 NU02
Directions: 4m E of Wooler. On B6348 in Chatton
Rooms: 3 en suite (1 GF) **S** £50-£65 **D** £86-£100
Notes: Wi-fi ⊗ ⚹ under 14yrs
Parking: 4
Closed: Nov-Feb

Built in 1875 and commanding excellent views over the open countryside, this imposing former manse stands on the edge of the pretty village of Chatton between the Cheviot Hills and the scenic North Northumberland Heritage Coast. The Old Manse is approached by a sweeping gravel drive bordered with lawns, roses and evergreen trees. Guests can relax in the secluded rear garden, with its patio, large fish pond, summerhouse and beautiful countryside views. Christine and Tony Lummis are welcoming hosts who do their utmost to ensure that The Old Manse feels like a home from home for all guests. The en suite accommodation is spacious, comfortable and well-equipped, and ranges from the Rosedale Suite with a four-poster bed, to the Buccleuch garden suite which has a sitting room and private patio, to the Mansfield Room with a king-size bed and slightly more contemporary decor. There's a lovely lounge with a stove for the colder months, and hearty breakfasts made from locally sourced produce are served in the elegant conservatory. When the weather is fine, tea and cake can be enjoyed outside on the decked terrace.

Recommended in the area
Alnwick Garden; Chillingham Castle and wild cattle; Bamburgh Castle

Chatton Park House

★★★★★ BED AND BREAKFAST

Address: CHATTON, NE66 5RA
Tel: 01668 215507
Fax: 01668 215446
Email: enquiries@chattonpark.com
Website: www.chattonpark.com
Map ref: 11 NU02
Directions: A1 onto B6348 signed Wooler & Chatton for 4m, on right
Rooms: 4 en suite **S** £100–£130 **D** £130–£170
Notes: Wi-fi ⊗ ⚲ under 18yrs
Parking: 4
Closed: Open all year

Exclusively for adults only, Chatton Park House sits in four acres of beautiful grounds, surrounded by stunning Northumberland countryside. There are four spacious guest rooms, two of which are suites, furnished to a very high standard and with every luxury you could wish for, including king- or super-king-size bed, music system, DVD player, fridge, robes and slippers. There are tennis courts in the grounds for guests to use, and plenty of open space to wander in and explore. Back inside the house, breakfast is served in the elegant dining room, with the vast choice including a 'Northumberland platter' of local bacon, sausages, black pudding and free-range eggs with all the trimmings, as well as mushrooms or tomatoes on toast, oak-smoked local kippers, porridge with locally produced honey, and toasted hot crumpets or warm croissants - it's no wonder the breakfast here has picked up many awards. Chatton Park House - winner of the AA Guest Accommodation of the Year award 2009/10 - is moments away from spectacular beaches, castles, stately homes and fabulous countryside, making it the perfect base for exploring this corner of the North East.

Recommended in the area
Cheviot Hills; Alnwick Castle; Berwick upon Tweed

Peth Head Cottage

★★★★ BED AND BREAKFAST

Address: Juniper, HEXHAM, NE47 0LA
Tel: 01434 673286
Fax: 01434 673038
Email: peth_head@btopenworld.com
Website: www.peth-head-cottage.co.uk
Map ref: 11 NY96
Directions: B6306 S from Hexham, 200yds fork right, next left. Continue 3.5m, house 400yds on right after Juniper sign
Rooms: 2 en suite **S** £30 **D** £60
Notes: ⊗
Parking: 2

This lovingly maintained rose-covered cottage dates back to 1825 and is popular for its warm welcome, idyllic setting, and home comforts. Tea and hand-made biscuits are offered on arrival, and the delicious home cooking is enjoyed at breakfast too, including freshly baked bread and delicious homemade preserves. The inviting sandstone cottage is set in peaceful, well-kept gardens. There are two bright, south-facing bedrooms, both overlooking the garden, with shower rooms en suite, a hairdryer, TV, radio alarm and hospitality trays. The relaxing lounge is heavily beamed and furnished with comfortable chairs. Peth Head Cottage is ideally situated for visiting Durham and Newcastle as well as nearby Roman sites, and there are plenty of opportunities for walking and cycling in the area. A wide range of tourist information and maps is on hand for visitors to browse through and plan the day. The owner, Joan Liddle, is an excellent host who knows how to ensure her guests have an enjoyable stay. There is private off-road parking.

Recommended in the area

Beamish Open Air Museum; Hadrian's Wall; the Northumberland coast; Durham Cathedral; Finchale Priory; Lanercost Priory

Pheasant Inn

★★★★ INN

Address: Stannersburn, FALSTONE NE48 1DD
Tel: 01434 240382
Fax: 01434 240382
Email: stay@thepheasantinn.com
Website: www.thepheasantinn.com
Map ref: 11 NY78
Directions: 1m S of Falstone. Off B6320 to Kielder Water, via Bellingham or via Hexham A69 onto B6320 via Wall-Wark-Bellingham
Rooms: 8 annexe en suite (1 fmly) (5 GF)
S £50-£60 **D** £90-£95
Notes: ⊗ **Parking:** 40 **Closed:** 4 days Xmas

Set close to the magnificent Kielder Water, this classic country inn, built in 1624, has exposed stone walls, original beams, low ceilings, open fires and a display of old farm implements in the bar. Run by the welcoming Kershaw family since 1985, the inn was originally a farmhouse and has been refurbished to a very high standard. The bright, modern en suite bedrooms, some with their own entrances, are all contained in stone buildings adjoining the inn and are set round a pretty courtyard. All the rooms, including one family room, are spotless, well equipped, and have tea and coffee facilities, hairdryer, colour TV and radio-alarm clock; all enjoy delightful country views. Delicious home-cooked breakfasts and evening meals are served in the bar or in the attractive dining room, or may be taken in the pretty garden courtyard if the weather permits. Irene and her son Robin are responsible for the traditional home cooking using local produce and featuring delights such as game pie and roast Northumbrian lamb, as well as imaginative vegetarian choices. Drying and laundry facilities are available and, for energetic guests, cycle hire can be arranged.

Recommended in the area

Hadrian's Wall; Scottish Borders region; Northumberland's castles and stately homes

Eshott Hall

★★★★★ ◉ GUEST ACCOMMODATION

Address: Eshott, MORPETH, NE65 9EN
Tel: 01670 787454
Fax: 01670 786011
Email: info@eshotthall.co.uk
Website: www.eshotthall.co.uk
Map ref: 11 NZ18
Directions: Eshott signed off A1. N of Morpeth
Rooms: 11 en suite
S £120-£210 **D** £120-£280
Notes: Wi-fi
Parking: 50
Closed: 23-27 Dec

Eshott Hall is an elegant 17th century country house offering boutique accommodation in a stunning countryside setting. Having achieved five AA stars and a Rosette in its first year of opening, Eshott Hall is the ideal place for a romantic or relaxing break. The décor cleverly blends stylish, contemporary furnishings with the historic ambience of the house. Each of the 11 bedrooms is individually designed, with luxurious statement beds and sumptuous fabrics. Some even have roll-top baths within the room, so you can sit back and enjoy a relaxing soak whilst looking out over the beautiful gardens. Guests are encouraged to make themselves at home, and the communal areas - such as the drawing room and library - offer the perfect environment in which to unwind. The gardens and woodland surrounding the hall are well worth exploring, and you may well come across a red squirrel too. The restaurant offers a superb fine-dining experience, with menus influenced by local and seasonal ingredients, many of which are grown in the hall's own kitchen garden. Free Wi-fi is available in the public areas.

Recommended in the area

Alnwick Castle & Garden; the Holy Island of Lindisfarne; Newcastle

Oxfordshire

Blenheim Palace

Upham House Bed & Breakfast

★★★★ BED AND BREAKFAST
Address: The Lanes, BAMPTON, OX18 2JG
Tel: 01993 852703 & 07946 625563
Email: pat@uphamhouse.co.uk
Website: www.uphamhouse.co.uk
Map ref: 3 SP30 **Directions:** A4095 between Faringdon & Brize Norton
Rooms: 2 (1 en suite) (1 pri facs)
S fr £40 **D** £65-£75
Notes: Wi-fi ⊗ ⚲ under 6yrs
Parking: 3
Closed: 18 Dec-5 Jan

Upham House is a charming, traditional-style Cotswold stone house built 11 years ago on the site of the proprietor's original kitchen garden. It sits within a Conservation Area in the village of Bampton, setting for many of the scenes in the hit TV series *Downton Abbey*. It's a quiet spot, well away from main roads and just a five-minute walk from the village centre, where there's a small range of shops and four pubs. Upham House provides well-appointed and tastefully decorated accommodation, with quality linen and towels, comfortable beds, TV, tea- and coffee-making facilities, Wi-fi and hairdryer. One bedroom is en suite, while the other has a private adjacent bathroom. Breakfasts are well worth getting up for, featuring top-notch local and organic produce wherever possible, including award-winning sausages from village butcher Patrick Strainge, bacon from Kelmscott (the summer home of William Morris), locally baked bread and home-made marmalade and jam. There is off-street parking for three cars. From Bampton it's just a short drive to the River Thames and Kelmscott Manor, eight miles to Burford - the 'gateway to the Cotswolds' - and 15 miles to Oxford.

Recommended in the area
Cotswold Wildlife Park & Gardens; Blenheim Palace; Buscot Park; Cotswold Woollen Mill

Burford House

★★★★★ GUEST ACCOMMODATION

Address: 99 High St BURFORD OX18 4QA
Tel: 01993 823151
Fax: 01993 823240
Email: stay@burfordhouse.co.uk
Website: www.burfordhouse.co.uk
Map ref: 3 SP21
Directions: A40 onto A361, on right half way down hill
Rooms: 8 en suite (1 fmly) (1 GF)
S £124-£186
D £159-£199
Notes: Wi-fi ⊗

Set in picturesque Burford, a famous Cotswolds market town with many specialist shops, this charming 17th-century house is a landmark on the High Street. Marked by its half-timbered and stone exterior, it is a beautiful building in a great location, offering guests quality, space and comfort. The en suite bedrooms, including one family suite and some rooms with four-posters, are individually decorated and furnished to a very high standard. The host of thoughtful extras includes Witney pure wool blankets, fine cotton bed linen, flat-screen TV/DVDs, bathrobes, Penhaligon's toiletries and complimentary mineral water. Wi-fi is available in all rooms. Guests are invited to make use of the two comfortable lounges, one furnished in contemporary style with a wood-burning stove and the other bright and airy with traditional furnishings and doors leading out to the wisteria-clad courtyard garden. Using fine-quality local produce, wonderful lunches and afternoon teas are available daily in the Centre Stage restaurant, with its theatre posters and pictures, while dinner is also available on Thursday, Friday and Saturday evenings. Morning coffee and afternoon tea may also be enjoyed in the lounges. A full bar service is available, and the house has a fine array of malt whiskies, cognacs and wines.

Recommended in the area

Ashmolean Museum; Batsford Arboretum; Blenheim Palace

Chowle Farmhouse Bed & Breakfast

★★★★ FARMHOUSE
Address: FARINGDON, SN7 7SR
Tel: 01367 241688
Email: info@chowlefarmhouse.co.uk
Website: www.chowlefarmhouse.co.uk
Map ref: 3 SU29
Directions: From Faringdon rdbt on A420, 2m W on right. From Watchfield rdbt 1.5m E on left
Rooms: 4 en suite (1 GF) **S** fr £65 **D** fr £85
Notes: Wi-fi
Parking: 10

This friendly, family-run farmhouse B&B makes an ideal base for visiting the Thames Valley and surrounding area. It's within easy reach of the Cotswolds, London, Bath and the south coast, while local attractions include The Ridgeway National Trail, Thames Path and many National Trust houses and gardens. All four double rooms are equipped with tea- and coffee-making facilities, flat-screen TV, CD player and a super-sized en suite bathroom with heated towel rail and either a bath or power shower - or both. The rooms are thoughtfully equipped with luxury toiletries, fluffy towels and hairdryers. Breakfast, served at individual tables, is prepared to order from fresh, locally sourced ingredients along with homemade preserves. The full English breakfast - with Chowle Farm's own home-produced eggs and bacon - is the house speciality, but there are lighter dishes and vegetarian options available. Facilities for guests to enjoy at Chowle Farmhouse include a heated pool (in summer), hot tub, and a spacious garden and patio area. There's also free Wi-fi and secure parking with CCTV.

Recommended in the area
Blenheim Palace; Kelmscott Manor; Buscot Park

The Miller of Mansfield

★★★★★ ◉ RESTAURANT WITH ROOMS

Address: High St, GORING, RG8 9AW
Tel: 01491 872829 **Fax:** 01491 873100
Email: reservations@millerofmansfield.com
Website: www.millerofmansfield.com
Map ref: 3 SU68 **Directions:** M40 junct 7, S on A329 towards Benson, A4074 towards Reading, B4009 towards Goring. Or M4 junct 12, S on A4 towards Newbury. 3rd rdbt onto A340 to Pangbourne. A329 to Streatley, right at lights onto B4009 into Goring
Rooms: 13 en suite (2 fmly) **S** £70-£130 **D** £80-£160
Notes: Wi-fi **Parking:** 2

The newly renovated Miller of Mansfield occupies a quiet Thames-side village setting, overlooking the Chiltern Hills. This former coaching inn offers sumptuous en suite rooms and suites, all distinctively styled and with all the home comforts guests could want, and more. There are flat-screen digital TVs, marble bathrooms, free-standing stone resin baths and/or high-pressure showers, fluffy robes, Egyptian cotton linen, organic latex mattresses and luxurious REN toiletries. Some rooms come with stunning antique French beds. The award-winning restaurant, with views over the terrace gardens, provides an informal and enjoyable eating experience. Diners can expect impressive modern British cuisine featuring local, free-range and organic produce, home-cured and smoked fish and meats, hand-rolled pasta, home-made breads, ice creams and sorbets, coupled with an exciting wine list - with many wines available by the glass - and a selection of local real ales in the bar. From breakfast, light meals and afternoon tea through to three-course dinners, the menus at the Miller change regularly to reflect the best of seasonal produce. Free high-speed internet access is available at the Wi-fi hotspot and there are also fully equipped meeting facilities for business travellers.

Recommended in the area

Basildon Park (NT); Beale Wildlife Park and Gardens; Henley-on-Thames

Corn Croft Guest House

★★★★ GUEST ACCOMMODATION

Address: 69-71 Corn St, WITNEY, OX28 6AS
Tel: 01993 773298
Fax: 01993 773298
Email: richardturner4@btconnect.com
Website: www.corncroft.co.uk
Map ref: 3 SP31
Directions: A40 to town centre, from Market Square into Corn Street, 400mtrs on left
Rooms: 11 en suite (1 fmly) (2 GF)
S £69 **D** £79
Notes: Wi-fi
Closed: 24-26 Dec

Corn Croft Guest House occupies a handsome old building at the quieter end of the town of Witney, though only two minutes' walk from the centre. It's a great base for visiting the Cotswolds and Oxford - which is only seven miles away - whether on business or for pleasure. Richard, the friendly proprietor, and his staff will make you feel at home, as will the comfortable, well-equipped, bright and airy and spotlessly clean accommodation. All 11 en suite bedrooms are furnished with Queen Anne and Jacobean-style pieces, including some four-poster beds, and come with tea- and coffee-making facilities, flat-screen TVs, and the odd little extra luxury such as fresh flowers, mineral water and chocolates. Substantial breakfasts based on top-notch local produce are served in the spacious dining room: take your pick from a first-class full English or an equally good continental breakfast. Corn Croft Guest House doesn't offer evening meals but the staff will happily recommend some good local restaurants and pubs.

Recommended in the area
Oxford; Blenheim Palace; The Cotswolds

Shropshire

Whitcliffe Common, Ludlow

Caro's Bed & Breakfast

★★★ BED AND BREAKFAST
Address: 1 Higher Netley, DORRINGTON, Shrewsbury, SY5 7JY
Tel: 01743 718790 & 07739 285263
Email: info@carosbandb.co.uk
Website: www.carosbandb.co.uk
Map ref: 6 SJ40
Directions: 1m SW of Dorrington. Exit A49 in Dorrington signed Picklescott, 1m left onto driveway by stone bridge, signed Higher Netley
Rooms: 2 en suite (1 fmly) **S** £35-£55 **D** £35-£55
Notes: Wi-fi ⊗ **Parking**: 4
Closed: 21-28 Dec

This charming cottage bed and breakfast in the foothills of Long Mynd is a perfect base for walking holidays. It's also an ideal place to stay for those wishing to explore Shropshire's many attractions, with the historic market towns of Shrewsbury and Ludlow and the Ironbridge Gorge World Heritage Site all within half-an-hour's drive. The cottage has lovely views across open countryside, a pretty garden where you can soak up the tranquil surroundings in summer, and a comfortable guest sitting room with roaring log fire in winter. There are two en suite rooms with king-size beds, one of which connects to a children's room with one single and one cot-size bed (a highchair, collapsible cot and toys are available to borrow too). Each double room has a flat-screen digital TV, radio, and tea- and coffee-making facilities. Breakfasts are based on locally sourced and homemade produce, including eggs from the chickens you can see roaming around in the next-door field, home-baked bread and marmalade, and fruits picked from the garden during the season. Packed lunches are available on request, as are homemade ready meals (prepared by the lady next-door) for families who wish to save money on going out to eat.

Recommended in the area
Ironbridge Gorge Museum; Stokesay Castle; Medieval towns of Shrewsbury and Ludlow

The Inn at Grinshill

★★★★  INN

Address: The High St, GRINSHILL,
Shrewsbury, SY4 3BL
Tel: 01939 220410
Fax: 01939 220397
Email: info@theinnatgrinshill.co.uk
Website: www.theinnatgrinshill.co.uk
Map ref: 6 SJ52
Directions: N of Shrewsbury on A49, after 7m turn left, Inn 500yds on left
Rooms: 6 en suite **S** fr £60 **D** £120
Notes: Wi-fi
Parking: 30

Surrounded by idyllic countryside and at the hub of the quintessentially English village of Grinshill, this charming old inn offers a true sense of history combined with a good dose of modern luxury. It's a graceful building dating from the Edwardian era, sitting in a lovely garden full of pretty roses in summer. Inside, the decor is a bold but successful mix of the traditional and the contemporary. The AA Rosette-awarded restaurant is colourful and vibrant, with an open kitchen so you can watch the chefs busily preparing your meal. Within the restaurant you'll find Bubbles Bar, where you can perch on a black barstool and take your pick from a range of sparkling wines, including champagne, prosecco and cava. Alternatively, the Elephant & Castle bar has a more traditional feel with its real ales and welcoming open fire. Upstairs the en suite bedrooms are individually designed in a luxurious and elegant style and finished to the highest standards. Think large baths, power-showers, and sumptuous pocket-sprung beds, along with all the technical mod-cons that you'd expect of a four-star inn. Fully sound-proofed floors ensure a peaceful night's sleep.

Recommended in the area

Stokesay Castle; The Ironbridge Gorge Museums; Severn Valley Railway

Broseley House

★★★★ GUEST HOUSE

Address: 1 The Square, Broseley,
IRONBRIDGE, TF12 5EW
Tel: 01952 882043 & 07790 732723
Email: info@broseleyhouse.co.uk
Website: www.broseleyhouse.co.uk
Map ref: 6 SJ60
Directions: 1m S of Ironbridge in Broseley town centre
Rooms: 7 en suite (2 fmly) (1 GF)
S £50-£60 **D** £70-£90
Notes: Wi-fi ❦ under 5yrs

This impressive and lovingly restored period townhouse, dating back to 1820, prides itself on being a friendly place to stay. It offers high quality decor throughout and a very personal service. The thoughtfully and individually furnished en suite bedrooms - including two family rooms, a twin and three doubles, one with a four-poster - come with all mod-cons, such as flat-screen TV, DVD player, fridge, i-Pod docking station, free Wi-fi, bathrobes, slippers and a well-stocked hospitality tray. Self-catering accommodation is also available. Comprehensive and award-winning breakfasts, ranging from a full English to lighter alternatives, are freshly cooked from local produce and served in the elegant dining room. Located in the centre of Broseley, just two miles from Ironbridge, Broseley House is convenient for touring the area, particularly on foot or by bike (with secure storage for bikes available). The town of Broseley has a variety of restaurants, pubs, takeaways and shops, which are all within easy walking distance.

Recommended in the area

Benthall Hall; Blists Hill Victorian Town; Buildwas Abbey

The Clive Bar & Restaurant with Rooms

★★★★★ ◉◉ RESTAURANT WITH ROOMS

Address: Bromfield, LUDLOW, SY8 2JR
Tel: 01584 856565 & 856665
Fax: 01584 856661
Email: info@theclive.co.uk
Website: www.theclive.co.uk
Map ref: 6 S057
Directions: 2m N of Ludlow on A49 in Bromfield
Rooms: 15 annexe en suite (9 fmly) (11 GF)
S £65-£90 **D** £90-£115
Notes: Wi-fi ⊗
Parking: 100
Closed: 25-26 Dec

Situated on the edge of the town of Ludlow, The Clive Bar & Restaurant with Rooms is a clever blend of the traditional and the contemporary. Originally an 18th century farmhouse, the main building has been developed to retain the original features of the bar, whilst giving the restaurant a more minimalist, 21st-century look and feel. All 15 en suite bedrooms are located in period outbuildings which have been tastefully converted to provide high quality, contemporary-style accommodation. The bedrooms are very well-equipped and some are suitable for families. There are many excellent restaurants in the foodie town of Ludlow, and The Clive Restaurant - holder of two AA Rosettes - certainly counts among them. The restaurant is renowned for its superb modern British cuisine, which is rooted in careful sourcing of fresh, local produce from the surrounding areas. The bar - with adjoining courtyard for the warmer months - offers less formal dining and a lighter menu. You'll find The Clive Bar & Restaurant with Rooms in Bromfield, two miles north of Ludlow. Ample parking is provided for guests.

Recommended in the area

Stokesay Castle; Ludlow Food Hall; Ludlow Race Course and Golf Club; Offa's Dyke

Number Twenty Eight

★★★★ BED AND BREAKFAST

Address: 28 Lower Broad St, LUDLOW, SY8 1PQ
Tel: 01584 875466
Email: enquiries@no28ludlow.co.uk
Website: www.no28ludlow.co.uk
Map ref: 6 S057
Directions: In town centre. Over Ludford Bridge into Lower Broad St, 3rd house on right
Rooms: 2 en suite **S** £65-£75 **D** £80-£90
Notes: Wi-fi ⊗ 🚭 under 16yrs
Closed: Nov-May

A property with a wealth of period character, this half-timbered, 16th-century town house is just a stroll from the centre of historic Ludlow with its world-class eateries, castle, famous market and many other attractions. The listed building is immaculately maintained and offers every modern comfort. Guests have the use of a cosy sitting room and in fine weather you can relax in the pretty courtyard or on the delightful roof terrace. The en suite bedrooms are well-equipped and come with flat-screen TV and Egyptian cotton bed linen, as well as many thoughtful extras such as home-made biscuits. Breakfasts are prepared to order and include freshly squeezed orange juice, fresh fruit salad, locally sourced bacon, sausage, eggs and breads, with a fish and vegetarian option available too. Number Twenty Eight doesn't offer evening meals but that shouldn't be a problem with some of the UK's - if not the world's - finest restaurants right on your doorstep.

Recommended in the area

Berrington Hall; Stokesay Castle; Ironbridge World Heritage Site

Soulton Hall

★★★★ GUEST ACCOMMODATION

Address: Soulton, WEM, SY4 5RS
Tel: 01939 232786
Fax: 01939 234097
Email: enquiries@soultonhall.co.uk
Website: www.soultonhall.co.uk
Map ref: 6 SJ52
Directions: From A49 between Shrewsbury & Whitchurch take B5065 towards Wem. Soulton Hall 2m E of Wem
Rooms: 4 en suite 3 annexe en suite (2 fmly) (3 GF)
S £44-£131 **D** £88-£142
Notes: Wi-fi **Parking:** 52

The Ashton family can trace their tenure of this impressive manor house back to the 1400s and 1500s, and much evidence of the building's age remains. The family and their staff offer excellent levels of personal service, with the care of guests given utmost importance. The welcoming entrance lounge leads into the well-stocked bar on one side and an elegant dining room on the other. Here, a good range of freshly prepared dishes, using local produce wherever possible, is served in a friendly and relaxed setting. After a meal, guests can retire to the lounge hall to enjoy coffee and liqueurs in front of a blazing log fire (the house has central heating as well as log fires during the winter). The bedrooms at Soulton Hall reflect the character of the house, with features like mullioned windows, exposed timbers and wood panelling. The converted carriage house across the garden offers ground-floor accommodation in two spacious double rooms, each with spa baths. Standing in its own grounds beyond the walled garden, Cedar Lodge provides a choice of a peaceful four-poster suite, or more modest family accommodation. Soulton Hall stands in 500 acres of open farmland, parkland and ancient oak woodland, which guests are welcome to explore.

Recommended in the area

Blists Hill Victorian Town, Ironbridge; China museum and ironworks, Ironbridge; Shrewsbury

Somerset

Glastonbury Tor

Dorian House

★★★★ GUEST ACCOMMODATION
Address: 1 Upper Oldfield Park, BATH, BA2 3JX
Tel: 01225 426336
Fax: 01225 444699
Email: info@dorianhouse.co.uk
Website: www.dorianhouse.co.uk
Map ref: 2 ST76
Directions: A36 onto A367 (Wells Rd), right into Upper Oldfield Park, 3rd building on left
Rooms: 13 en suite (4 fmly) (2 GF)
S £65-£95 **D** £65-£165
Notes: Wi-fi ⊗ **Parking:** 9
Closed: 25 & 26 Dec

This elegant Victorian property, built from Bath stone around 1880, has stunning views over the city. The house is just 10 minutes' walk from the centre and is also close to many fine gardens and pretty villages, making it a good base. Dorian House is owned by Tim Hugh, Principal Cellist with the London Symphony Orchestra, and his wife Kathryn. Music influences the overall character and ambience of the property, with bedrooms bearing names such as Vivaldi, Gershwin and Rossini. The house was extensively refurbished in 2009 and one new room, which contains a beautiful four-poster, has been named Slava in honour of the Russian cellist Rostropovich. Each of the en suite bedrooms, which feature opulent fabrics and stunning decor, have good views over Bath's famous Georgian Royal Crescent or the well-tended gardens. All provide a range of extras such as marble bathrooms with high-pressure showers, crisp cotton sheets, fluffy towels and hairdryers. The attractive lounge has an open fireplace, large comfortable sofas, a bar and views of the terraced gardens. Delicious breakfasts offer treats such as freshly baked croissants and fresh fruit juices, as well as the traditional full English. Parking is on a very steep incline but free.

Recommended in the area

Thermae Bath Spa; Bath Abbey; Westonbirt Arboretum

The Kennard

★★★★ GUEST ACCOMMODATION

Address: 11 Henrietta St, BATH, BA2 6LL
Tel: 01225 310472
Fax: 01225 460054
Email: reception@kennard.co.uk
Website: www.kennard.co.uk
Map ref: 2 ST76
Directions: A4 onto A36 (Bathwick St), 2nd right into Henrietta Rd & Henrietta St
Rooms: 12 (10 en suite) (2 GF)
S £65-£70 **D** £110-£150
Notes: Wi-fi ⊗ ⚭ under 8yrs
Closed: 1wk Xmas

A stay at The Kennard gives you the chance to enjoy the delights of a true Georgian town house. Built as a lodging house in 1794 - during the golden age of Bath's prosperity - The Kennard has been restored and refurbished over the years and is now run as a charming and friendly small guest house by Mary and Giovanni Baiano. All 12 bedrooms are thoughtfully and individually furnished in keeping with the period of the house, and all have en suite facilities, Wi-fi, flat-screen TVs and beverage trays. The original Georgian kitchen is these days a delightful breakfast room, where you can take your pick from the continental selection on the buffet table, followed by something hot fresh from the kitchen. Located just over Pulteney Bridge and only a short distance away from the railway station, The Kennard is ideally situated for visiting all of Bath's many attractions, including the abbey and Roman Baths. It also makes the perfect base for exploring the wider area: travel north to the picturesque villages of the Cotswolds; south to Glastonbury and Wells; or east to Stonehenge.

Recommended in the area

The Georgian city of Bath; Wells; Glastonbury

Marlborough House

★★★★ GUEST ACCOMMODATION
Address: 1 Marlborough Ln, BATH, BA1 2NQ
Tel: 01225 318175
Fax: 01225 466127
Email: mars@manque.dircon.co.uk
Website: www.marlborough-house.net
Map ref: 2 ST76
Directions: 450yds W of city centre, at A4 junct with Marlborough Ln
Rooms: 6 en suite (2 fmly) (1 GF)
S £75-£110 **D** £85-£135
Notes: Wi-fi **Parking:** 3
Closed: 24-26 Dec

Marlborough House is an enchanting guest house, run in a friendly and informal style by owner Peter Moore. This large and impressive stone Victorian house has well-proportioned, spacious rooms, elegantly refurbished to a very high standard. A fusion of antiques and contemporary furnishings best describes the style of the bedrooms, which are bright, airy and relaxing, and come with either a super-king or king-size bed. They are fully air-conditioned and equipped with new en suite bathrooms complete with complimentary organic toiletries and a hairdryer. There is a hospitality tray of organic teas and coffees in each room, a well-stocked mini-fridge, and a decanter of complimentary sherry, along with a flat-screen digital TV with Freeview channels, and free Wi-fi. Built in 1887, Marlborough House is conveniently situated for all of Bath's major attractions, such as the famous Royal Crescent, Circus, Assembly Rooms, Jane Austen Centre, guildhall, abbey, Roman Baths and Thermae Spa, which are all no more than 15 minutes' walk away.

Recommended in the area
Roman Baths; Bath Abbey tower tour; Thermae Bath Spa

Tasburgh House

★★★★★ GUEST ACCOMMODATION
Address: Warminster Rd, BATH, BA2 6SH
Tel: 01225 425096
Fax: 01225 463842
Email: stay@tasburghhouse.co.uk
Website: www.tasburghhouse.co.uk
Map ref: 2 ST76
Directions: On N side of A36, next to Bathampton Ln junct
Rooms: 12 en suite (3 fmly) (2 GF)
S £85-£100 **D** £120-£180
Notes: Wi-fi ⊗ **Parking:** 16
Closed: 21 Dec-14 Jan

Tasburgh House is an award-winning 12-bedroom guest house, located just over half-a-mile from the centre of Bath. The house sits in seven acres of beautiful gardens extending down to the Kennet and Avon Canal, and has stunning views over the Avon Valley and Bath city centre. If you're looking for luxury at an affordable price, complimentary parking and somewhere to relax away from the bustle of the busy city, then you can't go wrong here. Enjoy a glass of wine or bubbly out on the terraces, listen to the relaxing sounds of the fountain and watch the boats go by. Tasburgh House offers a range of tastefully decorated rooms with all the facilities you would expect to make your stay comfortable and enjoyable. Your welcoming and knowledgeable hosts, Sue and Toni, will greet you with homemade chocolate brownies on arrival, and will go out of their way to make you feel at home, offering advice on things to see and do in the area, and making bookings for you if required. The award-winning breakfast is well worth getting up for, with a choice of continental or a full English. Groups of four or more can take advantage of gourmet meals, a picnic in the meadow or a barbecue on the terrace.

Recommended in the area
World Heritage City of Bath; walking along the Kennet and Avon Canal; Roman Baths & Pump Rooms; Southgate Shopping Centre; Bath Music Festival; Bath Golf Club; boat & cycle hire

Blackmore Farm

★★★★ FARMHOUSE
Address: Blackmore Ln, Cannington,
BRIDGWATER, TA5 2NE
Tel: 01278 653442
Fax: 01278 653427
Email: dyerfarm@aol.com
Website: www.dyerfarm.co.uk
Map ref: 2 ST23 **Directions:** 3m W of Bridgwater, left at Bridgwater Mowers (Cannington) into Blackmore Ln. Farm 1m on left
Rooms: 3 en suite 2 annexe en suite (1 fmly) (2 GF)
S £48-£55 **D** £90-£100
Notes: Wi-fi ⊗ **Parking:** 10

Step back in time at this Grade I listed 15th-century manor house, which was named AA Guest Accommodation of the Year for England 2011-2012. The old house retains many period features including oak beams, stone archways and a medieval chapel, and is surrounded by beautiful rolling countryside. There's a range of accommodation to choose from at Blackmore Farm, with the rooms in the main house offering views across to the Quantock Hills, along with a real sense of history thanks to the original roof trusses and a cob and lime plaster wall. That's not to say you won't find every modern comfort you could wish for too. Alternatively, you can stay in the Cider Press or Courtyard rooms - located in the tastefully converted farm buildings - which are comfortable, modern and flexible enough to suit all types of guest, including families and disabled people. The hearty breakfasts, based on lots of fresh, home-produced ingredients, are a highlight of any stay at this friendly and welcoming B&B.

Recommended in the area
Cheddar Gorge; Wells Cathedral; The Quantock Hills

Tarr Farm Inn

★★★★★ ◉ INN

Address: Tarr Steps, Exmoor National Park,
DULVERTON, TA22 9PY
Tel: 01643 851507
Fax: 01643 851111
Email: enquiries@tarrfarm.co.uk
Website: www.tarrfarm.co.uk
Map ref: 2 SS92
Directions: 4m NW of Dulverton. Off B3223 signed Tarr Steps, signs to Tarr Farm Inn
Rooms: 9 en suite (4 GF) **S** £95 **D** £150
Notes: Wi-fi 🐾 under 14yrs
Parking: 10

Set in its own 40 acres, 16th century Tarr Farm Inn sits just above Tarr Steps and the River Barle in the heart of the stunning Exmoor National Park. Only seven miles from Dulverton, the journey to Tarr Farm Inn takes you through beautiful wooded valleys and across the open moorland of Winsford Hill, with fabulous views of Wales, Devon and Dartmoor. Each of the nine bedrooms is spacious and tastefully decorated in a fresh, contemporary style, with every modern comfort you could wish for, including power showers, full-size baths, fluffy bathrobes and towels and Egyptian cotton sheets. There are DVD players in every room, along with broadband access, an iron and ironing board, mini-bar, tea- and coffee-making facilities, homemade biscuits and more. When it comes to dining in, why wouldn't you? Tarr Farm Inn has picked up an AA Rosette for the high quality of its cuisine, with the kitchen making full use of the abundant local larder - including Exmoor lamb, Devon Red Ruby beef, Cornish seafood, and locally shot game and venison - in classic dishes with a contemporary twist.

Recommended in the area

Exmoor National Park; North Devon coast; numerous National Trust properties

Roman baths with Bath Abbey behind

Tudor Cottage

★★★★ GUEST ACCOMMODATION
Address: PORLOCK, TA24 8HQ
Tel: 01643 862255 & 07855 531593
Email: bookings@tudorcottage.net
Website: www.tudorcottage.net
Map ref: 2 SS84
Directions: M5 junct 25, A358, A39 through Minehead. 5m, follow signs for Allerford & Bossington. 1m, 1st house on left
Rooms: 3 (1 en suite) (2 pri facs) **S** £50 **D** £70-75
Notes: Wi-fi ⊗ ⚠ under 10yrs
Parking: 3

A charming 15th century cottage is the setting for this delightful bed and breakfast in the National Trust village of Bossington, within the Exmoor National Park. The three guest bedrooms come with en suite or private facilities, TV with Freeview, DVD player, Wi-fi, hospitality tray, mini-bar and hairdryer, and all have lovely views over the paddock and Bossington Hill. At breakfast there's an extensive menu to choose from, with everything prepared from fresh, local produce. Tudor Cottage is in a wonderfully tranquil setting, surrounded by beautiful countryside and with many walks from the doorstep - the sea is just 10 minutes away on foot. For wildlife lovers, the drive up Porlock Hill shouldn't be missed: here you should spot Exmoor ponies and, if you're particularly lucky, red deer. The cottage is just one mile from Porlock with its many shops, pubs and restaurants, but if you choose to eat in, pre-booked evening meals can be provided, as well as packed lunches. Tudor Cottage is licensed and offers a good range of wines, spirits and beers to enjoy with a meal in the dining room, or whilst relaxing in the lounge or the beautiful garden.

Recommended in the area

South West Coast Path; Exmoor National Park; Porlock; star-gazing

Cannards Grave Farmhouse

★★★★ GUEST ACCOMMODATION
Address: Cannards Grave,
SHEPTON MALLET, BA4 4LY
Tel: 01749 347091 **Fax:** 01749 347091
Email: sue@cannardsgravefarmhouse.co.uk
Website: www.cannardsgravefarmhouse.co.uk
Map ref: 2 ST64
Directions: On A37 between Shepton Mallet
& The Bath and West Showground, 100yds from
Highwayman pub towards showground on left
Rooms: 4 en suite 1 annexe en suite (2 fmly) (1 GF)
S £40-£50 **D** £60-£70
Notes: Wi-fi ⊗ **Parking:** 6

Charming host Sue Crockett offers quality accommodation at this welcoming 17th-century farmhouse. The bedrooms are spotlessly clean and have lots of thoughtful extras, including hospitality trays with mineral water, biscuits and mints, and fridges with fresh milk. There's a spacious four-poster room, plus a double, twin and two family rooms (one is actually a family annexe with its own entrance, two interconnecting twin rooms and a small self-catering area). The rear-facing rooms have far-reaching countryside views, and all have double-glazed windows which effectively block out any noise from the main road. Superb full English breakfasts, along with a range of cereals, fruit, yoghurts, croissants and toast, are served in the garden conservatory, and there is a comfortable lounge to relax in. Cannards Grave Farmhouse is ideally situated for those visiting the Shepton Mallet area on business, as well as for leisure travellers exploring the beautiful countryside, towns and villages of the West Country. The farmhouse is just two minutes' drive from the Bath and West Showground, making it an ideal base for event exhibitors or visitors.

Recommended in the area
Bath and West Showground; historic Wells; Glastonbury Tor; City of Bath

Lower Farm

★★★★ FARMHOUSE
Address: Thornfalcon, TAUNTON, TA3 5NR
Tel: 01823 443549
Email: doreen@titman.eclipse.co.uk
Website: www.thornfalcon.co.uk
Map ref: 2 ST22
Directions: M5 junct 25, 2m SE on A358, left opposite Nags Head pub, farm signed 1m on left
Rooms: 2 (1 en suite) (1 pri facs) 9 annexe (7 en suite) (2 pri facs) (2 fmly) (7 GF)
S £45-£50 **D** £70-£75
Notes: Wi-fi ⊗ ⚹ under 5yrs
Parking: 10

This charming thatched 15th century Somerset longhouse, run by Doreen and husband John, is full of character and surrounded by lovely gardens and open fields. Beamed ceilings and inglenook fireplaces testify to its age. The bedrooms are split between the thatched farmhouse and a converted granary and byre, situated in an attractive courtyard setting. All rooms are en suite or have private facilities, and are furnished to a high standard with hospitality trays, televisions, hairdryers and Wi-fi available. A hearty breakfast is served in the farmhouse kitchen/breakfast room, and features locally produced bacon and sausages, as well as eggs from Lower Farm's own free-range hens, all cooked on the Aga. Even the jams are homemade by Doreen, using soft and orchard fruits from the farm. There's a comfortable sitting room where guests can relax in front of a wood burning stove during the cooler months. Lower Farm is ideally located for visiting the county town of Taunton - just four miles away - and touring Somerset's many attractions.

Recommended in the area

Hestercombe Gardens; Willow & Wetlands visitor centre; Quantock Hills; West Somerset Railway

Crown & Victoria

★★★★ ● INN

Address: Farm St, TINTINHULL, Yeovil, BA22 8PZ
Tel: 01935 823341
Fax: 01935 825786
Email: info@thecrownandvictoria.co.uk
Website: www.thecrownandvictoria.co.uk
Map ref: 2 ST41
Directions: Off A303, signs for Tintinhull Gardens
Rooms: 5 en suite
Notes: Wi-fi
Parking: 60

The Crown and Victoria country inn stands in the heart of the pretty village of Tintinhull. In days gone by, as well as being the village pub, the inn was also a private school - lessons took place where the existing bar is situated. Today, above the new restaurant, the unfussy bedrooms are light and airy and very well equipped with hairdryers, TVs with DVD players, tea- and coffee-making facilities, and wireless broadband internet access. The staff ensure you are well cared for. The contemporary bar and restaurant offers a successful combination of traditional pub atmosphere and quality dining. Carefully presented dishes are available for lunch and dinner under the direction of head chef, Stephen Yates. The menu ranges from traditional English dishes such as steak and ale pie to the more elaborate pan-roasted breast of duck on a bed of spinach with a potato rösti, plum and port jus. The extensive wine list includes 10 fine house wines and there is a choice of local real ales. Relax in the garden with a drink or a light meal when the weather is kind, or enjoy a candlelit dinner in the conservatory with lovely garden views.

Recommended in the area

Tintinhull House Garden (NT); Montacute House (NT); Barrington Court (NT); Yeovil; Fleet Air Arm Museum, Yeovilton

Double-Gate Farm

★★★★ FARMHOUSE
Address: Godney, WELLS, BA5 1RZ
Tel: 01458 832217
Fax: 01458 835612
Email: doublegatefarm@aol.com
Website: www.doublegatefarm.com
Map ref: 2 ST54
Directions: A39 from Wells towards Glastonbury, at Polsham right signed Godney/Polsham. 2m to x-rds, continue to farmhouse on left after inn
Rooms: 3 en suite 4 annexe en suite (4 fmly) (4 GF)
S £60-£85 **D** £70-£120
Notes: ⊗ **Parking:** 9 **Closed:** 20 Dec-5 Jan

A special welcome awaits you, not just from the owner but from Jasper and Paddy, the friendly retrievers, at this lovely old farmhouse situated on the banks of the River Sheppey on the Somerset Levels. There are good views of Glastonbury Tor and the Mendip Hills, as well as fishing at the bottom of the garden, and cycle rides from the farm on the quiet roads which abound with birds and wildlife. Guests can play table tennis or snooker in the games room, or watch their own DVDs in the well-equipped en suite bedrooms. Telephone and internet access are now available in all guest rooms. New to Double-Gate Farm are some luxury riverside suites (£50-55pppn) suitable for two to four guests, with spacious bedrooms with fridges, ceiling fans, mood lighting and access onto an extensive patio. Each of these large suites can be adapted for disabled use (NAS 3). Double-Gate Farm is well-known for its beautiful summer flower garden and home-grown tomatoes and fruit. Excellent breakfasts are served in the dining room with its panoramic views of the garden and meadow. The options are extensive - take your pick from cereals, juices, yoghurts, compotes, local cheeses, homemade bread, a full farmhouse breakfast, kippers and freshly-made pancakes.

Recommended in the area
Wells Cathedral and Bishop's Palace; Cheddar Gorge; Bath; Glastonbury

North Wheddon Farm

★★★★ 🛏 🍽 FARMHOUSE

Address: WHEDDON CROSS, TA24 7EX
Tel: 01643 841791
Email: rachael@go-exmoor.co.uk
Website: www.go-exmoor.co.uk
Map ref: 2 SS93
Directions: 500yds S of village x-rds on A396. Pass Moorland Hall on left, driveway next right
Rooms: 3 (2 en suite) (1 pri facs)
S £33-£38.50 **D** £66-£77
Notes: Wi-fi
Parking: 5

North Wheddon Farm sits on a south-facing hillside within the Exmoor National Park, offering fabulous, far reaching views. Built in 1840, the listed farmhouse has the feel of a Georgian country house, with its high ceilings and large open fires. Guests are invited to explore the lovely grounds, complete with a tranquil stream, a waterfall and a paddock crossed with natural springs. The bedrooms are light and airy and attractively furnished, with all mod cons such as tea- and coffee-making facilities, TV and DVD players. The Snug provides a cosy place to relax during the day and is also the setting for breakfast - that is, unless it's warm enough to enjoy breakfast in the sunny garden. North Wheddon Farm is renowned for its excellent traditional cooking, which guests can enjoy further in the evenings when a three-course dinner is served, accompanied by a choice of wines. Whatever cannot be produced on the farm is sourced from trusted local suppliers. From home-smoked bacon to breads baked in the Aga, you certainly won't go hungry. The farm provides the ideal base for touring the area, with fantastic beaches and stunning scenery right on the doorstep.

Recommended in the area

Dunster Castle; West Somerset Railway; Dunkery Beacon

Staffordshire

Lichfield Cathedral

The Church Farm

★★★★ FARMHOUSE
Address: Holt Ln, KINGSLEY,
Stoke-on-Trent, ST10 2BA
Tel: 01538 754759
Email: thechurchfarm@yahoo.co.uk
Website: www.bandbatthechurchfarm.co.uk
Map ref: 6 SK04
Directions: From A52 in Kingsley into Holt Ln,
150mtrs on right opposite school drive
Rooms: 3 en suite **S** £35 **D** £55-£60
Notes: Wi-fi ✪
Parking: 6

The Church Farm, a listed 18th-century farmhouse situated in the quaint village of Kingsley, is still a working dairy farm and family home. It sits amid 100 acres of farmland and makes a good base for exploring the Potteries and the Peak District. It provides friendly, relaxed accommodation in a number of beautiful, individually decorated rooms, complete with original antique furniture. There's a lounge with a log fire where guests can put their feet up during the winter season and relax. The thoughtfully equipped en suite bedrooms within the main house are stylishly furnished, and guests are provided with a range of little extras. Breakfast is not to be missed, as you will be offered a hearty Staffordshire farmhouse plate of locally sourced produce, including free-range eggs from the owners' hens, all served at individual tables overlooking the cottage gardens. Church Farm's scented garden is a haven for birds and butterflies during the summer, and you can wander down the paths that lead from the house to the beautiful Churnet Valley.

Recommended in the area

Alton Towers; Peak District National Park; Churnet Valley Steam Railway

Netherstowe House

★★★★ GUEST HOUSE
Address: Netherstowe Ln, LICHFIELD, WS13 6AY
Tel: 01543 254270
Fax: 01543 419998
Email: reception@netherstowehouse.com
Website: www.netherstowehouse.com
Map ref: 6 SK10
Directions: A38 onto A5192, 0.3m on right, turn onto Netherstowe Ln. Take 1st left & 1st right down private drive
Rooms: 9 en suite 8 annexe en suite (2 fmly) (4 GF)
D £85-£120 **Notes:** Wi-fi ⊗
Parking: 35

Netherstowe House is a charming boutique guest house set in a beautiful country estate - the perfect retreat for leisure and business guests alike. The house is a stunning Georgian Grade II listed building, surrounded by tranquil formal grounds, resplendent in verdant shades at any time of the year. Netherstowe has the elegance of a fine old country house, along with every modern luxury you could possibly desire. Guests can enjoy the many stylishly decorated public rooms, conference facilities, gardens, gym, fine-dining restaurant, steakhouse brasserie and cocktail bar throughout their stay. All the guest accommodation at Netherstowe House is en suite, with lots of little extra touches to make you feel welcome, such as complimentary Wi-fi, flat-screen TVs with Freeview, luxury toiletries, memory foam pillows, and a superb selection of refreshments including home-made biscuits. The bedding is of the highest quality, and fresh fluffy towels await you after a refreshing shower or bath. There's secure private parking, and a well-appointed gymnasium. The restaurant is elegant and formal, with crisp white linen and efficient yet discreet service. Breakfast and dinner are a real treat, with a wide range of delicacies prepared from fine local and seasonal produce.

Recommended in the area
Lichfield Cathedral; The National Forest; Fradley Junction

Suffolk

Dunwich

The Chantry

★★★★ GUEST ACCOMMODATION
Address: 8 Sparhawk St,
BURY ST EDMUNDS, IP33 1RY
Tel: 01284 767427
Fax: 01284 760946
Email: chantry1987@btinternet.com
Website: www.chantryhotel.com
Map ref: 4 TL86
Directions: From cathedral S into Crown St, left into Sparhawk St
Rooms: 11 en suite 3 annexe en suite (1 fmly) (1 GF)
S £77-£107.50 **D** £97-£117
Notes: Wi-fi **Parking:** 16

The Chantry is situated in the heart of the medieval grid pattern of streets that make up central Bury St Edmunds, just a few minutes' walk from the cathedral, Theatre Royal, restaurants and shops. It is a Grade II listed Georgian townhouse dating from 1780, with an adjoining Tudor annex dating from the 16th century. The 14 en suite guest rooms are individually decorated in a traditional style to an extremely high standard, and with evident attention to detail. Superior rooms come with genuine antique beds, while deluxe doubles have lounge areas and large walk-in showers in the en suite. The off-road car park provides a space for each bedroom, and free internet access is available throughout the building. The Chantry is only open to residents, so you can be assured that the cosy and relaxing lounge bar and the restaurant are exclusively for the use of guests. Bury St Edmunds is an historical gem with fine buildings, public gardens, a Georgian theatre and lots of independent shops and restaurants. There is also a modern side to the town, with a new shopping centre and a state-of-the-art music and performance venue.

Recommended in the area

Abbey Gardens and ruins; Theatre Royal (NT); Ickworth House Park & Gardens (NT)

Clarice House

★★★★★ ◉ GUEST ACCOMMODATION
Address: Horringer Court, Horringer Rd, BURY ST EDMUNDS, IP29 5PH
Tel: 01284 705550
Fax: 01284 716120
Email: bury@claricehouse.co.uk
Website: www.claricehouse.co.uk
Map ref: 4 TL86
Directions: 1m SW from town centre on A143 towards Horringer
Rooms: 13 en suite **S** £80-£100 **D** £120-£160
Notes: ⊗ ⛔ under 5yrs **Parking:** 85
Closed: 24-26 Dec & 31 Dec-1 Jan

This large neo-Jacobean mansion is set in 20 acres of landscaped grounds just a short drive from Bury St Edmunds. The emphasis here is on rest and relaxation, with unlimited use of the extensive spa and leisure facilities included in your stay. For the active there's a 20-metre indoor swimming pool, a fully equipped gym, and a jogging track through woodland (which has been classified a Site of Special Scientific Interest). If that all sounds like too much hard work, there's always the spa bath, sauna and steam rooms to unwind in, plus you can take your pick from a number of health and beauty treatments available at an extra charge. The bedrooms at Clarice House are spacious and well-equipped and each is individually designed and comfortably furnished. When it comes to dining, head to the AA Rosette-awarded restaurant for some well-presented modern European cooking, with the regularly changing menu offering the likes of chicken Caesar salad alongside smoked haddock risotto, and chargrilled fillet steak. Breakfast is equally good, with the options including a full English, and smoked Suffolk ham with fresh basil, sliced tomato and melted brie on granary toast.

Recommended in the area

Bury St Edmunds; Abbey Gardens; Ickworth House, Park and Gardens (NT)

The George

★★★★ RESTAURANT WITH ROOMS
Address: The Green, CAVENDISH, Sudbury, CO10 8BA
Tel: 01787 280248
Email: thegeorgecavendish@gmail.com
Website: www.thecavendishgeorge.co.uk
Map ref: 4 TL84
Directions: A1092 into Cavendish, The George next to village green
Rooms: 5 en suite (1 fmly) **S** £50 **D** £65-£85
Notes: Wi-fi
Closed: 25 Dec & 1 Jan

This restaurant with rooms on the edge of the village green has been welcoming travellers through its doors since the 16th century. These days it presents a smart face to the world with its cream and grey frontage, hanging baskets and topiary trees outside the front door, but it still retains bags of period character. The main emphasis at The George is on good food, and that's reflected in the award in 2010 of one AA Rosette. The menu changes frequently depending on availability of seasonal produce, and offers a wide range of dishes to suit all tastes and budgets. Many of the ingredients used by the kitchen are from The George's own garden, including salad leaves, beetroot, edible flowers, tomatoes and herbs. The George has five double en suite bedrooms, each with its own unique charm - think exposed beams, sash windows and views of the village green and church. All rooms have double or king-size beds, and the largest can be made into a twin or family room with extra beds or a cot. Co-owners Lewis Bennet and Bonnie Steel offer a warm welcome to all their guests and pride themselves in offering excellent customer service.

Recommended in the area
Lavenham; Clare; Long Melford

Sandpit Farm

★★★★ BED AND BREAKFAST
Address: Bruisyard, SAXMUNDHAM, IP17 2EB
Tel: 01728 663445
Email: smarshall@aldevalleybreaks.co.uk
Website: www.aldevalleybreaks.co.uk
Map ref: 4 TM36
Directions: 4m W of Saxmundham. A1120 onto B1120, 1st left for Bruisyard, house 1.5m on left
Rooms: 2 en suite **S** £40-£60 **D** £65-£90
Notes: Wi-fi
Parking: 4
Closed: 24-26 Dec

This delightful Grade II listed farmhouse set in 20 acres of grounds, with the River Alde meandering along its boundary, is ideally located for visiting the Suffolk coast, the Aldeburgh Festival, Minsmere RSPB Reserve, and for exploring Suffolk's beautiful and unspoilt countryside. An excellent choice of restaurants and pubs are in easy reach. The elegant and comfortable en suite bedrooms are well-equipped and enjoy lovely country views; one is located in its own wing of the house. There is a cosy sitting room for relaxing and a sunny south facing terrace in the beautiful garden for soaking up the tranquil rural setting. There's a lovely wild flower orchard too, and guests are invited to work up a sweat on the hard tennis court if they're so inclined.

A hearty breakfast, cooked in the Aga by Susie and served in the attractive dining room, includes fresh free-range eggs from the resident chickens, and plenty of other local and homemade produce. It's wonderfully easy to relax and unwind in this idyllic and welcoming home - so much so that you may find it hard to leave.

Recommended in the area
Framlingham; Minsmere RSPB Reserve; Sutton Hoo (NT)

Sibton White Horse Inn

★★★★ ◉ INN
Address: Halesworth Rd, SIBTON,
Nr Saxmundham, IP17 2JJ
Tel: 01728 660337
Email: info@sibtonwhitehorseinn.co.uk
Website: www.sibtonwhitehorseinn.co.uk
Map ref: 4 TM36 **Directions:** From A12 in Yoxford take A1120 signed Sibton & Peasenhall. 3m, in Peasenhall turn right opposite butcher's shop. White Horse 600mtrs
Rooms: 6 annexe en suite (3 GF)
S £60-£75 **D** £65-£90 **Notes:** Wi-fi ⌘ under 12yrs
Parking: 50 **Closed:** 26-27 Dec

This attractive and popular freehouse is tucked away off the beaten track in the heart of the glorious Suffolk countryside, yet just five miles from the A12 and only 10 miles from the heritage coast. The Sibton White Horse was built during the 16th century and retains all of its original Tudor charm, including beamed ceilings, exposed brickwork and open fires. These days run by husband and wife team Neil and Gill Mason, it's the perfect haven for travellers seeking first-class overnight accommodation, with the added benefit of an AA Rosette-awarded restaurant (serving lunch and dinner seven days a week) and a well-stocked bar. There are many cosy corners in the pub to sit and enjoy a real ale, a glass of fine wine or a full meal.

The six bedrooms are in a peaceful annex adjacent to the main building and provide all the comforts and facilities you'd expect from a four-star inn, including TV with Freeview and Wi-fi. Breakfast is served in the pub's dining room and includes fresh fruit salad, homemade muesli, a full English breakfast with sausages and bacon from the local butcher, a choice of fresh, locally landed fish, and homemade bread and preserves.

Recommended in the area
Southwold; Aldeburgh; RSPB Minsmere

Sutherland House

★★★★★ ◉◉ RESTAURANT WITH ROOMS

Address: 56 High St, SOUTHWOLD, IP18 6DN
Tel: 01502 724544
Email: enquiries@sutherlandhouse.co.uk
Website: www.sutherlandhouse.co.uk
Map ref: 4 TM57
Directions: A1095 into Southwold, on High St on left after Victoria St
Rooms: 4 en suite (1 fmly) **D** £140-£250
Notes: Wi-fi ⊗
Parking: 1

Sutherland House restaurant with rooms sits in Southwold's High Street, just a few hundred yards from the delightful beach, and is one of the oldest and most historically important buildings in the town. The period features of the Grade II* listed house - such as oak beams, exposed brickwork and open fireplaces - date back to 1455, and somehow blend well with the contemporary furnishings and sumptuous fabrics. The stylish en suite bedrooms come with king-size beds, flat-screen TVs and DVD players with a choice of films. Whether you're looking for the perfect base for a short break exploring the Suffolk Heritage Coast, a celebratory evening meal in the two AA Rosette seafood restaurant, or just a leisurely lunch in the walled garden, Sutherland House is a comfortable and welcoming place with a relaxed, informal atmosphere. The kitchen team at Sutherland House makes every effort to source ingredients that are seasonal and local, and this is backed up by the food miles printed on the regularly changing menu.

Recommended in the area

Southwold Railway; Walberswick; Electric Picture Palace

Surrey

The Castle keep, Guildford

Hatsue Guest House

★★★★ GUEST ACCOMMODATION

Address: 17 Southwell Park Rd,
CAMBERLEY, GU15 3PU
Tel: 01276 22160 & 07791 267620
Fax: 01276 671415
Email: welcome@hatsueguesthouse.com
Website: www.hatsueguesthouse.com
Map ref: 3 SU86
Directions: M3 junct 4, A331 N, A30 E, at Arena sports centre turn right. At T-junct, turn right, 2nd house on left before church
Rooms: 5 en suite **S** £60 **D** £70
Notes: Wi-fi ⊗ **Parking:** 5

Hatsue Guest House is close to Camberley town centre, with the train station, Vue cinema, shops, supermarkets and restaurants all within five minutes' walk. Despite its central location, the guest house, built in 1928, is a peaceful place to stay, with a large, secluded, cottage-style garden. The five bedrooms (one twin, two double and two single) are all en suite, extremely comfortable and spotlessly clean. Each room comes well-equipped with internet point and free Wi-fi, TV with Freeview, DVD player (with a selection of films to borrow), fridge, tea- and coffee-making facilities, hairdryer and telephone. There is plenty of off-street parking for guests. Prices include a generous full English breakfast or any other dish of your choice from the menu. Within 500 yards is the entrance to the Royal Military Academy, while nearby are Windsor and Ascot, Virginia Water, and Wentworth and Sunningdale golf courses. Heathrow is 30 minutes away by car and there is a direct train service to Gatwick. Your hosts, Hatsue and Michael, are always happy to deal with any special requests and aim to make Hatsue Guest House a comfortable home away from home.

Recommended in the area

Windsor; The Savill Garden; Virginia Water

Brighton House

★★★★ GUEST ACCOMMODATION
Address: 52 Regency Square, BRIGHTON, BN1 2FF
Tel: 01273 323282
Email: info@brighton-house.co.uk
Website: www.brighton-house.co.uk
Map ref: 3 TQ30
Directions: Opposite West Pier
Rooms: 16 en suite (2 fmly)
S £50-£65 **D** £105-£130
Notes: ⊗ ✱ under 12yrs

This charming Regency townhouse is perfectly placed for all of Brighton's attractions, including the beach, The Brighton Centre and shopping in The Lanes. Arrangements have been made with nearby car parks for the benefit of guests arriving by car. The smartly furnished bedrooms all have high quality beds and linens, Wi-fi access, hairdryer, tea- and coffee-making facilities and fans for summer use. Double rooms come in a choice of small, standard and superior, and there are single, twin and triple rooms available. The continental-style buffet breakfast offers a broad choice of primarily organic and locally sourced produce, including smoked wild salmon, local organic eggs and cheese, a selection of cereals, fresh or soya milk, and organic fruits and juices. Owners Christine and Lucho try to minimise their impact on the environment without compromising on the comfort of guests. Electricity supplies are from renewable sources (including wind), a new extension to the kitchen has a sedum roof, and recycling is taken seriously, with packaging kept to a minimum, arrangements made with a local recycling co-operative, and bio-degradable waste processed through a wormery. Children under the age of 12 cannot be accommodated at Brighton House.

Recommended in the area
Brighton Pavilion; Brighton Pier; Kipling Gardens

Five

★★★★ GUEST ACCOMMODATION
Address: 5 New Steine, BRIGHTON, BN2 1PB
Tel: 01273 686547
Fax: 0871 522 7472
Email: info@fivehotel.com
Website: www.fivehotel.com
Map ref: 3 TQ30
Directions: On A259 towards E, 8th turn on left into square
Rooms: 10 en suite **S** £45-£70 **D** £70-£140
Notes: Wi-fi ⊗ ⚓ under 5yrs

Five is a smartly turned out Georgian townhouse overlooking a classic Regency Square. Centrally located a few steps from the beach and pier, Five is just a short stroll away from the famous Lanes with their many independent shops and eating places, while the Royal Pavilion and conference centre are also close by. There are 10 stylish and comfortable bedrooms with a contemporary look, all en suite and some with fantastic far-reaching views. The front rooms all have large sash windows with plantation shutters, and all rooms benefit from complimentary Wi-fi, flat-screen TV with Freeview, and DVD player (you can take your pick of films from the free DVD library). Some rooms also come with i-Pod docking stations and tea- and coffee-making facilities. Breakfasts are a sociable affair when guests get together at a large table in the bay fronted dining room. The ingredients are all locally sourced, including eggs, bacon, berries, cereals, muffins, organic juices, yoghurts, jams and honey. If you need any advice on local attractions, your experienced and friendly hosts will be only too happy to help.

Recommended in the area

Brighton Pier; Brighton Pavilion; shopping in The Lanes

New Steine

★★★★ GUEST ACCOMMODATION

Address: 10-11 New Steine, BRIGHTON, BN2 1PB
Tel: 01273 695415 & 681546
Fax: 01273 622663
Email: reservation@newsteinehotel.com
Website: www.newsteinehotel.com
Map ref: 3 TQ30
Directions: A23 to Brighton Pier, left into Marine Parade, New Steine on left after Wentworth St
Rooms: 20 (16 en suite) (4 pri facs) (4 fmly) (2 GF)
S £29.50-£59 **D** £57.50-£119
Notes: Wi-fi under 4yrs

The New Steine is an elegant and fashionable five-storey Georgian townhouse in the centre of Brighton, just off the seafront, and within walking distance of Brighton Pier. With a modern design that exudes warmth and style, and a hint of French influence, the New Steine offers exceptional value accommodation suited to both leisure and corporate guests. Decorated in a contemporary fashion in shades of chocolate, cream and red, the chic bedrooms are equipped with free Wi-fi, desk space, hairdryers, flat-screen LCD TVs, tea- and coffee-making facilities and luxury toiletries. Meals can be taken in the on-site New Steine Bistro, a cosy Parisian-style restaurant offering homemade French cuisine along with more classic British dishes. The kitchen makes the most of top quality produce from farms in Sussex for both its evening menu and award-winning breakfasts. With high standards of service and a friendly, relaxed atmosphere, the New Steine is the perfect base for exploring all that Brighton has to offer.

Recommended in the area

The Royal Pavilion; Devil's Dyke; Brighton Museum & Art Gallery

Regency Lansdowne Guest House

★★★ GUEST ACCOMMODATION

Address: 45 Lansdowne Place, BRIGHTON, BN3 1HF
Tel: 01273 321830 **Fax:** 01273 777067
Email: regencylansdowne@aol.com
Website: www.regencylansdowne.co.uk
Map ref: 3 TQ30
Directions: A23 to Brighton Pier, right onto A259, 1m right into Lansdowne Place, house on left before Western Rd
Rooms: 7 (5 en suite) (2 pri facs) **S** £30-£55 **D** £46-£89
Notes: Wi-fi ⊗ **Closed:** 20-27 Dec

This welcoming, family-run guesthouse boasts a central location within easy walking distance of Brighton's many shops and restaurants, and just 150 metres from the seafront. Despite being right in the heart of things, the Regency Lansdowne is in a quiet setting in Brighton's Brunswick Town Conservation Area. The elegant Grade II listed townhouse offers exceptionally clean accommodation, with bright, fresh and airy rooms all with en suite facilities, LCD flat-screen television with Freeview channels, and tea- and coffee-making facilities. Breakfast is a continental-style affair, with a selection of cheeses, cereals, fresh fruit, yoghurts, fresh croissants, brioche and cakes to choose from. For guests planning an early start - or a late night - breakfast can be provided in your room. For those guests travelling by public transport, the Regency Lansdowne could hardly be more convenient - it's less than 80 metres from the frequent bus routes on Western Road, and is equidistant from Brighton and Hove railway stations.

Recommended in the area

Brighton Pier; The Lanes; Brighton Marina

Tovey Lodge

★★★★★ GUEST ACCOMMODATION
Address: Underhill Ln, DITCHLING, BN6 8XE
Tel: 08456 120544
Fax: 08456 120533
Email: info@sussexcountryholidays.co.uk
Website: www.sussexcountryholidays.co.uk
Map ref: 4 TQ31
Directions: From Ditchling N on Beacon Rd. 0.5m, left into Underhill Ln, 100yds, 1st drive on left
Rooms: 5 en suite (4 fmly) (2 GF)
D £80-£155
Notes: Wi-fi
Parking: 28

At Tovey Lodge, not only can you enjoy three acres of lovely gardens and great views of the South Downs, but the added bonus of an indoor swimming pool, sauna and hot tub. The guest accommodation in this large family home comprises three luxurious junior suites on the first floor and two equally high quality bedrooms on the ground floor. Each is spacious and stylishly decorated, and has fabulous views of the gardens and the South Downs National Park, including Ditchling Beacon. All have a flat-screen TV with Freeview, DVD player, free Wi-fi and tea- and coffee-making facilities. Some rooms are suitable for families. Guests are encouraged to relax in the large lounge with its inglenook fireplace and two zones - one for those who want to read in quiet and the other with a 50-inch plasma-screen TV. The lounge backs onto a lovely patio where you can enjoy the tranquillity of the garden on warmer days. The lavishly decorated dining room is the setting for a full English or continental breakfast, as well as for pre-booked lunches or dinner parties for up to 16 people (Tovey Lodge is licensed to serve alcohol).

Recommended in the area
South Downs National Park; Wings Place; St Margaret's Church

The Manse B&B

★★★★★ BED AND BREAKFAST

Address: 7 Dittons Rd, EASTBOURNE, BN21 1DW
Tel: 01323 737851
Email: anne@themansebb.com
Website: www.themansebb.com
Map ref: 4 TV69
Directions: A22 to town centre railway station, into Old Orchard Rd, right into Arlington Rd
Rooms: 3 en suite **S** £55-£60 **D** £80-£92
Notes: Wi-fi
Parking: 2

Originally built in 1906 as a Presbyterian manse, this character property in the Arts and Crafts style retains many of its original features, such as stained-glass windows, oak panelling and oak floors. The property benefits from a quiet location, yet is just a five-minute stroll from Eastbourne's lively town centre, with its many shops, theatres, pubs and restaurants. The start of the South Downs is within a 10-minute stroll and there are many lovely walks and places to visit in the nearby area. Inside, the spacious, beautifully decorated en suite bedrooms provide armchairs, digital TVs, DVD/CD players, Wi-fi access, hospitality trays and fridges. Guests can enjoy a good night's sleep in king- or super-king-size beds with deep pocket-sprung mattresses. The wide selection of breakfast options, many of them locally sourced, homemade, and free-range and/or organic, is served in the south-facing dining room, which has French doors leading to the rear garden. Guests can relax in the garden if the weather is fine, or otherwise there's a comfortable sitting room. Off-street and unrestricted street parking is available.

Recommended in the area

South Downs and Beachy Head; Charleston (home of the Bloomsbury Group); Michelham Priory

Barn House Seaview B&B

★★★★★ BED AND BREAKFAST
Address: Warren Rd, Fairlight, HASTINGS &
ST LEONARDS, TN35 4AN
Tel: 01424 813821
Email: enquiries@seaviewbnb.co.uk
Website: www.seaviewbnb.co.uk
Map ref: 4 TQ80
Directions: From Hastings on A259, right into
Fairlight Rd to Battery Hill. Right at Warren Rd
Rooms: 3 en suite (1 fmly) **S** £80-£100 **D** £100-£160
Notes: Wi-fi
Parking: 6

Barn House Seaview B&B is a friendly, family-run business, offering luxury accommodation in the coastal village of Fairlight, in an Area of Outstanding Natural Beauty. Built in the 16th century, Barn House sits in 14 acres of private meadows and woodlands, with extensive sea and countryside views. It has been refurbished to the highest standard and offers three elegant guest rooms, along with a one-bedroom cottage with its own private garden and terrace. Guests can relax after a busy day of sightseeing or beachcombing in the comfortable lounge or the reading room, or perhaps in the beautiful gardens and terraces. Top-notch breakfasts are served around a large table in the light and airy breakfast room. The village of Fairlight is right on the edge of the Hastings Country Park Nature Reserve, and half-an-hour from the historic towns of Rye, Battle, Hastings and Camber Sands. It is under two hours from London, Heathrow and Gatwick a rports, and under one hour from Folkstone and Dover.

Recommended in the area

Camber Sands and Winchelsea beaches; Battle Castle; Chapel Down Vineyard, Tenterden

Mermaid Street, Rye

The Cloudesley

★★★★ GUEST ACCOMMODATION
Address: 7 Cloudesley Rd, HASTINGS &
ST LEONARDS, TN37 6JN
Tel: 01424 722759 & 07969 048757
Email: info@thecloudesley.co.uk
Website: www.thecloudesley.co.uk
Map ref: 4 TQ80
Directions: A21 (London Rd) onto A2102,
left into Tower Rd. Right into Cloudesley Rd, house at top on left
Rooms: 5 en suite **S** £70 **D** £140
Notes: Wi-fi ⊗ 🐾

The Cloudesley is an award-winning eco-friendly guest house with five opulent bedrooms and two dedicated holistic therapy rooms. Guests can take their pick from a range of relaxing and health-boosting treatments, including aromatherapy, shiatsu, reiki, reflexology, and deep tissue, Swedish, hot stone and holistic massage. Proprietor Shahriar Mazandi is a globally syndicated photographer and Chelsea Flower Show gold medalist, so it's little surprise that the stylishly designed house is decorated throughout with stunning photographs, or that the small town garden is so well utilised - figs, apples, pears, strawberries and blueberries are all grown here (and offered to guests during the season), along with several varieties of mint for tea, plus sage, rosemary, oregano and other herbs for cooking. The Cloudesley is a special place to stay, not just because of the chemical-free toiletries in the bathrooms, the solar hot water, wood-burning stoves, the many books on art, photography, gardening and history, the original furniture, the limewashed walls, the gourmet breakfasts and the sumptuous beds, but because it has a calming, peaceful and wonderfully relaxing atmosphere in which you can't fail to unwind and de-stress. There are no TVs but there is free Wi-fi.

Recommended in the area

Bodiam Castle; Bateman's (NT); Herstmonceux Castle; Great Dixter House & Gardens

Parkside House

★★★★ GUEST ACCOMMODATION
Address: 59 Lower Park Rd, HASTINGS &
ST LEONARDS, TN34 2LD
Tel: 01424 433096
Email: bkentparksidehse@aol.com
Map ref: 4 TQ80
Directions: A2101 to town centre,
right at rdbt, 1st right
Rooms: 5 (4 en suite) (1 pri facs) (1 fmly)
S £35-£50 **D** £55-£70
Notes: Wi-fi ⊗

Parkside House is in an elevated position in a quiet conservation area opposite the beautiful and extensive Alexandra Park, with its lakes, tennis courts, bowling green and many other recreational activities. The house is also a convenient 15-minute walk from the town centre and seafront, and there is plenty of unrestricted parking outside. The elegant Victorian house retains many of its original features whilst benefitting from every modern amenity, including free Wi-fi. The rooms are stylishly furnished, with many antique pieces, and are generously equipped with flat-screen TVs and DVD players, hairdryers, styling tongs, bathrobes and tea- and coffee-making facilities. Expect high standards of hospitality, cleanliness and comfort, along with a lovely informal, friendly and welcoming atmosphere. In the mornings you can choose from a full and varied menu including a traditional English or continental-style breakfast, served at individual tables in the elegant dining room. There's also an inviting and spacious lounge where guests can relax, complete with real fire in winter.

Recommended in the area
Battle Abbey; Bodiam Castle (NT); Michelham Priory

Holly Grove

★★★★ BED AND BREAKFAST

Address: Spinney Lane, Little London, HEATHFIELD, TN21 0NU
Tel: 01435 863375 & 07814 398854
Email: andy.christie@btconnect.com
Website: www.hollygrovebedandbreakfast.co.uk
Map ref: 4 TQ52
Directions: A267 to Horam, turn right at Little London garage into Spinney Lane, proceed to bottom of lane
Rooms: 3 (2 en suite) (1 pri facs) (1 fmly) (2 GF)
Notes: Wi-fi
Parking: 7

Holly Grove enjoys a very quiet rural location in the heart of East Sussex, close to Heathfield, Horam and the village of Waldron, with easy access to many local attractions. The house sits in over two acres of garden, with lots of areas to sit and relax, and a heated outdoor swimming pool which is usually open from May to October, depending on the weather. At Holly Grove guests will enjoy the luxury, comfort and warm welcome offered by the Christie family - and that includes their three dogs and three cats. All the bedrooms are appointed to a very high standard, with flat-screen TVs with full Sky channels, tea- and coffee-making facilities and many thoughtful extras. There is a separate lounge/dining room for the sole use of guests, with a lovely roaring log fire to welcome you in from the cold during the winter. Breakfast is served in the dining room, or if the weather is fine, you can take it on the patio or on the decked terrace beside the swimming pool. Evening meals can be pre-arranged, or crockery can be provided should you wish to order a take-away.

Recommended in the area

Bentley Wildfowl and Motor Museum; Glyndebourne; Bateman's (NT)

Cleavers Lyng Country House

★★★★ GUEST ACCOMMODATION
Address: Church Rd, HERSTMONCEUX, BN27 1QJ
Tel: 01323 833644
Email: cleaverslyng@btinternet.com
Website: www.cleaverslyng.co.uk
Map ref: 4 TQ61
Directions: Exit A271 at Herstmonceux, into Chapel Row leading into Church Rd, 1.5m on right
Rooms: 4 en suite (1 fmly) **S** fr £60 **D** fr £75
Notes: Wi-fi
Parking: 10

Cleavers Lyng is a Grade II listed country house of considerable charm and character dating back to 1577. The house is situated in a quiet country lane, just a five-minute walk to Herstmonceux Castle or 1.5 miles from Herstmonceux village, and benefits from panoramic uninterrupted views over the Pevensey flats towards the South Downs. Cleavers Lyng is in an ideal location for visiting the Sussex Weald, 1066 Country and the South Downs, along with the many local beaches. The house sits in one-and-a-half acres of landscaped gardens, ablaze with colour during the spring and summer months. The double bedrooms are all en suite and individually furnished to a high standard. Each room comes with a 22-inch flat-screen TV with integrated DVD/CD player, iron and ironing board, radio alarm and hospitality tray. Some rooms also have a fridge, and free Wi-fi is available. One room benefits from a balcony and a super-king-size bed, although it can be converted to a twin. The entire house is strictly non-smoking. When it comes to dining out you're spoilt for choice: the village has a bistro, two pubs and two restaurants to take your pick from.

Recommended in the area
Sussex Weald; South Downs; local beaches

The Blacksmiths Arms

★★★★ INN

Address: London Rd, Offham, LEWES, BN7 3QD
Tel: 01273 472971
Email: blacksmithsarms@shineadsl.co.uk
Website: www.theblacksmithsarms-offham.co.uk
Map ref: 4 TQ41
Directions: 1m N of Lewes. On A275 in Offham
Rooms: 4 en suite **S** fr £50 **D** £65-£95
Notes: Wi-fi ⊗
Parking: 22

Nestled beneath the Sussex Downs just outside Lewes, this charming 18th-century inn is in an Area of Outstanding Natural Beauty, and is a great base for touring the south coast. Each of the high-quality, comfortable double bedrooms at the Blacksmiths Arms features an en suite bathroom, flat-screen TV and tea- and coffee-making facilities. All have been refurbished and are stylishly decorated. Downstairs, open log fires and a warm, relaxed atmosphere welcome you to the cosy bar, where excellent dinners and hearty breakfasts are freshly cooked to order. Evening diners can choose from the inventive brasserie-style menu, which draws from only the best local produce wherever possible, including fresh fish and seafood landed at local ports. Dishes here are much more than pub food, and might include roast local estate free-range venison, wild sea bass fillets on a seafood risotto with a lobster velouté drizzle, or 'Auntie Kate's fresh crispy roast duckling'. Bernard Booker, the owner and chef, has won awards for his seafood dishes. Award-winning, locally brewed Harveys Sussex Bitter is properly served in superb condition: another indication that they like to do things properly here.

Recommended in the area

Brighton; South Downs Way; Sheffield Park Gardens; Bluebell Railway; Glyndebourne Opera House

Manor Farm Oast

★★★★★ BED AND BREAKFAST

Address: Windmill Ln, RYE, TN36 4WL
Tel: 01424 813787 & 07866 818952
Fax: 01424 813787
Email: manor.farm.oast@lineone.net
Website: www.manorfarmoast.co.uk
Map ref: 4 TQ92 **Directions:** 4m SW of Rye. A259 W past Icklesham church, left at x-rds into Windmill Ln, after sharp left bend, left (follow sign) into orchards **Rooms:** 3 (2 en suite) (1 pri facs) (1 fmly)
S £85-£105 **D** £105
Notes: Wi-fi ⊗ under 11yrs **Parking:** 8
Closed: 23 Dec-15 Jan

Built in 1860 and surrounded by farmland on the edge of Icklesham, Manor Farm Oast is ideal for a quiet break. The oast house has been thoughtfully and tastefully converted to retain its original features both inside and out, with the double bedroom in one tower completely circular. All rooms come with tea- and coffee-making facilities, TV, king-size or twin beds, and either an en suite or private bathroom. Proprietors Kate and Syd Mylrea offer an extremely friendly welcome and pride themselves on their first-class service. Kate is passionate about food, so you can be assured that the full Sussex breakfast prepared from locally sourced produce (including her own homemade sausages) - or an alternative such as Manx kippers or Hastings smoked haddock with poached egg - will be just about as good as it gets. A five-course dinner can also be provided on Fridays and Saturdays (from November to March) if booked in advance. Manor Farm Oast is right in the heart of 1066 Country, with Rye, Winchelsea, Battle and Hastings all within easy reach. Backpacks and maps are available to lend to guests keen to explore by foot or by bike.

Recommended in the area

Battle Abbey; historic Rye; Ellen Terry's House (NT)

Ab Fab Rooms

★★★★ 🛏 BED AND BREAKFAST

Address: 11 Station Rd, Bishopstone,
SEAFORD, BN25 2RB
Tel: 01323 895001 & 07713 197915
Fax: 0705 360 3204
Email: stay@abfabrooms.co.uk
Website: www.abfabrooms.co.uk
Map ref: 4 TV49
Rooms: 3 en suite **S** £55-£65 **D** £70-£80
Notes: Wi-fi ⊗
Parking: 2

Situated in Bishopstone, close to the train station and on the outskirts of the pretty Sussex town of Seaford, Ab Fab Rooms is just a short walk from sandy beaches and the South Downs, making it an ideal base for visiting local sights and attractions. The stylish, contemporary en suite bedrooms enjoy stunning views of the end of Seaford Bay and on to the ferry port of Newhaven and beyond. Each room offers a superior level of comfort and amenities, such as fluffy towels, TV/DVDs and well-stocked hospitality trays, which include such treats as home-baked biscuits and cakes. One room has a chocolate brown leather bed and tub chairs in which to relax. Breakfast, served in the garden conservatory, is a special feature and includes home-made jams and marmalade alongside local Sussex produce. Sunsets in this part of the world are spectacular, and the friendly owners are happy to provide sunset picnic baskets, packed with delicious home-made food, for guests to sit back and enjoy on the beach. They'll even chill the wine beforehand. Guest parking is available.

Recommended in the area

Brighton & Hove; Glyndebourne; Charleston Farmhouse

The Avondale

★★★ GUEST ACCOMMODATION
Address: Avondale Rd, SEAFORD, BN25 1RJ
Tel: 01323 890008
Fax: 01323 490598
Email: info@theavondale.co.uk
Website: www.theavondale.co.uk
Map ref: 4 TV49
Directions: In town centre, off A259 behind war memorial
Rooms: 14 (8 en suite) (4 fmly) **S** £35-£45 **D** £65-£85
Notes: Wi-fi ⊗

The Avondale is conveniently positioned for both the town centre and the seafront, with Seaford Leisure Centre close by and Brighton, Eastbourne, the South Downs and many other places of interest within easy reach. Guests frequently comment on how well they sleep in the spotlessly clean bedrooms. The beds are certainly comfortable, but the friendly service, relaxed atmosphere and fresh flowers also play their part in the home-from-home experience. Jane and Martin Home and their experienced staff spare no effort in making your stay relaxing and enjoyable, offering a perfect blend of modern comforts and traditional courtesy and service. All bedrooms are accessible by stair-lift and eight rooms have en suite facilities.

Each room has free Wi-fi access, a hospitality tray, complimentary toiletries, radio and TV, with a DVD player on request. An inviting lounge is available during the day for guests' use, and breakfast is served at individual tables in the spacious dining room. Guests appreciate the quality and choice at breakfast, and dinners and hot/cold buffets featuring home-cooked local produce can be provided by arrangement. There are also plenty of good pubs and restaurants in the area.

Recommended in the area

Beachy Head Countryside Centre; Firle Place; Alfriston Clergy House (NT)

West Sussex

Beach huts at Littlehampton

Angmering Manor

★★★★ GUEST ACCOMMODATION

Address: High St, ANGMERING, BN16 4AG
Tel: 01903 859849
Fax: 01903 783268
Email: angmeringmanor@thechapmansgroup.co.uk
Website: www.relaxinnz.co.uk
Map ref: 3 TQ00
Directions: Follow A27 towards Portsmouth, exit A280, follow signs for Angmering
Rooms: 17 en suite (3 fmly) (4 GF)
S £70-£99 **D** £99-£139
Notes: Wi-fi ⊗
Parking: 25

Angmering Manor is an outstanding restaurant and bar with guest accommodation situated in a tranquil setting in the heart of Angmering village in West Sussex. Thought to have been built in the 16th century by missionaries, it has recently been completely refurbished throughout and combines first-class facilities with exceptional service. Each thoughtfully decorated en suite bedroom is individually designed and furnished to the highest standard - think rich fabrics, flat-screen TVs, crisp Egyptian cotton sheets and personal slippers and bathrobes for every guest. Wi-fi is available throughout. The fine-dining restaurant offers an a la carte menu created by Angmering Manor's award-winning chef. Full leisure facilities are also available, including a heated indoor swimming pool, mini-gym, sauna and spa with a dedicated on-site therapist providing a wide range of treatments. The manor is within easy reach of Brighton, Chichester and Arundel, and an ideal base for visitors to Goodwood racecourse.

Recommended in the area

Brighton; Arundel Castle & Cathedral; The South Downs

The Town House

★★★★ ◉◉ RESTAURANT WITH ROOMS
Address: 65 High St, ARUNDEL, BN18 9AJ
Tel: 01903 883847
Email: enquiries@thetownhouse.co.uk
Website: www.thetownhouse.co.uk
Map ref: 3 TQ00
Directions: A27 to Arundel, into High Street, establishment on left at top of hill
Rooms: 4 en suite **S** £75 **D** £95-£130
Notes: Wi-fi ⊗
Closed: 2wks Feb & 2wks Oct

The Town House sits at the top of Arundel's High Street in a prime position opposite the castle. It is a splendid Grade II listed Regency building dating from around the 1800s. The dining room has a spectacular carved ceiling, which is much older than the rest of the house: it originated in Florence and is a beautiful example of late Renaissance architecture. All of the en suite bedrooms here are sympathetically and tastefully decorated and all benefit from TV, hairdryer and tea- and coffee-making facilities. The restaurant, which holds two AA Rosettes, is equally stylish, although also very informal with a friendly, relaxed feel. Chef Lee Williams, who runs The Town House with his wife Katie, offers a diverse menu based on seasonal Sussex produce, including locally caught lobster and crab during the summer months. All the bread served is freshly baked on the premises. Dinner, bed and breakfast rates are available on Tuesdays, Wednesdays and Thursdays. The Town House is just a few minutes' walk from Arundel's many antiques shops, boutiques, the cathedral and the pretty River Arun.

Recommended in the area

Glorious Goodwood; Arundel Castle; Chichester Theatre

Moorings

★★★★ GUEST ACCOMMODATION

Address: 4 Selden Rd, WORTHING, BN11 2LL
Tel: 01903 208882
Email: themooringsworthing@hotmail.co.uk
Website: www.mooringsworthing.co.uk
Map ref: 3 TQ10
Directions: 0.5m E of pier off A259 towards Brighton
Rooms: 7 en suite (1 fmly) (1 GF)
S £35-£45 **D** £60-£85
Notes: Wi-fi ⊗

The Moorings is situated in a quiet side street just off the Brighton Road to the east of Worthing town centre, and is very handy for the seafront. It's just 10 minutes' walk to the shops, five minutes to the indoor swimming pool, hospital and bowling greens, and even less to the beach. The Moorings offers a warm and friendly welcome and a comfortable and relaxed atmosphere. Rooms are spacious, individually decorated in co-ordinating colours, and come with en suite bathrooms, TV, tea- and coffee-making facilities and free Wi-fi. There's also secure parking for bicycles and motorcycles, monitored by CCTV and behind high gates. Breakfast is a highlight of any stay, and includes your choice of cereals, fruits and yoghurts from the buffet, followed by a full English or your selection from a range of hot dishes such as free-range eggs on toast, beans on toast, kipper fillets and porridge. The Moorings' owner, Sarah, will do her utmost to make your stay as enjoyable as possible - it's no wonder she made it into the top 25 in the AA Friendliest Landlady of the Year Award 2011.

Recommended in the area

Highdown Gardens; Worthing Pier; the South Downs

Warwickshire

Peacock Garden, Warwick Castle

Chapel House Restaurant With Rooms

★★★★★ ● RESTAURANT WITH ROOMS
Address: Friar's Gate, ATHERSTONE, CV9 1EY
Tel: 01827 718949
Fax: 01827 717702
Email: info@chapelhouse.eu
Website: www.chapelhouse.eu
Map ref: 3 SP39
Directions: A5 to town centre, right into Church St. Right into Sheepy Rd, left into Friar's Gate
Rooms: 11 en suite
Notes: Wi-fi ⊗
Closed: Etr wk, Aug BH wk & Xmas wk

In a quiet cul-de-sac and surrounded by a pretty walled garden next to the church in the centre of Atherstone, Chapel House is in a delightfully peaceful spot. It was built in 1728 as the dower house to Atherstone Hall, home of the Bracebridge family, and Florence Nightingale used to stay here when visiting her friends and benefactors. These days converted into an elegant hotel, Chapel House welcomes 21st century guests with 11 superbly equipped and beautifully furnished bedrooms, which are split between the first and second floors. All rooms have en suites with power-showers, LCD digital televisions with plenty of channels including radio, and free Wi-fi. The restaurant, with a marble fireplace and lovely views over the garden and patio, has well-spaced, smartly-appointed tables, polished silver cutlery and classical background music providing a relaxed and welcoming atmosphere. The menu offers a modern take on classic French cooking, with dishes simply prepared to let the natural flavours of the ingredients - which are mostly sourced locally - shine through.

Recommended in the area

Twycross Zoo; National Exhibition Centre; Mallory Park

Holly End Bed & Breakfast

★★★★ BED AND BREAKFAST

Address: London Rd,
SHIPSTON ON STOUR, CV36 4EP
Tel: 01608 664064
Email: hollyend.hunt@btinternet.com
Website: www.holly-end.co.uk
Map ref: 3 SP24
Directions: 0.5m S of Shipston on Stour on A3400
Rooms: 3 (2 en suite) (1 pri facs)
S £50-£60 **D** £75-£95
Notes: Wi-fi ⊗ 🚫 under 9yrs
Parking: 6

Holly End provides top-drawer accommodation on the edge of the Cotswolds, midway between Moreton-in-Marsh and Stratford-upon-Avon. Whether your preferences lie with long country hikes and exploring quaint Cotswold villages, or discovering the history and culture of Shakespeare country, Holly End is suitably placed for both. This delightful family home, immaculately maintained and spotlessly clean, is just a short walk from the centre of Shipston on Stour. Shipston, once an important sheep market town, was also a major stopping point for coaches, and many of the inns in the High Street date from that era. Holly End's spacious, comfortable bedrooms - king-size, twin and double - with subtle soft furnishings and décor, have well-equipped bathrooms, while dormer windows add extra character. You can pamper yourself with The Sanctuary spa products provided in each room. Digital televisions and tea- and coffee-making facilities are also provided. A comprehensive freshly cooked English breakfast uses the best of local produce (organic wherever possible). Afternoon tea or sherry and snacks are offered on arrival. There is a beautiful sunny garden with a lawn and patio dotted with many container plants.

Recommended in the area

Stratford-upon-Avon; Hidcote Manor (NT); Warwick Castle; Cotswold Falconry Centre; Cotswolds

Ambleside

★★★★ GUEST HOUSE
Address: 41 Grove Rd,
STRATFORD-UPON-AVON, CV37 6PB
Tel: 01789 297239
Fax: 01789 295670
Email: peter@amblesideguesthouse.com
Website: www.amblesideguesthouse.com
Map ref: 3 SP25
Directions: 250mtrs from town centre on A4390 opposite Firs Gdns
Rooms: 7 (5 en suite) (2 pri facs) (2 fmly) (2 GF)
S £30-£45 **D** £55-£85
Notes: Wi-fi ⊗ ⌘ under 7yrs **Parking:** 9

Ambleside is a comfortable guest house in the heart of Stratford-upon-Avon, where owners Ruth and Peter provide a warm welcome. A refurbishment has left the house in sparkling condition, and the accommodation can suit every need. Choose from the family rooms, one of which is situated on the ground floor, a double, twin or singles. Many rooms have shower rooms en suite, and each is equipped with a TV, hairdryer and hospitality tray. Ironing facilities are also available. Breakfast is served in the bright and spacious dining room, which looks out over the charming front patio garden. The menu offers plenty to suit all tastes and appetites, and the traditional full English and vegetarian alternative are always freshly cooked. Ambleside stands opposite the attractive gardens of Firs Park and is just a short stroll from the town centre, where there is a good choice of restaurants, cafés and inns. As well as the Shakespeare attractions, Stratford-upon-Avon offers a wide range of shops, and there are town trails to help guide you around its many ancient buildings. Ambleside guests can also benefit from free on-site parking and free Wi-fi.

Recommended in the area

Shakespeare's birthplace; The Royal Shakespeare, Swan and Courtyard theatres; Anne Hathaway's Cottage; Warwick Castle; Warwick

Arden Way Guest House

★★★ GUEST HOUSE

Address: 22 Shipston Rd,
STRATFORD-UPON-AVON, CV37 7LP
Tel: 01789 205646
Fax: 01789 205646
Email: info@ardenwayguesthouse.co.uk
Website: www.ardenwayguesthouse.co.uk
Map ref: 3 SP25
Directions: On A3400, S of River Avon, 100mtrs on left
Rooms: 6 en suite (1 fmly) (2 GF)
S £35-£55 **D** £58-£74
Notes: Wi-fi ⊗ **Parking:** 6

Arden Way is a friendly, family-run guest house close to all the amenities of the town centre and just a few minutes from Stratford's famous theatres. To the back of the house is a large garden with a summer house, while at the front there is plenty of parking reserved for guests to use. The en suite bedrooms are attractively furnished and all have flat-screen TVs with Freeview, Wi-fi access and tea- and coffee-making equipment. A hearty breakfast is served in the dining room overlooking the garden, and special diets are catered for on request. Arden Way is a fantastic base for any Shakespeare buff. The guest house is a mere 100 metres away from the Clopton Bridge, which is the main route into the town centre, or alternatively there's a pretty walk along the riverbank to Holy Trinity Church, where Shakespeare is buried. From the church you can take an interesting route through the town, visiting three Shakespeare properties along the way.

Recommended in the area

Shakespeare properties; The Cotswolds; Warwick Castle

Wiltshire

Stonehenge

The George & Dragon

★★★★ ◉◉ RESTAURANT WITH ROOMS

Address: High St, ROWDE, SN10 2PN
Tel: 01380 723053
Email: thegandd@tiscali.co.uk
Website: www.thegeorgeanddragonrowde.co.uk
Map ref: 2 ST96
Directions: 1.5m from Devizes on A350 towards Chippenham
Rooms: 3 (2 en suite) (1 pri facs) (1 fmly)
D £55-£115
Notes: Wi-fi
Parking: 15

A 16th-century coaching inn, the George & Dragon retains many original features, including exposed beams with the carved Tudor rose and large open fireplaces. Wooden floors, antique rugs and candlelit tables create a warm atmosphere in the bar and restaurant. The inn is located on the village high street in Rowde which is only a couple of miles from Devizes and not far from the Caen Hill lock flight on the Kennet & Avon Canal. Accommodation is provided in individually designed bedrooms, furnished with large double beds made up with luxurious linens. Two of the bedrooms are en suite while the third has its own private bathroom. All are equipped with flat-screen televisions with DVD players, iPod stations and tea- and coffee-making facilities. The inn has two AA Rosettes for its food, so dining in the bar or restaurant should not be missed. The house speciality is fresh fish delivered daily from Cornwall, but a full a la carte is offered featuring local produce, meats and game and is available in both the restaurant and bar. Events are held throughout the year, including the likes of summer barbecues, wine and cheese tastings, games nights and charity quizzes.

Recommended in the area

Bowood House & Gardens; Roman Baths & Pump Room; Stonehenge

The Old House

★★★★ GUEST ACCOMMODATION

Address: 161 Wilton Rd, SALISBURY, SP2 7JQ
Tel: 01722 333433
Fax: 01722 335551
Map ref: 3 SU12
Directions: 1m W of city centre on A36
Rooms: 7 en suite (1 fmly)
S £45-£65 **D** £65-£110
Notes: Wi-fi ⊗ 🚸 under 7yrs
Parking: 10

The Old House is full of character with traditional beams and brick walls dating back to the 16th century. It is elegantly furnished to provide excellent accommodation in-keeping with the building's period charms. All the spacious bedrooms - which are split between the ground and first floor - have en suite facilities and are tastefully decorated and well-equipped. Guests are invited to relax after a busy day of sightseeing in the large and comfortable residents' lounge, or in the attractive mature garden to the rear of the house if the weather is fine. All food is freshly prepared and home-cooked. It's an easy stroll from The Old House to the centre of Salisbury, with its stunning cathedral and lovely walks by the River Avon. The railway station, with a direct line to London Waterloo, is also just a short walk away. Stonehenge and The New Forest are half-an-hour by car, and the wonderful city of Bath, historic Portsmouth and the seaside resort of Bournemouth are all within easy travelling distance. Free parking and Wi-fi is provided.

Recommended in the area
Stourhead (NT); Heale Garden; Wilton House

Ardecca

★★★★ GUEST ACCOMMODATION
Address: Fieldrise Farm, Kingsdown Ln, Blunsdon
SWINDON SN25 5DL
Tel: 01793 721238 & 07791 120826
Email: chris-graham.ardecca@fsmail.net
Website: www.ardecca-bedandbreakfast.co.uk
Map ref: 3 SU18
Directions: A419 onto B4019 to Blunsdon/Highworth, then into Turnpike Rd at Cold Harbour pub, left into Kingsdown Ln
Rooms: 4 (4 pri facs) (1 fmly) (4 GF) (no smoking)
S fr £40 **D** £60-£85
Notes: Wi-fi ⊗ 𝕨 under 6yrs **Parking:** 5

Ardecca (the name is an amalgamation of the names Rebecca and Richard, the owners' children) has been the family home of Chris and Graham Horne for over 25 years. The large modern bungalow is immaculate inside and out and sits in 16 acres of pastureland on the edge of Blunsdon village. It's a quiet rural setting, within easy reach of Swindon and Cirencester, the Cotswolds and the Marlborough Downs. The bungalow offers spacious first-class accommodation in a friendly and relaxed atmosphere created by Chris and Graham. The bedrooms are larger than average and equipped with modern amenities including Wi-fi access, TV, hairdryer, radio alarm and tea- and coffee-making facilities. A full English breakfast is provided and freshly cooked evening meals are available by arrangement. Alternatively, your hosts will be happy to point you in the direction of one of the many good pubs and restaurants in the area. During your stay you can relax on the patio in the garden, explore the immediate area on public footpaths leading through the meadows, or perhaps take part in an on-site arts and crafts workshop. Ample parking is available. Please note that credit cards are not accepted.

Recommended in the area

Cotswold Water Park; STEAM (Museum of the Great Western Railway); Avebury; Stonehenge; Royal Wootton Bassett

Worcestershire

Broadway Tower

Boot Inn

★★★★ INN

Address: Radford Rd, FLYFORD FLAVELL,
Worcester, WR7 4BS
Tel: 01386 462658
Fax: 01386 462547
Email: enquiries@thebootinn.com
Website: www.thebootinn.com
Map ref: 2 SO95
Directions: In village centre, signed from A422
Rooms: 5 annexe en suite (2 GF)
S £50-£65 **D** £65-£95
Notes: Wi-fi
Parking: 30

An inn has occupied this site since the 13th century, though 'The Boot' itself, as it is called locally, dates from the Georgian period. It provides an ideal base for anyone wishing to explore Stratford-upon-Avon, the Cotswolds or the Malvern Hills. The award-winning inn has undergone modernisation, yet has managed to retain much of its historic charm. The comfortable bedrooms in the converted coach house, furnished in antique pine, are equipped with practical extras such as tea- and coffee-making facilities, TV with Freeview, CD player, iPod dock and free Wi-fi, and all have modern bathrooms. Two rooms have disabled access. Guests can relax and indulge in the range of options available at this family-run pub, which prides itself on its friendly staff and lively atmosphere. Traditional ales and an extensive wine list complement the varied and imaginative menus, which are adapted according to availability of ingredients, with everything from sandwiches to bar meals to full carte on offer. The excellent cooking here, based on fine local produce, can be enjoyed in the cosy public areas, which include an attractive restaurant and a light and airy conservatory, or on the shaded patio during the summer.

Recommended in the area
Worcester Cathedral; Stratford-upon-Avon; Evesham

The Dewdrop Inn

★★★★ INN

Address: Bell Ln, Lower Broadheath, WORCESTER, WR2 6RR
Tel: 01905 640012
Fax: 01905 640265
Email: enquiries@thedewdrop-inn.co.uk
Website: www.thedewdrop-inn.co.uk
Map ref: 2 SO85
Directions: From A44 follow signs for Elgar Birthplace Museum, 0.5m past museum turn right at x-rds. 800yds on left
Rooms: 7 en suite (7 GF) **S** £69 **D** £90
Notes: Wi-fi **Parking:** 40

The Dewdrop Inn occupies a lovely semi-rural location in the parish of Lower Broadheath near Worcester, only a few minutes' walk from the birthplace of composer Sir Edward Elgar (now a museum dedicated to his life and work). As well as being the perfect stopover for fans of Elgar's music, The Dewdrop Inn is ideally located for walkers, cyclists and anglers, and for riding and motor sports enthusiasts as it's only a short journey to Worcester Racecourse and the Chaddesley Hill Climb. Chef Tim Hoare, who runs the inn with his wife Annelene, has devised seasonal bar and a la carte menus using lots of fresh, local produce. There's also a great value set menu available at lunch and dinner, a popular carvery on Sundays, and a wide selection of wines, real ales, beers, lagers and soft beverages to choose from. The Dewdrop Inn has seven well-appointed and spotlessly clean en suite bedrooms, with supremely comfortable beds. After a peaceful night's sleep, set yourself up for the day ahead with a hearty full English breakfast - or a continental if you prefer - in the lovely restaurant.

Recommended in the area

The Elgar Birthplace Museum & Visitor Centre; Worcester Porcelain Museum; Witley Court & Gardens

Abberley Hall Clock Tower

East Riding of Yorkshire

Selwicks Bay, Flamborough

Burton Mount Country House

★★★★★ GUEST ACCOMMODATION

Address: Malton Rd, Cherry Burton,
BEVERLEY, HU17 7RA
Tel: 01964 550541
Email: pg@burtonmount.co.uk
Website: www.burtonmount.co.uk
Map ref: 7 TA03
Directions: 2m NW of Beverley. B1248 for Malton, 2m right at x-rds, house on left
Rooms: 3 en suite
Notes: Wi-fi ⊗ 🚫 under 12yrs
Parking: 20

Burton Mount is a charming country house three miles from Beverley, set in more than two acres of delightful gardens and woodland. The three en suite bedrooms are well-equipped with TVs, hairdryers, tea- and coffee-making facilities and bathrobes. An excellent, Aga-cooked Yorkshire breakfast - or a lighter continental if you prefer - is served in the morning room, along with home-made preserves and fresh bread. In summer, guests can relax on the outdoor terrace, while in the cooler months log fires blaze in the elegant drawing room and the comfortable sitting room. The lovely dining room, with French windows opening onto the terrace, is the setting for pre-booked lunches and dinners. The magnificent dining table can comfortably seat up to 22 people, making it ideal for a special celebration or simply a dinner party with friends or family. Expect excellent traditional home cooking using plenty of local produce, along with friendly and attentive service from proprietors the Greenwood family. Burton Mount Country House makes an ideal base for people visiting Beverley on business, as well as leisure travellers exploring picturesque East Yorkshire.

Recommended in the area
Beverley Minster; Bishop Burton horse trials; Wilberforce house

The Royal Bridlington

★★★★ GUEST ACCOMMODATION
Address: 1 Shaftesbury Rd,
BRIDLINGTON, YO15 3NP
Tel: 01262 672433
Fax: 01262 672118
Email: info@royalhotelbrid.co.uk
Website: www.royalhotelbrid.co.uk
Map ref: 7 TA16
Directions: A615 N to Bridlington (Kingsgate), right into Shaftesbury Rd
Rooms: 14 (13 en suite) (1 pri facs) 4 annexe en suite (7 fmly) (4 GF) **S** £46-£50 **D** £72-£80
Notes: Wi-fi ⊗ **Parking:** 7

The Royal Bridlington occupies a prime spot, just 100 yards from Bridlington's beautiful South Beach and just a short walk along the promenade from The Spa theatre and conference centre. It also makes the perfect base for exploring further afield, with easy access to the entire East Yorkshire coast and the Yorkshire Wolds. The thoughtfully furnished bedrooms, including singles, doubles, twins and family rooms, are en suite and very well-equipped. Some rooms have self-catering facilities and many have sea views. There are some rooms on the ground floor with level access to the bar and restaurant. Free Wi-fi is available throughout the building. Spacious public areas include a dining room where breakfasts and dinners are served, a light and airy conservatory/TV room, and a well-stocked bar with open fire. There is also a large, well maintained garden area. The Royal Bridlington can offer function and conference facilities and also holds sequence, ballroom and line dance events. Patchwork and quilting retreats and golf packages can also be arranged.

Recommended in the area
RSPB Bempton Cliffs; MV Yorkshire Belle coastal cruises; Burton Agnes Hall

North Yorkshire

North York Moors at Levisham

Maypole Farm B&B

★★★ BED AND BREAKFAST
Address: 14 Wistowgate, CAWOOD, Selby, YO8 3SH
Tel: 01757 268849
Email: bookings@maypole-farm.co.uk
Website: www.maypole-farm.co.uk
Map ref: 7 SE53
Rooms: 3 en suite **S** £40 **D** £70
Notes: Wi-fi ⊗
Parking: 3

This 19th century farmhouse B&B is right in the heart of the historic village of Cawood, just 20 minutes from York with all its many attractions, and a short drive from Selby. There are three delightful themed rooms, including the 'Africa room', decked out with African-style fabrics and artifacts, and the 'garden room' with views over the pretty walled gardens. All are en suite and have TVs, DVD players, hairdryers, and tea- and coffee-making facilities. Free internet access is available. There's a lovely conservatory where you can relax and read the newspaper or a good book, or perhaps enjoy a game of pool. After a comfortable and peaceful night's sleep, take your pick from a continental or full English breakfast, prepared using local produce and served in the cosy dining room. For evening meals, there are three pubs in the village, or otherwise you can take a drive to York and choose from one of the city's many good restaurants. Whether your stay at Maypole Farm is for business or pleasure, you can be assured of a warm welcome and great service from hands-on owners.

Recommended in the area

Historic city of York; National Railway Museum; Castle Howard

Ashfield House

★★★★★ 🛏 🍽 GUEST ACCOMMODATION

Address: Summers Fold, GRASSINGTON, Skipton, BD23 5AE
Tel: 01756 752584
Fax: 07092 376562
Email: sales@ashfieldhouse.co.uk
Website: www.ashfieldhouse.co.uk
Map ref: 6 SE06
Directions: B6265 to village centre, from main street left into Summers Fold
Rooms: 7 en suite 1 annexe en suite
S £65-£110 **D** £95-£125
Notes: Wi-fi ⊗ 🚭 under 5yrs **Parking:** 8

This well-maintained 17th-century house is tucked away down a private lane with its own walled gardens, making it the perfect place to simply get away from it all. Ashfield House was once a row of miners' cottages, but today it provides luxurious accommodation and exceptional hospitality, along with the charm and character of a Grade II listed building. There are smart furnishings throughout, from the delightful and well-equipped en suite bedrooms, to the cosy lounges with honesty bar. Dine in style at breakfast time with the likes of home-made yoghurt, marmalade, granola, and own-recipe sausages, while in the evenings you can expect some excellent home-cooking, which has justly earned Ashfield House an AA Dinner Award. There's a large, tranquil garden to relax in if the weather is fine, and plenty of private parking. Ashfield House is within easy reach of the many attractions of the North Yorkshire Dales, and your friendly hosts Joe and Elizabeth will happily provide advice on what to see and do.

Recommended in the area
Skipton Castle; Bolton Abbey; Pennine boat trips

Shelbourne House

★★★★ GUEST ACCOMMODATION
Address: 78 Kings Rd, HARROGATE, HG1 5JX
Tel: 01423 504390
Email: sue@shelbournehouse.co.uk
Website: www.shelbournehouse.co.uk
Map ref: 7 SE35
Directions: Follow signs to International Centre, over lights by Holiday Inn, premises on right
Rooms: 8 en suite (2 fmly) **S** £40-£45 **D** £68-£90
Notes: Wi-fi ⊗
Parking: 1

Shelbourne house is a Victorian family home which has been transformed into a beautiful boutique style B&B. Located in the heart of town, it's an ideal base for exploring Harrogate and the Yorkshire Dales. Owners Sue and Neil have created a homely atmosphere at Shelbourne House and offer a very friendly welcome - it's no wonder many guests return year after year. Only the finest quality locally sourced Yorkshire produce is served each morning at breakfast, with the options ranging from a hearty full English to scrambled eggs with smoked salmon, and fresh Whitby kippers. Early breakfasts can be arranged for those who need an early start, while packed lunches and evening bites can also be provided on request. The bedrooms at Shelbourne House have recently undergone an extensive refurbishment and are tastefully decorated to an extremely high standard and spotlessly clean. Guests are invited to relax in the lavish Baroque-style guest lounge in front of a real fire during the winter months, and to enjoy the lovely grounds when the weather allows. Shelbourne House guests also benefit from free parking.

Recommended in the area
Harrogate Turkish Baths and Spa; Fountains Abbey & Studley Royal Estate; Harlow Carr

Capple Bank Farm

★★★★ BED AND BREAKFAST
Address: West Witton, LEYBURN, DL8 4ND
Tel: 01969 625825 & 07836 645238
Email: julian.smithers@btinternet.com
Website: www.capplebankfarm.co.uk
Map ref: 6 SE19
Directions: A1 to Bedale, onto A684 to Leyburn, towards Hawes, through Wensley, 1st left in West Witton. Up hill, left bend, gates straight ahead
Rooms: 2 en suite **S** £60 **D** £90
Notes: ⊗ ⚹ under 10yrs
Parking: 6

Capple Bank Farm sits overlooking the Dales village of West Witton, with panoramic views extending for 50 miles over the stunning surrounding countryside. Whether your plan is to spend your stay walking, touring or simply relaxing, you're sure to leave with happy memories. Having been recently converted and refurbished, Capple Bank Farm offers a high standard of accommodation with two very comfortable bedrooms - one king-size and one super-king or twin - with bath and separate shower en suite. Both bedrooms have TV, tea- and coffee-making facilities, hairdryer and high quality linen. There's a comfortable drawing room to relax in, and breakfast is taken in the large dining room/kitchen and features plenty of locally produced ingredients, including the farm's own eggs. Fishcakes and kedgeree are specialities of the house. Capple Bank Farm is close to Bolton Castle and Aysgarth Falls and is ideal for exploring Wensleydale, Swaledale, Coverdale, Nidderdale and the nearby towns of Bedale, Leyburn, and Richmond.

Recommended in the area
Bolton Castle; Wensleydale; Aysgarth Falls

River House

★★★★ GUEST HOUSE

Address: MALHAM, Skipton, BD23 4DA
Tel: 01729 830315
Email: info@riverhousehotel.co.uk
Website: www.riverhousehotel.co.uk
Map ref: 6 SD96
Directions: Off A65, N to Malham
Rooms: 8 en suite (1 GF) **S** £45-£75 **D** £70-£80
Notes: Wi-fi under 9yrs
Parking: 5

A warm Yorkshire welcome awaits you from owners Ann and Alex at this attractive guest house in the beautiful Dales village of Malham. The location could hardly be much more perfect, with stunning limestone scenery all around and a multitude of walking and cycling routes running past the front door. Local attractions include the stunning natural amphitheatre of Malham Cove, the peaceful and intriguing Janet's Foss waterfall, the impressive Goredale Scar and the popular Malham Landscape Trail. Parts of River House date back to 1664 and today it successfully combines modern facilities with period elegance. The eight en suite bedrooms - including a twin on the ground floor - are individually decorated, some with baths as well as showers, and all have heated towel rails, large fluffy towels and luxury toiletries. River House is a member of Deliciously Yorkshire, so you can expect lots of locally sourced produce on your plate at breakfast and dinner (a three-course menu is available in the evenings from Tuesday to Saturday). A guest lounge with wood burning stove, a licensed bar, free wireless internet, board games and reading material, and secure cycle storage, complete the picture at this award-winning bed and breakfast.

Recommended in the area

Gordale Scar; Settle to Carlisle Railway; Skipton Castle

Bank Villa

★★★★ GUEST HOUSE

Address: MASHAM, Ripon, HG4 4DB
Tel: 01765 689605
Email: stay@bankvilla.com
Website: www.bankvilla.com
Map ref: 7 SE28
Directions: Enter on A6108 from Ripon, property on right
Rooms: 5 en suite (1 fmly) **S** fr £55 **D** £65-£95
Notes: Wi-fi ⊗ under 5yrs
Parking: 6

Perfectly situated at the entrance to the picturesque Dales market town of Masham, Bank Villa is a delightful Georgian house sitting in an acre of lovely terraced gardens. Owners Liz and Graham offer comfort with style in their historic home, along with the warmest of welcomes. The accommodation is immaculate and beautifully presented, and all the rooms have their own individual character, along with comfortable beds, crisp white linen and generous fluffy white towels. Pride is taken in serving locally sourced and homegrown produce, both at breakfast and in the evenings (when pre-booking is essential). All that historic Masham has to offer is a short stroll away, while Bank Villa is also an ideal base for exploring the Yorkshire Dales and Moors with their breathtaking scenery, many stately homes, ruined castles and abbeys, and friendly towns and villages. For a different day out you can take a tour around a local brewery - such as Black Sheep and Theakston, right on the doorstep in Masham - or perhaps visit a chocolatier or cheese factory. Wherever your interests lie, Liz and Graham will be happy to point you in the right direction.

Recommended in the area
Masham; Harrogate; York; Black Sheep Brewery; Yorkshire Dales

Filey

17 Burgate

★★★★★ GUEST ACCOMMODATION
Address: 17 Burgate, PICKERING, YO18 7AU
Tel: 01751 473463
Email: info@17burgate.co.uk
Website: www.17burgate.co.uk
Map ref: 7 SE78
Directions: From A170 follow sign to Castle. 17 Burgate on right
Rooms: 5 en suite **S** £70-£110 **D** £83-£120
Notes: Wi-fi ✗ under 10yrs
Parking: 7
Closed: Xmas

17 Burgate is an elegant Georgian townhouse between the Market Place and the castle in the historic market town of Pickering - gateway to the North Yorkshire Moors. The house has been sympathetically renovated to retain all of its 17th-century period charm, whilst providing modern-day travellers with everything they might need for a comfortable and relaxing stay. All five individually designed rooms have a flat-screen TV with Freeview, DVD player (take your pick from the DVD library), MP3 station, dressing gowns, spa cosmetics, a selection of herbal infusions and ground coffee. Free Wi-fi is available throughout the house. Guests are welcome to relax in the lounge with its honesty bar, comfortable settees and roaring log fire in winter or, during the summer months, in the secluded garden, perhaps with a bottle of chilled wine or afternoon tea. The award-winning breakfasts - featuring lots of locally sourced produce - ensure a great start to every day, while excellent customer service and easy access to all of North Yorkshire's attractions complete the picture.

Recommended in the area

Pickering; Castle Howard; North Yorkshire Moors National Park

Low Skibeden House

★★★ FARMHOUSE

Address: Harrogate Rd, SKIPTON, BD23 6AB
Tel: 01756 793849
Website: www.lowskibeden.co.uk
Map ref: 6 SD95
Directions: 1m E of Skipton on right before A59/A65 rdbt, set back from road
Rooms: 4 (2 en suite) (2 fmly)
S £40–£56 **D** £64–£68
Notes: ⊗ ⼤ under 14yrs
Parking: 4

Surrounded by open countryside on the edge of the Yorkshire Dales National Park and enjoying fine views, Low Skibeden B&B is a fine-looking stone-built 16th-century farmhouse. It's just a mile away from the attractive old town of Skipton, with its open-air markets, medieval castle and Leeds-Liverpool canal basin. Hosts Heather and Bill Simpson offer a warm and friendly welcome, with every guest offered tea or coffee and cake on arrival. The four en suite bedrooms are traditionally furnished and provide accommodation suitable for families, couples or single travellers. There is a spacious and comfortable lounge with TV where guests are invited to enjoy evening drinks, and a separate dining room which is the setting for hearty farmhouse breakfasts. There's plenty of safe parking and guests can enjoy the large garden if the weather allows. Low Skibeden B&B is perfectly situated for exploring the Yorkshire Dales villages of Malham and Grassington, as well as the Bolton Abbey estate, Fountains Abbey, Brimham Rocks, Newby Hall, Harlow Carr and Ripley Castle.

Recommended in the area

Bolton Abbey; Harrogate; York

Spital Hill

★★★★★ GUEST ACCOMMODATION

Address: York Rd, THIRSK, YO7 3AE
Tel: 01845 522273
Fax: 01845 524970
Email: spitalhill@spitalhill.entadsl.com
Website: www.spitalhill.co.uk
Map ref: 7 SE48
Directions: 1.5m SE of town, set back 200yds from A19, driveway marked by 2 white posts
Rooms: 3 (2 en suite) (1 pri facs) 2 annexe en suite (1 GF) **S** £70-£75 **D** £110-£120
Notes: Wi-fi ⊗ under 12yrs
Parking: 6

This peaceful house with lovely furnishings, set in one-and-a-half acres of garden and surrounded by parkland, makes the perfect stopover for anyone travelling the A1. The original parts of the house date from Georgian times, with the remainder built in the Victorian era. Bedrooms are comfortable with large warm bathrooms and lots of extras, from Penhaligon's toiletries to bathrobes. Robin and Ann Clough are passionate about hospitality. Ann produces an excellent set dinner each evening as an optional extra, which is served in the candlelit dining room, complemented by wines from a short list. Proceedings might begin with roast figs wrapped in pancetta with a salad dressed in a raspberry vinaigrette, or a warm salad of smoked mackerel, bacon and potato, while main course might be noisettes of lamb on a garlicky sauce, or in-season game served traditionally. A local cheese board with freshly baked soda bread, and homemade ice cream with a glug of Pedro Ximinez sherry, may follow. Leaf teas, various infusions and coffee with homemade fudge provide the perfect finale to a memorable evening.

Recommended in the area
York; Harrogate; Castle Howard

Corra Lynn

★★★★ GUEST ACCOMMODATION
Address: 28 Crescent Av, WHITBY, YO21 3EW
Tel: 01947 602214
Fax: 01947 602214
Map ref: 7 NZ81
Directions: Corner A174 & Crescent Av
Rooms: 5 en suite (1 fmly) **D** fr £75
Notes: ⊗ **Parking:** 5
Closed: 21 Dec-14 Feb

Bruce and Christine Marot have a passion for what they do, mixing traditional values of cleanliness, comfort and friendly service with a modern style. The house, which has been operating as a B&B since the 1940s, is in a prominent corner position just off one of the main roads through the town and is just a short walk away from the shops, the sandy beach and the picturesque harbour. There are five bedrooms, including a family room, and each is individually furnished and colourfully decorated. All the rooms are thoughtfully equipped with TV, radio-alarm and hospitality tray. The delightful dining room, with plenty of light flooding in through a large bay window, and a wall adorned with clocks, really catches the eye. There's a bar in here and it's also the setting for some hearty breakfasts, including the full works traditional English and an alternative option for vegetarians. The menu changes with the seasons, but you can be assured that the produce is always of the highest quality. There s plenty of off-street parking and a lovely, award-winning garden complete with water feature.

Recommended in the area
Whitby Abbey; Captain Cook Memorial Museum; Robin Hood's Bay

Estbek House

★★★★ ◉◉ 🍴 RESTAURANT WITH ROOMS
Address: East Row, Sandsend, WHITBY, YO21 3SU
Tel: 01947 893424
Fax: 01947 893625
Email: info@estbekhouse.co.uk
Website: www.estbekhouse.co.uk
Map ref: 7 NZ81
Directions: From Whitby take A174. In Sandsend, left into East Row
Rooms: 4 (3 en suite) (1 pri facs)
S £90 **D** £125
Notes: Wi-fi ⊗ 🚫 under 14yrs
Parking: 6

Estbek house, a beautiful Georgian establishment located in a small coastal village north-west of Whitby, is a restaurant with rooms that specialises in seafood. Here, diners can indulge themselves in the first-floor restaurant while listening to the relaxing sound of breaking waves from the nearby Yorkshire Moors coastline. Chef/co-proprietor Tim Lawrence has nearly 30 years' experience of seafood cookery and he and his team present a range of mouth-watering dishes, including non-fish alternatives, on daily-changing menus. Over 250 wines - representing probably the largest collection of Australian wines in the UK (with many from New Zealand too) - are offered on the blackboard in the bar, with several available by the glass.

Surroundings in the restaurant are modern and stylishly simple - airy and bright by day, thoughtfully lit in the evenings. When the weather allows, diners may eat outside in the flower-bordered courtyard. On the ground floor is a small bar and breakfast room, while above are the four individually decorated and luxurious en suite bedrooms. Each has its own name - such as Florence or Eva - and character, and comes with a wealth of thoughtful extras including flat-screen TV, CD/radio-alarm, hairdryer, tea- and coffee-making facilities and complimentary guest pack.

Recommended in the area
Mulgrave Castles; Mulgrave Woods; Cleveland Way

Ascot House

★★★★ GUEST ACCOMMODATION
Address: 80 East Pde, YORK, YO31 7YH
Tel: 01904 426826
Fax: 01904 431077
Email: admin@ascothouseyork.com
Website: www.ascothouseyork.com
Map ref: 7 SE65
Directions: 0.5m NE of city centre. Off A1036 Heworth Green onto Mill Ln, 2nd left
Rooms: 12 en suite (3 fmly) (2 GF)
S £60-£80 **D** £70-£90
Notes: Wi-fi **Parking:** 13
Closed: 21-28 Dec

This Victorian villa was built for a prominent family in 1869 close to the city centre. The owners have retained many original features, yet they have improved the building to provide modern standards of comfort. Most of the spacious rooms on the ground and first floors have period furniture and four-poster or canopy beds. The top-floor rooms have now been completely refurbished and come with superb bathrooms; all rooms have hospitality trays, hairdryers, radio-alarms and TVs. The curved stained-glass window on the landing is a particularly attractive feature. There is a spacious and comfortable lounge where you can relax, watch television or enjoy a drink from the Butler's Pantry. Tea and coffee are also served in the lounge throughout the day. Delicious traditional, vegetarian and continental breakfasts are served in the dining room: the generous portions are sure to set you up for the day. Ascot House is a welcoming property that can be reached from the city by bus in just a few minutes, or by a short brisk walk. It has an enclosed car park, and the public park next door has two tennis courts and two bowling greens. A nearby pub serves good food, and there are also many restaurants, wine bars and theatres within walking distance.

Recommended in the area

Jorvik Viking Centre; National Railway Museum; York Minster

The Heathers

★★★★ GUEST ACCOMMODATION
Address: 54 Shipton Rd, Clifton-Without, YORK, YO30 5RQ
Tel: 01904 640989 **Fax:** 01904 640989
Email: aabbg@heathers-guest-house.co.uk
Website: www.heathers-guest-house.co.uk
Map ref: 7 SE65
Directions: N of York on A19, halfway between A1237 ring road & York city centre
Rooms: 6 (4 en suite) (2 pri facs) (1 fmly)
S £52-£126 **D** £56-£130
Notes: Wi-fi ⊗ ⛔ under 10yrs **Parking:** 9
Closed: Xmas

The Heathers guest house, close to the centre of York, is a large 1930s house which has been updated over the years to provide comfortable accommodation along with the very warmest of welcomes. Owners Heather and Graham Fisher continue to refurbish the guest house on a yearly basis. The bedrooms vary in size but all benefit from either en suite or private facilities, and each has been individually designed using quality fabrics and furniture. All rooms come with digital TV, Wi-fi, hairdryer and refreshments, including tea- and coffee-making facilities. The light and airy breakfast room looks out on a large, well-tended rear garden, which is regularly visited by local birds and wildlife. There's also a large lounge for guests to relax in. Off-street parking is guaranteed here, which is a special bonus in busy York. For those who wish to leave their car at The Heathers - and aren't up to walking into the city centre, just over a mile away - there's a frequent bus service that runs past the front door.

Recommended in the area

North York Moors; Castle Howard; Ryedale Folk Museum

West Yorkshire

Rochdale Canal

Shibden Mill

★★★★ ◉◉ INN

Address: Shibden Mill Fold, Shibden,
HALIFAX, HX3 7UL
Tel: 01422 365840
Fax: 01422 362971
Email: enquiries@shibdenmillinn.com
Website: www.shibdenmillinn.com
Map ref: 6 SE02
Directions: 3m NE of Halifax off A58
Rooms: 11 en suite (1 GF) **S** £81-£133 **D** £100-£158
Notes: Wi-fi
Parking: 100

The Shibden Mill Inn has won many awards - including four AA stars and two Rosettes for its cuisine - and it's not difficult to see why. This stunning 17th-century inn sits in West Yorkshire's picturesque Shibden Valley and offers luxurious guest accommodation, having been tastefully restored and refurbished by its current owners, Simon and Caitlin Heaton. The pair have achieved a successful marriage of original period features with modern-day creature comforts. There are 11 individually styled guest rooms, each with free Wi-fi, flat-screen TV and DVD player. When it comes to the inn's other major draw - the food - the menu features a wide variety of locally sourced, seasonal produce, and everything is prepared freshly to order by Shibden Mill's talented kitchen team. To accompany your meal there's a great selection of Cask Marque accredited real ales, plus some excellent wines, and it's all served in a delightfully cosy setting of low beamed ceilings and open fires - or, if the weather is kind, perhaps in the tranquil garden with the Red Beck millstream running past. The Shibden Mill Inn offers the perfect haven to escape, whether for a weekend break or a longer stay exploring the beautiful Yorkshire Dales.

Recommended in the area
Shibden Hall; Yorkshire Dales; Leeds shopping

The Huddersfield Central Lodge

★★★★ GUEST ACCOMMODATION
Address: 11/15 Beast Market,
HUDDERSFIELD, HD1 1QF
Tel: 01484 515551
Fax: 01484 432349
Email: angela@centrallodge.com
Website: www.centrallodge.com
Map ref: 6 SE11
Directions: In town centre off Lord St. Follow signs for Beast Market from ring road
Rooms: 9 en suite 13 annexe en suite (2 fmly) (6 smoking) **S** £53-£59 **D** £70
Notes: Wi-fi **Parking:** 50

The Huddersfield Central Lodge is a family-run operation with a reputation for outstanding service and a friendly welcome. It's right in the heart of Huddersfield town centre, within walking distance of the university, town hall, library and train and bus stations. Some of the smart, spacious bedrooms are in the main building, while others, many with kitchenettes, are situated across a courtyard. All are en suite and well-equipped with flat-screen TVs with Freeview, tea tray and ironing facilities. Free Wi-fi is available to all guests. Public rooms include a fully licensed bar with two plasma-screen TVs and a conservatory. The lodge's award-winning breakfast is based on local and organic produce. For evening meals ask about 'Woks Cooking'. There are some smoking rooms available on request, and children and pets are welcome. The reception is open 24 hours and there's also a night porter. All major cards are accepted, and corporate rates, accounts and discounts are available (ask for details and see the website for the latest offers).

Recommended in the area

Galpharm Stadium; Holmfirth; National Coal Mining Museum for England

Channel Islands

The Panorama

★★★★★ GUEST ACCOMMODATION

Address: La Rue du Crocquet, ST AUBIN, Jersey, JE3 8BZ
Tel: 01534 742429
Fax: 01534 745940
Email: info@panoramajersey.com
Website: www.panoramajersey.com
Map ref 15 **Directions:** In village centre
Rooms: 14 en suite (3 GF) **S** £48-£78 **D** £96-£156
Notes: Wi-fi ⊗ ⚲ under 18yrs
Closed: mid Oct-mid Apr

The Panorama is aptly named indeed, with its spectacular views across St Aubin's Bay. A long established favourite with visitors, not least because of the genuinely warm welcome, it is situated on a pretty seafront street. Inside are antiques aplenty, including a number of elegant fireplaces, and a collection of over 500 teapots. A feature of the recently upgraded bedrooms is the luxurious pocket-sprung beds, most well over six feet long. Breakfast, which is always cooked to order, is another draw, with dishes such as 'grand slam' and 'elegant rarebit' among the inventive choices on the lengthy menu. For lunch or dinner there are many restaurants in close proximity, providing ample opportunity to sample the best produce that Jersey has to offer. Many are within walking distance, and the owners will happily make recommendations. The Panorama makes a good base for walking, cycling (a cycle track along the promenade leads to St Helier) or travelling around the island by bus. Day trips by boat are available to the neighbouring islands of Guernsey, Herm and Sark, and also to St Malo in Brittany. The accommodation is unsuitable for children.

Recommended in the area

Picturesque village of St Aubin; railway walk to Corbière; Beauport and Les Creux Country Park

River Tweed at Dryburgh

Callater Lodge Guest House

★★★★ GUEST HOUSE
Address: 9 Glenshee Rd, BRAEMAR, AB35 5YQ
Tel: 013397 41275
Email: info@hotel-braemar.co.uk
Website: www.callaterlodge.co.uk
Map ref: 14 NO19
Directions: Next to A93, 300yds S of Braemar centre
Rooms: 6 en suite (1 fmly) **S** fr £40 **D** fr £78
Notes: Wi-fi ⊗
Parking: 6
Closed: Xmas

A warm welcome is assured at Callater Lodge, a 19th century Victorian villa, which stands in spacious, attractive grounds where you can often spot red squirrels and many species of birds. Sink into deep leather chairs after a day spent walking, climbing, playing golf, cycling, sightseeing, fishing or even ski-ing. The guest house is licensed, so you can sit back and relax with your favourite tipple. The individually styled en suite bedrooms are tastefully furnished, and come with flat-screen TV with Freeview, and tea- and coffee-making facilities. Free Wi-fi is available throughout the house. A wide choice is offered at breakfast, and later, soup of the day, snacks and sandwiches are served. There is a drying room available for hanging up wet clothing, and storage facilities for bicycles, golf clubs, skis, etc. Callater Lodge provides easy access to some of Scotland's wildest areas and is the perfect base from which to explore the Cairngorm National Park and Royal Deeside. The friendly owners are always happy to advise guests on what to see and do.

Recommended in the area

Balmoral Castle; Cairngorm National Park; Glenshee Ski Centre, Cairnwell

Glenburnie House

★★★★ GUEST HOUSE
Address: The Esplanade, OBAN, PA34 5AQ
Tel: 01631 562089
Fax: 01631 562089
Email: graeme.strachan@btinternet.com
Website: www.glenburnie.co.uk
Map ref: 9 NM82
Directions: On Oban seafront. Follow signs for Ganavan
Rooms: 12 en suite (2 GF) **S** £55-£60 **D** £90-£110
Notes: Wi-fi ⊗ ⛔ under 12yrs
Parking: 12
Closed: Dec-Feb

Sitting right on The Esplanade in Oban, Glenburnie offers an unrivalled seafront location with spectacular views across Oban Bay and Kerrera Island. This Victorian house provides a tranquil retreat, yet is only a 10-minute stroll from the centre of Oban - perfect for those wanting the best of both worlds. Glenburnie has been in the Strachan family since 1968 and continues to be a favoured place to stay in Oban. From the moment you step inside the front door you know you have arrived somewhere very special. The 12 en suite rooms are individually designed, with beautiful fabrics and colour schemes, whilst retaining many of the house's original features. Breakfast time at Glenburnie is a special treat, with a delicious home-cooked Scottish breakfast served in the lovely dining room complete with spectacular sea views. Those same views can be enjoyed from some of the bedrooms and from the conservatory-style porch whilst relaxing with a newspaper or a good book.

Recommended in the area

Mccaig's Tower; Dunstaffnage Castle; trips to the Isle of Mull

Craigadam

★★★★ 🛏 🍴 GUEST HOUSE

Address: Craigadam, CASTLE DOUGLAS, DG7 3HU
Tel: 01556 650233 & 650100
Fax: 01556 650233
Email: inquiry@craigadam.com
Website: www.craigadam.com
Map ref: 10 NX76 **Directions:** From Castle Douglas E on A75 to Crocketford. In Crocketford turn left on A712 for 2m. House on hill
Rooms: 10 en suite (2 fmly) (7 GF)
S £60-£94 **D** £94-£110
Notes: Wi-fi **Parking:** 12
Closed: Xmas & New Year

This working estate on the edge of the Galloway Hills is the place to head to for an authentic Scottish culinary experience. Farmers and hoteliers Richard and Celia Pickup produce their own organic beef and lamb and also have their own trout loch and smoker. What's more, Craigadam has sporting access to 25,000 acres of shooting and stalking, with pheasants and partridges reared on the estate and shoots arranged in season. Celia is an expert game cook and has won many awards for her country cuisine, which is served in the elegant wood-panelled dining room, opening out onto the pretty courtyard. However, it's not all about the food at Craigadam - the rooms are wonderful too. Each suite is designed along a particular theme, such as the 'Scottish traditional' suite with its tartan canopied bed (what else?), and the 'Macintosh' which is superbly styled after its namesake. The sunny lounge has views over the Galloway Hills and is a comfortable place to relax. There's also a billiards room with a full-size table and an extensive honesty bar.

Recommended in the area

Henry Moore/Roden statues; Drumlandrig Castle; Threave Gardens

Elmview

★★★★★ GUEST ACCOMMODATION
Address: 15 Glengyle Ter, EDINBURGH, EH3 9LN
Tel: 0131 228 1973
Email: nici@elmview.co.uk
Website: www.elmview.co.uk
Map ref: 10 NT27
Directions: 0.5m S of city centre. Exit A702 (Leven St) into Valleyfield St, one-way to Glengyle Terrace
Rooms: 3 en suite (3 GF) **S** £70-£105 **D** £90-£130
Notes: Wi-fi ⊗ ⚑ under 15yrs
Closed: Dec-Feb

'Luxury' is sometimes an overused word, but in the case of Elmview it is entirely appropriate. Nici and Robin Hill's house has been converted into a top-class establishment, with three spacious and quiet bedrooms, all with en suite shower-rooms, and all furnished and equipped to include everything a guest could want, including wonderfully comfortable king-size beds. Elmview is situated in the heart of Edinburgh in a delightful Victorian terrace within easy walking distance of Edinburgh Castle, Princes Street (just one kilometre away), the universities, theatres and the Edinburgh International Conference Centre. Fresh flowers, complimentary sherry, Wi-fi and elegant, traditional furnishings all add to the homely feel. Elmview faces The Meadows, a large urban park, where there's a 36-hole pitch and putt golf course which is free to use (Robin will happily lend you a no. 9 putter, iron and balls). While the high quality accommodation at Elmview is worth checking in for alone, the highlight of your stay is likely to be the excellent breakfast taken at one large table.

Recommended in the area

Edinburgh Castle; Edinburgh old town; Museum of Scotland; Royal Mile

Kew House

★★★★★ GUEST ACCOMMODATION

Address: 1 Kew Ter, Murrayfield,
EDINBURGH, EH12 5JE
Tel: 0131 313 0700
Fax: 0131 313 0747
Email: info@kewhouse.com
Website: www.kewhouse.com
Map ref: 10 NT27
Directions: 1m W of city centre A8
Rooms: 6 en suite (1 fmly) (2 GF)
S £79-£96 **D** £94-£194
Notes: Wi-fi ⊗ **Parking:** 6
Closed: approx 5-23 Jan

Kew House forms part of a listed Victorian terrace dating from 1860, located a mile west of the city centre, convenient for Murrayfield Rugby Stadium, and just a 15-minute walk from Princes Street. Regular bus services from Princes Street pass the door. The house is ideal for both business travellers and holidaymakers, with secure private parking. While many period features have been retained, the interior design is contemporary, and the standards of housekeeping are superb. Expect complimentary sherry and chocolates on arrival, and you can order supper in the lounge. Full Scottish breakfast with an alternative vegetarian choice is included in the room tariff, and light snacks, with room service, are available all day. Bedrooms, including some on the ground floor, are en suite and well-equipped with remote control TV with digital channels, direct-dial telephones, modem points, hairdryers, trouser presses, fresh flowers and tea- and coffee-making facilities. The superior rooms also have their own fridge. Kew House also offers a luxurious serviced apartment accommodating up to three people.

Recommended in the area

Edinburgh Castle; Edinburgh International Conference Centre; Murrayfield Rugby Stadium

23 Mayfield

★★★★★ GUEST ACCOMMODATION
Address: 23 Mayfield Gardens,
EDINBURGH, EH9 2BX
Tel: 0131 667 5806
Fax: 0131 667 6833
Email: info@23mayfield.co.uk
Website: www.23mayfield.co.uk
Map ref: 10 NT27
Directions: A720 bypass S, follow city centre signs. Left at Craigmillar Park, 0.5m on right
Rooms: 9 en suite (2 fmly) (2 GF)
S £75-£110 **D** £90-£170
Notes: Wi-fi ⊗ **Parking:** 10

This family-run guest house, just a mile from the city centre, was named 'AA Guest Accommodaton of the Year' for Scotland in 2012. A detached Victorian villa dating from 1868, it retains many original features and is furnished in a timelessly elegant style. Guests can relax and unwind in the Club Room complete with Chesterfield sofas, Georgian chess board, hand-made oversized Connect Four, selection of CDs, a laptop and a collection of old and rare books, some of which date back to the 1740s. The bedrooms are spacious and stylishly designed with handcrafted solid mahogany furniture, and each has its own individual features. One room has a Jacobean-style, hand-carved four-poster bed and a Bose sound system, while the family room comes with a Nintendo Wii. All rooms have wonderfully comfortable beds with pocket-sprung mattresses, high quality linen, bathrobes, large LCD televisions, desks, radio/alarms, sea kelp toiletries, hairdryers and generously-stocked hospitality trays. Mountain bikes are available to hire and there's also a hot tub for guests' use. The breakfasts - which have picked up an AA Breakfast Award - are well worth getting up for, with the extensive menu including a full Scottish, pancakes with blueberries, Loch Fyne smoked salmon, traditional-style porridge, and even Scottish fillet steak.

Recommended in the area

Edinburgh Castle; Holyrood Palace; Princes Street

Southside

★★★★ GUEST HOUSE

Address: 8 Newington Rd, EDINBURGH, EH9 1QS
Tel: 0131 668 4422
Fax: 0131 667 7771
Email: info@southsideguesthouse.co.uk
Website: www.southsideguesthouse.co.uk
Map ref: 10 NT27
Directions: E end of Princes St into North Bridge to Royal Mile, continue S, 0.5m, house on right
Rooms: 8 en suite (1 GF)
S £68-£85 **D** £90-£180
Notes: Wi-fi ⊗ ⚠ under 10yrs

Built in 1867, Southside Guest House is an elegant Victorian sandstone terraced house in the centre of Edinburgh, only a few minutes' walk from Holyrood Park and The Meadows. The Royal Mile and Edinburgh Castle are only a 20-minute walk away. Your hosts, Lynne and her Italian husband Franco, have been involved at managerial level in the hospitality trade for many years and take great pleasure in welcoming guests from all over the world to Southside. The house offers individually designed, stylish, well-equipped accommodation. All bedrooms are en suite and provide free Wi-fi, direct-dial telephone, TV with Freeview and DVD player. Two of the rooms have four-poster beds and comfortable sofas, and there is also a new self-contained penthouse apartment. Breakfast is a very important part of the experience at Southside, with a menu offering an outstanding selection including smoked salmon, cheeses, fresh fruits, daily hot specials and Buck's Fizz. Complimentary car parking is available nearby, which needs to be reserved at the time of booking.

Recommended in the area

Edinburgh Castle; The Palace of Holyroodhouse; Princes Street shops and gardens

Ashcroft Farmhouse

★★★★★ GUEST HOUSE

Address: East Calder, LIVINGSTON, EH53 0ET
Tel: 01506 881810
Fax: 01506 884327
Email: scottashcroft7@aol.com
Website: www.ashcroftfarmhouse.com
Map ref: 10 NT06
Directions: On B7015, off A71, 0.5m E of East Calder, near Almondell Country Park
Rooms: 6 en suite (2 fmly) (6 GF)
S £55-£60 **D** £80-£90
Notes: Wi-fi ⊗ ⚑ under 12yrs
Parking: 8

Derek and Elizabeth Scott have been running their B&B business for almost 50 years, and are as full of energy and enthusiasm as when they first began. Ashcroft Farmhouse is a modern bungalow set in beautiful award-winning landscaped gardens. Located just outside East Calder and only 10 miles from Edinburgh, it's ideally situated for exploring the city without the problems of parking (the bus goes from just outside the gates into town, or there's a Park & Ride not far away). The bedrooms (named after famous Scottish golf courses) have recently been refurbished and updated, with new bedding, carpets, and curtains. The rooms are smart and well equipped, offering hospitality trays, dressing gowns and complimentary toiletries, with fresh fluffy towels every day. Wireless internet access is available and all bedrooms have flat-screen digital TVs with Freeview. There's a DVD library available for guests in the cosy lounge, and the breakfasts are excellent, featuring home-made sausages and the best of local produce, including award-winning haggis, bacon and black pudding, all served at individual tables in the dining room. Many guests return year after year to this friendly and welcoming establishment where nothing is too much trouble.

Recommended in the area

The Giant Pandas at Edinburgh Zoo; Edinburgh Castle and shops; Glasgow, Stirling and Perth

The Spindrift

★★★★ 🛏 🍽 GUEST HOUSE

Address: Pittenweem Rd, ANSTRUTHER, KY10 3DT
Tel: 01333 310573
Fax: 01333 310573
Email: info@thespindrift.co.uk
Website: www.thespindrift.co.uk
Map ref: 11 NO50
Directions: Enter town from W on A917, 1st building on left
Rooms: 8 (7 en suite) (1 pri facs) (2 fmly)
S £40-£80 **D** £66-£80
Notes: Wi-fi 🚭 under 10yrs **Parking:** 12
Closed: Xmas-late Jan

The Spindrift is an imposing stone-built Victorian home, now a friendly, comfortable guest house which offers a warm, welcoming atmosphere and good value for money. Inside, many of the building's original features have been carefully restored. There are eight individually furnished, spacious bedrooms, all brightly decorated and with en suite or private facilities. One of the bedrooms, the Captain's Cabin, is rather unique: it was created by the original owner of the house, a tea clipper captain called John Smith, to resemble a ship master's cabin, with its small east-facing window looking towards Anstruther harbour. On the ground floor of the house, the elegantly furnished guest lounge has a well-stocked honesty bar, and is the perfect place to relax over a pre-dinner drink, whether you're dining in or out in one of the many local restaurants. In the morning, enjoy a well presented Scottish breakfast made from locally sourced ingredients, before taking a stroll around the picturesque fishing village of Anstruther, or perhaps exploring the wider area by car in this beautiful part of Fife.

Recommended in the area

Scottish Fisheries Museum; St Andrew's; East Neuk coastal villages

The Peat Inn

★★★★★ ◉◉◉ RESTAURANT WITH ROOMS
Address: PEAT INN, KY15 5LH
Tel: 01334 840206
Fax: 01334 840530
Email: stay@thepeatinn.co.uk
Website: www.thepeatinn.co.uk
Map ref: 11 NO40
Directions: At junct of B940 & B941,
5m SW of St Andrews
Rooms: 8 annexe en suite (3 fmly) (8 GF)
S £150 **D** £195
Notes: Wi-fi ⊗ **Parking:** 24
Closed: 25-26 Dec, 2wks Jan

Geoffrey and Katherine Smeddle took over this celebrated restaurant with rooms in 2006. Since then the couple have continued to build on The Peat Inn's fine reputation, gaining many awards including AA Restaurant of the Year for Scotland 2010/2011. The inn has existed on this spot since the 1700s and has been tastefully renovated to provide three small dining rooms offering an intimate setting for lunch or dinner. To complement the excellent food there is a wine list which is almost as legendary as the menus. With Geoffrey at the heart of the kitchen and Katherine heading up a dedicated front of house team, every effort is made to ensure all guests enjoy a memorable experience. Eight luxury suites, set around a delightful private garden with views over adjoining farmland, offer the opportunity for a very special night away. Each suite is individually designed, with the bedroom and living room on separate levels, and is sumptuously furnished with rich fabrics, deep carpets and elegant Italian marble bathrooms. After a refreshing night's sleep there'll be no need to get dressed for breakfast, with a selection of homemade continental goodies delivered to your suite.

Recommended in the area
St Andrews; Edinburgh; Falkland Palace

Craiglinnhe House

★★★★ GUEST HOUSE

Address: Lettermore, BALLACHULISH, PH49 4JD
Tel: 01855 811270
Email: info@craiglinnhe.co.uk
Website: www.craiglinnhe.co.uk
Map ref: 13 NN05
Directions: From village A82 onto A828, Craiglinnhe 1.5m on left
Rooms: 5 en suite **S** £48-£55.50 **D** £60-£85
Notes: Wi-fi ⊗ 🚭 under 13yrs
Parking: 5
Closed: 24-26 Dec

Craiglinnhe is a charming Victorian villa built in 1885. The house sits in attractive gardens right on the shore of Loch Linnhe close to Ballachulish and Glencoe, and is surrounded by spectacular mountain and coastal scenery. In the last few years the house has been upgraded and refurbished, with the end result being a happy combination of Victorian charm and modern day comforts. Craiglinnhe boasts wonderful views of the Ardgour hills and Loch Linnhe, which you can enjoy from the cosy sitting room with its coal fire during the winter months, as well as from your comfortable, well-equipped and stylish bedroom. If you're staying during the spring or summer, you might be treated to some fabulous sunsets, while for wildlife enthusiasts, there are otters, seals and red squirrels to be spotted in the area. A three-course set menu is offered in the evenings by prior arrangement. The menu changes daily, with everything freshly prepared and a good dose of imagination evident in owner David Hughes' cooking. To complement your meal there is a range of wines, malt whiskies, spirits and soft drinks to choose from.

Recommended in the area

Glencoe; Fort William; whisky distilleries

The Ghillies Lodge

★★★★ BED AND BREAKFAST

Address: 16 Island Bank Rd, INVERNESS, IV2 4QS
Tel: 01463 232137 & 07817 956533
Email: info@ghillieslodge.com
Website: www.ghillieslodge.com
Map ref: 13 NH64
Directions: 1m SW from town centre on B862, pink house facing river
Rooms: 3 en suite (1 GF) **S** £40-£55 **D** £62-£72
Notes: Wi-fi ⊗
Parking: 4

Built in 1847, Ghillies Lodge occupies one of the finest riverside locations in Inverness. Situated on the banks of the Ness, overlooking the Ness Islands, its tranquil setting is just one mile from the city centre, with a gentle 10-minute walk along the river path bringing you to many good restaurants. The lodge retains all of its Victorian charm and character, with carefully chosen antiques and paintings giving it an elegant look. The individually designed en suite bedrooms come with all mod-cons including flat-screen TV, CD player, free Wi-fi and amenity trays with many thoughtful extras. Ghillies Lodge is ideal for both leisure and business travellers, with private parking and ample secure storage for cycles and golf equipment. Ghillies Lodge has a long established reputation for a warm and friendly welcome and personal service, with guests returning time and time again. Inverness is an ideal base for touring the Highlands, and there is plenty to see and do in the vicinity of Ghillies Lodge. There are over 25 golf courses within an hour's drive, river and loch fishing, walking, and many attractions to visit including Loch Ness, Culloden Battlefield and Cawdor Castle.

Recommended in the area

Loch Ness; Speyside distilleries; Isle of Skye

Moyness House

★★★★ GUEST ACCOMMODATION
Address: 6 Bruce Gardens, INVERNESS, IV3 5EN
Tel: 01463 233836
Fax: 01463 233836
Email: stay@moyness.co.uk
Website: www.moyness.co.uk
Map ref: 13 NH64
Directions: Off A82 (Fort William road), almost opposite Highland Regional Council headquarters
Rooms: 6 en suite (1 fmly) (2 GF)
S £60-£85 **D** £69-£105
Notes: Wi-fi ⊗ ⚓ under 5yrs
Parking: 10

Built in 1880, this gracious villa, once the home of acclaimed Scottish author Neil Gunn, has been sympathetically restored to its full Victorian charm by Jenny and Richard Jones, and has many fine period details. The six stylish en suite bedrooms, named after Gunn's novels, are enhanced by contemporary amenities and thoughtful extra touches. Breakfasts served in the elegant dining room include a wide range of delicious Scottish dishes, as well as vegetarian and healthy options, using fresh local produce. The inviting sitting room overlooks the garden to the front, and a pretty walled garden to the rear is a peaceful retreat in warm weather. Free wireless internet connection is available throughout the house. Moyness House has ample parking within the grounds, and is well located in a quiet residential street, less than 10 minutes' walk from the city centre where there are several highly recommended restaurants, the Eden Court Theatre and delightful riverside walks. Jenny and Richard are happy to advise on local restaurants and to make dinner reservations for their guests. They will also be glad to provide touring advice and help guests make the most of their stay in the beautiful Highlands.

Recommended in the area
Culloden Battlefield; Loch Ness and the Caledonian Canal; Urquhart Castle and Cawdor Castle

Trafford Bank

★★★★★ GUEST HOUSE

Address: 96 Fairfield Rd, INVERNESS, IV3 5LL
Tel: 01463 241414
Email: enquiries@inverness
hotelaccommodation.co.uk
Website: www.traffordbank.co.uk
Map ref: 13 NH64
Directions: Off A82 at Kenneth St, Fairfield Rd 2nd left, 600yds on right
Rooms: 5 en suite (2 fmly) **S** £75-£98 **D** £98-£125
Notes: Wi-fi
Parking: 10

Luxurious accommodation and Highland hospitality go hand-in-hand at this guest house, located within walking distance of the city centre and the Caledonian Canal. Trafford Bank was built in 1873 and was once the local bishop's home. Proprietor Lorraine Freel's flair for interior design has produced a pleasing mix of antique and contemporary; some furnishings she has designed herself. The dining room chairs are a special feature, and there is unusual lighting and original art throughout the house. The bright bedrooms are individually themed; all are en suite and have enticing extras like Arran Aromatics products and organic soap from the Strathpeffer Spa Soap Company. Each bedroom is superbly decorated and comes with fine bed linen, hairdryer, Fairtrade tea and coffee, flat-screen digital TV, DVD player, CD/radio alarm, iPod docking station and silent fridge. Breakfast is prepared using the best Highland produce and served on Anta pottery in the stunning conservatory. There are two spacious lounges and the house is surrounded by mature gardens that guests are welcome to enjoy. Wi-fi is available throughout the house.

Recommended in the area

Cawdor Castle; Culloden Battlefield (NTS); Loch Ness; Moniack Castle (Highland Winery)

Glen Muick, Cairngorms National Park

Corriechoille Lodge

★★★★ GUEST HOUSE

Address: SPEAN BRIDGE, PH34 4EY
Tel: 01397 712002
Website: www.corriechoille.com
Map ref: 13 NN28
Directions: Off A82 signed Corriechoille, 2.5m, left at fork (10mph sign). At end of tarmac, turn right up hill & left
Rooms: 4 en suite (2 fmly) (1 GF)
S £42-£48 **D** £64-£76
Notes: Wi-fi ⊗ ⛔ under 7yrs
Parking: 7
Closed: Nov-Mar

This former fishing lodge dating from the 18th century is in a peaceful and secluded position above the River Spean. Well away from any main roads, Corriechoille, which has been extensively renovated over the years, sits in around six acres of its own grounds and enjoys uninterrupted mountain views. River, mountain pass and hill walks can all be started from the front door. The en suite bedrooms are all spacious and well-equipped, and look out towards the mountains or the woods. There's also a large guests' sitting-room with fantastic views and a relaxed atmosphere. Free Wi-fi is available throughout the lodge. In the evenings a three-course set dinner is served (advance bookings are essential), featuring dishes carefully prepared from ingredients sourced locally, including produce from the garden (the lodge even has its own resident hens, hence the wonderfully fresh eggs at breakfast). Corriechoille also has a drinks license, so you can take your pick from a good range of wines, spirits and single malt whiskies on the list.

Recommended in the area

Glenfinnan Monument; Viaduct & Station Museum; Ben Nevis footpath/Glen Nevis; Creag Meagaidh; Aonach Mor cable car

Tigh Na Leigh Guesthouse

★★★★★ 🛏 🍽 GUEST ACCOMMODATION

Address: 22-24 Airlie St, ALYTH, PH11 8AJ
Tel: 01828 632372
Fax: 01828 632279
Email: bandcblack@yahoo.co.uk
Website: www.tighnaleigh.co.uk
Map ref: 14 NO24
Directions: In town centre on B952
Rooms: 5 en suite (1 GF) **S** £44-£50 **D** £88-£129
Notes: Wi-fi 🐾 under 12yrs
Parking: 5
Closed: Dec-Feb

Previous winner of the AA 'Guest Accommodation of the Year for Scotland' award, this guest house in the heart of the country town of Alyth is an absolute delight. Tigh Na Leigh is Gaelic for 'the house of the doctor or physician', and although it may look rather sombre from the outside, the property is superbly modernised and furnished with an eclectic mix of modern and antique furniture. The large, luxurious and individually decorated bedrooms, one of which is on the ground floor, are very well equipped. All rooms have spa baths as well as TV/DVD players, tea- and coffee-making facilities, hairdryer and bathrobes. For extra luxury, one room has a grand four-poster, while the suite has its own lounge with a very comfortable sofa. The public rooms comprise three entirely different lounges, one with a log fire for cooler evenings, another a large TV lounge, and the third a reading room with brochures, maps and guides detailing the activities available in the area. Wi-fi is available throughout the house. The superb home-cooked dinners have an international flavour and, like the hearty breakfasts, are all made from the best of Scottish produce - vegetables come from the kitchen garden or surrounding organic farms where possible. Meals are served in the huge conservatory/dining room overlooking the spectacular landscaped garden.

Recommended in the area
Scone Palace; Glamis Castle; Dunkeld Cathedral

Gilmore House

★★★★ BED AND BREAKFAST
Address: Perth Rd, BLAIRGOWRIE, PH10 6EJ
Tel: 01250 872791
Fax: 01250 872791
Email: jill@gilmorehouse.co.uk
Website: www.gilmorehouse.co.uk
Map ref: 14 NO14
Directions: On A93 S
Rooms: 3 en suite **D** £60-£80
Notes: Wi-fi
Parking: 3
Closed: Xmas

Situated in the pretty Perthshire town of Blairgowrie, Gilmore House is an award-winning bed and breakfast. Built in 1899, this deceptively spacious late-Victorian detached house offers three comfortable bedrooms - a king, a twin and a super-king - with all modern conveniences and superb en suite facilities. An unexpected surprise is the upstairs sun lounge, where guests are invited to sit back and relax and take advantage of the huge array of books and local information. There is also a very large ground floor lounge with deep, comfortable sofas and a delightful window seat. The dining room looks out over the front garden and is the setting for a freshly prepared Perthshire breakfast, with an extensive range of dishes to choose from. When it comes to dining out, a short stroll into town will bring you to a great selection of eating establishments and independent shops. Blairgowrie is the perfect base for your holiday, and with so much to see and do in Perthshire - including nearby Glamis Castle, Scone Palace and Dunkeld for starters - one night simply isn't enough.

Recommended in the area
Glamis Castle; Blair Castle; Perth Races

Fauhope House

★★★★★ 🛏 GUEST HOUSE

Address: Gattonside, MELROSE, TD6 9LU
Tel: 01896 823184
Fax: 01896 823184
Email: info@fauhopehouse.com
Map ref: 11 NT53
Directions: 0.7m N of Melrose over River Tweed.
N off B6360 at Gattonside 30mph sign (E)
up long driveway
Rooms: 3 en suite **S** £70 **D** £90-£110
Notes: ⊗
Parking: 10

Fauhope House is a fine example of the Arts and Crafts style of architecture of the 1890s, designed by Sidney Mitchell, who was also responsible for Edinburgh's Ramsey Gardens property. It is perched high on a hillside on the edge of the village of Gattonside, and provides the kind of breathtaking views of the River Tweed and the Eildon Hills that have inspired artists and writers down the years. It offers discerning guests comfortable seclusion and the space to relax, yet is just a 10-minute walk from the Borders town of Melrose, with its shops, restaurant and small theatre. A short drive will take you to Abbotsford, home of Sir Walter Scott, and the Robert Adam-designed Mellerstain House. The hospitality provided by experienced host Sheila Robson is first-class, and the delightful country house boasts a splendid interior, furnished to the highest possible standard. Stunning floral displays enhance the overall interior design, and lavish drapes and fine furniture grace the drawing room and the magnificent dining room, where full Scottish or a continental breakfast is served. The generously sized bedrooms are luxurious and superbly equipped, with many thoughtful extras. Fauhope House was named AA 'Guest Accommodation of the Year for Scotland' 2008/2009.

Recommended in the area
Melrose Abbey; Roxburghe Golf Course; River Tweed; Fantastic walks

26 The Crescent

★★★★★ GUEST HOUSE

Address: 26 Bellevue Crescent, AYR, KA7 2DR
Tel: 01292 287329
Fax: 01292 201003
Email: enquiries@26crescent.co.uk
Website: www.26crescent.co.uk
Map ref: 9 NS32
Directions: Exit A79 at rdbt, 3rd exit into King St. Left into Bellevue Crescent
Rooms: 5 en suite **S** £45-£50 **D** £55-£80
Notes: Wi-fi

26 The Crescent was built in 1898 at the height of Victorian splendour. Its location amidst an impressive row of imposing terraced houses allows guests complete peace and quiet, yet it's only a short walk from Ayr's busy shopping centre and seafront. Ayr Race Course, Burns Cottage and the famous Turnberry and Royal Troon golf courses are approximately 20 minutes from the guest house by car (parking is available on the street right outside). The en suite accommodation at 26 The Crescent comes in a range of sizes, including rooms with four-poster and king-size beds. All are well-equipped and tastefully and traditionally furnished. Breakfast is served in the dining room at individual tables (a packed breakfast can be provided for guests with an early departure), and the extensive choice includes fresh juices and fruit, cereals, porridge with cream, a full Scottish breakfast or smoked salmon and scrambled eggs, natural smoked haddock and poached eggs, or smoked kippers, along with a selection of teas and cafetiere coffee. When it comes to eating out, you'll be spoilt for choice, with a large number of restaurants and bars within a couple of minutes' walk.

Recommended in the area

Burns Cottage; Dumfries House; Culzean Castle

Daviot House

★★★★ GUEST HOUSE
Address: 12 Queens Ter, AYR, KA7 1DU
Tel: 01292 269678
Email: daviothouse@hotmail.com
Website: www.daviothouse.com
Map ref: 9 NS32
Directions: Exit A719 into Wellington Sq & Bath Place, turn right
Rooms: 6 (5 en suite) (1 pri facs) (1 fmly) (1 GF)
S £25-£40 **D** £46-£65
Notes: Wi-fi

A warm welcome awaits you in this charming Victorian family home only a stone's throw from Ayr Beach. Daviot House is also just a few minutes' walk from the town centre with its good selection of shops, while Ayr's best restaurants and bars - with something to suit all tastes and pockets - are all within easy walking distance. Keen golfers are spoilt for choice with several courses nearby, with the option to book rounds through Golf South Ayrshire or via Daviot House's own agent. With flexible sleeping arrangements and the ability to accommodate 12 people, Daviot House certainly provides an ideal base for a golfing holiday. Bedrooms are bright and modern, and equipped with thoughtful extras. In the dining room, guests congregate around one big table to start the day with a superb, hearty breakfast, chosen from an extensive menu. Begin with cereals, yoghurts and fresh fruit, followed by a hot dish, cooked to order. Take your pick from a traditional Scottish breakfast, or something a little different such as eggs Benedict, omelettes, pancakes or scrambled eggs and smoked salmon.

Recommended in the area

Burns Cottage; Royal Troon & Turnberry golf courses; Culzean & Country Park

Rissons at Springvale

★★★ RESTAURANT WITH ROOMS

Address: 18 Lethame Rd, STRATHAVEN, ML10 6AD
Tel: 01357 521131 & 520234
Fax: 01357 521131
Email: rissons@msn.com
Website: www.rissonsrestaurant.co.uk
Map ref: 10 NS74
Directions: A71 into Strathaven, W of town centre off Townhead St
Rooms: 10 en suite (1 fmly) (1 GF)
S £42.50-£45 **D** £75-£80
Notes: Wi-fi ⊗ **Parking:** 10
Closed: 1st wk Jan

A small family-run restaurant with rooms, Rissons at Springvale is a little gem in the heart of the quiet village of Strathaven. The restaurant has a warm and friendly atmosphere, and is the setting for co-proprietor Scott Baxter's simple but accomplished Scottish cooking. You can dine in the stylish restaurant or the adjoining conservatory, and then relax in the comfortable and spacious lounge complete with wood-burning stove. Scott and Anne Baxter have refurbished Rissons at Springvale in recent years, and the result is 10 well-equipped bedrooms offering a mixture of single, double, twin and family accommodation. All rooms are en suite and simply but tastefully decorated. Excellent breakfasts are served in the restaurant, and on Sundays you can always rise a little later and indulge in brunch before you leave - the menu features the likes of 'green eggs and ham' (homemade crumpets, poached eggs, leg ham and herb hollandaise), and 'fat Elvis' (three hot pancakes, bacon, grilled banana and maple syrup). Whether you're looking for bed and breakfast accommodation or a longer stay including dinner, Rissons - located near the shopping area of Strathaven Common Green and Strathaven Park - fits the bill perfectly.

Recommended in the area
Glasgow; Edinburgh; Ayrshire coast; Clyde Valley

Bo'mains Farm

★★★★ GUEST HOUSE

Address: Bo'ness, LINLITHGOW, EH49 7RQ
Tel: 01506 822188 & 822861
Fax: 01506 824433
Email: bunty.kirk@onetel.net
Website: www.bomains.co.uk
Map ref: 10 NS97
Directions: A706, 1.5m N towards Bo'ness, left at golf course x-rds, 1st farm on right
Rooms: 6 (4 en suite) (1 pri facs) (1 fmly)
Notes: Wi-fi
Parking: 12

Bo'mains is a working arable farm offering high quality B&B accommodation and genuinely warm hospitality in a prime spot midway between Edinburgh and Glasgow at the gateway to the Highlands. There are six comfortably and traditionally furnished guest bedrooms - most with en suite shower rooms - within the modern farmhouse. All are well-equipped with satellite TV, CD and radio/alarm clock, hospitality tray, free Wi-fi, luxury toiletries and hairdryer. Almost all of the rooms have fantastic views of the surrounding countryside: one looks out towards the historic town of Linlithgow, while others face the Firth of Forth. Breakfasts at Bo'mains are of the memorable kind, with the choice of freshly cooked dishes including a traditional Scottish, grilled kippers, smoked salmon with scrambled egg and vine tomatoes, pancakes with scrambled egg, bacon and maple syrup, or oatcakes with a selection of cheeses. Fresh fruit, porridge, cereals and yoghurt are also offered, and vegetarian and special diets can be catered for. The conservatory is a lovely spot to relax with the papers or a good book, whilst taking in the views of Heather Island, the River Forth and the hills beyond.

Recommended in the area

Bo'ness & Kinneil Railway; Linlithgow Palace; Hopetoun House

WALES

Dolbadarn Castle ruins, Llanberis

Sarnau Mansion

★★★★ GUEST ACCOMMODATION
Address: Llysonnen Rd, CARMARTHEN, SA33 5DZ
Tel: 01267 211404
Fax: 01267 211404
Email: d.fernihough@btinternet.com
Website: www.sarnaumansion.co.uk
Map ref: 1 SN42
Directions: 5m W of Carmarthen. Exit A40 onto B4298, becomes Bancyfelin road (signed Bancyfelin), Sarnau Mansion on right
Rooms: 4 (3 en suite) (1 pri facs)
S £45-£50 **D** £75-£80
Notes: ⊗ ✿ under 5yrs **Parking:** 10

This fine Grade II listed Georgian country house, dating from 1765, is set in the heart of the Carmarthen countryside in 16 acres of grounds complete with a large pond, landscaped gardens, tennis court and a walled garden. Ideally situated for the many attractions and beaches of south and west Wales, and only four miles from the market town of Carmarthen, it is a delightful place to return to each evening. Many original features have been retained, and the public areas are both comfortable and elegant. The oak floored sitting room, with Chesterfields and a log fire, has French windows leading out into the garden. The dining room, where guests are seated at separate tables, is an elegant space with a feature original Welsh slate fireplace. Here, freshly cooked breakfasts are served using local produce and Sarnau Mansion's own free-range eggs, while in the evenings a set two- or three-course menu is available. Bedrooms are large and attractively furnished, with equally spacious bathrooms, and all have stunning rural views. Sarnau Mansion is only 15 minutes' drive from the National Botanic Gardens of Wales and Aberglasney Gardens.

Recommended in the area
National Botanic Garden of Wales; Aberglasney Gardens; Dylan Thomas Boathouse, Laugharne

Allt Y Golau Farmhouse

★★★★ FARMHOUSE
Address: Allt Y Golau Uchaf,
FELINGWM UCHAF, SA32 7BB
Tel: 01267 290455
Email: alltygolau@btinternet.com
Website: www.alltygolau.com
Map ref: 1 SN52
Directions: A40 onto B4310, N for 2m. 1st on left after Felingwm Uchaf
Rooms: 3 (2 en suite) (1 pri facs) (2 GF)
S £45 **D** £68
Notes: ⊗ **Parking:** 3
Closed: 20 Dec-2 Jan

Beautifully renovated by owners Colin and Jacquie Rouse, this Georgian stone farmhouse offers the epitome of gracious country living and a welcome that earned Jacquie a place in the finals of the AA 'Friendliest Landlady of the Year' Awards in 2008. The owners are knowledgeable about the heritage and nature of the area, and are always happy to advise guests on how to get the best out of their visit. The setting of the farmhouse, with views over the Tywi Valley towards the Black Mountain, is glorious, and the two acres of gardens include a fine orchard. Snowdrops, daffodils and bluebells carpet the ground in spring, and ducks, geese, turkeys, and the hens that provide the breakfast eggs roam free here. Inside the house there are cosy sofas and easy chairs around the lovely old fireplace in the lounge. The traditional dining room features one big elm table and an eclectic display of antiques, including a stately grandfather clock. Breakfast here is a real highlight, with home baking and the finest local produce accompanying those fresh eggs. The bright, comfortable bedrooms are in traditional style, with pine furniture and patchwork quilts.

Recommended in the area
National Botanic Garden of Wales; Aberglasney Gardens; Dynefwr Castle and Park

Coedllys Country House

★★★★★ BED AND BREAKFAST
Address: Coedllys Uchaf, Llangynin,
ST CLEARS, SA33 4JY
Tel: 01994 231455 **Fax:** 01994 231441
Email: coedllys@btinternet.com
Website: www.coedllyscountryhouse.co.uk
Map ref: 1 SN21 **Directions:** A40 St Clears rdbt, take 3rd exit, at lights turn left. After 100yds turn right, 3m to Llangynin, pass village sign. 30mph sign on left, turn immediately down track (private drive)
Rooms: 3 en suite 1 annexe en suite (1 fmly) (1 GF)
S £62-£67.50 **D** £90-£140
Notes: Wi-fi 🐾 under 12yrs **Parking:** 6 **Closed:** Xmas

Set in 11 acres of grounds, Coedllys is the ultimate country hideaway, tucked away in a tranquil spot and surrounded by farmland with far-reaching views and a pretty woodland dell. Guests are invited to amble around and enjoy the abundant wildlife. Owners Valerie and Keith Harber are serious about conservation and nature and they provide a refuge for countless animals, including sheep, donkeys and ponies. Inside, this large, beautiful house has been tastefully restored to provide elegant bedrooms with antique furniture and luxurious fabrics, as well as a host of thoughtful extras such as chocolates, fruit, flowers and magazines alongside soft bathrobes, slippers, flat-screen TV/DVD, free Wi-fi, iPod dock, comfortable sofas and large, inviting antique beds - all of which combine to make a stay here truly memorable. Energetic guests are welcome to make use of the fitness suite, or they can simply relax in the hydro swimming pool (available April-September only) and sauna. An extensive breakfast menu, from lighter choices through to a full English, uses the finest local produce, including free-range eggs from Coedllys' own chickens.

Recommended in the area
Dylan Thomas Boathouse, Laugharne; Millennium Coastal Path; National Botanical Gardens

Afon View Guest House

★★★★ GUEST HOUSE
Address: Holyhead Rd, BETWS-Y-COED, LL24 0AN
Tel: 01690 710726
Fax: 01690 710726
Email: welcome@afon-view.co.uk
Website: www.afon-view.co.uk
Map ref: 5 SH75
Directions: On A5, 150yds E of HSBC bank
Rooms: 7 en suite (1 fmly) **S** £45 **D** £75-£95
Notes: Wi-fi ⊗ ⚑ under 4yrs
Parking: 7
Closed: 23-26 Dec

Open countryside stretches away towards thick woodland behind this charming stone-built Victorian house, giving the impression that it's miles away from anywhere. However, Afon View is actually just a short stroll from the shops, restaurants, pubs and the station in one of the loveliest villages in North Wales. Inside, there are lots of original Victorian features, along with a comfortable lounge warmed by an open fire in the winter. There are seven en suite bedrooms to choose from, all with lovely views across the valley towards Mount Garmon, and recently refurbished to a high standard. The accommodation includes a four-poster bedroom, doubles with a king-size bed, and a luxury double complete with corner bath. All come with a generous hospitality tray, high quality toiletries and free Wi-fi access. Afon View is a cosy place to return to after a day of exploring, and along with plenty of books, maps and friendly advice, there's safe undercover storage for bikes, drying room facilities and ample private parking.

Recommended in the area

Snowdon Mountain Railway; Conwy Castle; Portmeirion

Cwmanog Isaf Farm

★★★★ FARMHOUSE
Address: Fairy Glen, BETWS-Y-COED, LL24 0SL
Tel: 01690 710225 & 07808 421634
Email: h.hughes165@btinternet.com
Website: www.cwmanogisaffarmholidays.co.uk
Map ref: 5 SH75
Directions: 1m S of Betws-y-Coed off A470 by Fairy Glen Hotel, 500yds on farm lane
Rooms: 3 (2 en suite) (1 pri facs) (1 GF)
S £45-£60 **D** £62-£75
Notes: ⊗ ⛔ under 15yrs
Parking: 4
Closed: 15 Nov-1 Mar

Hidden away with stunning views of the Conwy Valley, yet only a 20-minute stroll from the Victorian village of Betws-y-Coed, Cwmanog Isaf is a working sheep farm set in 50 acres of undulating land which encompasses the renowned Fairy Glen Gorge. Guests staying in the 200-year-old traditional farmhouse are invited to meander through the enchanting riverside woodland leading to the gorge, with its wealth of wildlife including otters, kingfishers, goosanders and many more. Cwmanog offers a double en suite bedroom, a double/twin with private bathroom, and a ground-floor double en suite with its own lounge. All are tastefully and comfortably furnished and equipped with flat-screen TVs, hospitality trays and hairdryers.

At breakfast, which is served at individual tables, you can look forward to a varied menu of freshly cooked dishes prepared from high quality local and homemade produce, including free-range eggs from the farm. Cwmanog Isaf offers the perfect relaxing base for visiting the many attractions of North Wales and Snowdonia.

Recommended in the area
Bodnant Garden (NT); Fairy Glen; Portmeirion

Penmachno Hall

★★★★★ 🛏 GUEST ACCOMMODATION

Address: Penmachno, BETWS-Y-COED, LL24 0PU
Tel: 01690 760410
Fax: 01690 760410
Email: stay@penmachnohall.co.uk
Website: www.penmachnohall.co.uk
Map ref: 5 SH75
Directions: 4m S of Betws-y-Coed. A5 onto B4406 to Penmachno, over bridge, right at Eagles pub signed Ty Mawr. 500yds at stone bridge
Rooms: 3 en suite **D** £85-£100
Notes: Wi-fi ⊗ **Parking:** 5
Closed: Xmas & New Year

Penmachno Hall, a lovingly restored Victorian rectory, is situated in over two acres of mature grounds in the secluded Glasgwm Valley in Snowdonia National Park. With its breathtaking views and quiet forest tracks leading to waterfalls, the valley is a haven of tranquillity within easy reach of bustling Betws-y-Coed. This is an establishment that prides itself on catering for the visitor's every need. Stylish decor and quality furnishings highlight the many original features throughout the ground-floor areas, while the bedrooms come with a wealth of thoughtful extras, and each benefits from panoramic views. The spacious morning room has comfortable sofas and large bay windows overlooking the garden; it houses a large collection of books, maps, walking guides and tourist information, as well as games and puzzles. The slightly more formal dining room is the venue for evening meals, served dinner-party style around a central table (by special request - contact the owners or see the website for further details). Penmachno Hall is fully licensed and offers a carefully selected wine list. A range of spirits, along with local ales and ciders, is available from the honesty bar in the dining room.

Recommended in the area

Snowdon; Bodnant Garden (NT); Portmeirion; Welsh Highland Railway

St Govans Chapel, Pembrokeshire Coast National Park

Abbey Lodge

★★★★ GUEST HOUSE
Address: 14 Abbey Rd, LLANDUDNO, LL30 2EA
Tel: 01492 878042
Email: enquiries@abbeylodgeuk.com
Website: www.abbeylodgeuk.com
Map ref: 5 SH78
Directions: A546 to N end of town, onto Clement Av, right onto Abbey Rd
Rooms: 4 en suite **S** £45 **D** £75
Notes: Wi-fi ⊗
Parking: 4
Closed: Dec-1 Mar

Built in 1840 and set in a quiet leafy avenue within easy walking distance of the promenade, Abbey Lodge retains all the charm of a Victorian townhouse. This Grade II listed building is under the personal supervision of Dennis and Janet, who welcome guests with a complimentary pot of tea or coffee in the comfortable lounge; they will even meet you from the train. The pretty walled garden that shelters beneath the Great Orme is the perfect place to relax. The charming en suite bedrooms are well-equipped with hospitality trays, hairdryers, TV, magazines, books, towels and bathrobes. Free Wi-fi is available throughout the house. A collection of local interest books and maps is available to help guests plan excursions. Breakfast is mostly sourced from the farmers' market, and packed lunches can be ordered. Abbey Road is quiet, yet only five minutes' walk from the pier and the Victorian High Street with a good choice of shops, cafés and a variety of restaurants.

Recommended in the area

Bodnant Garden (NT); Conwy Castle; Snowdonia Mountains

Can-Y-Bae

★★★★ GUEST ACCOMMODATION

Address: 10 Mostyn Crescent, Central Promenade, LLANDUDNO, LL30 1AR
Tel: 01492 874188
Fax: 01492 868255
Email: canybae@btconnect.com
Website: www.can-y-baehotel.com
Map ref: 5 SH78
Directions: A55 junct 10, A470, signed Llandudno/Promenade. Can-Y-Bae on seafront promenade between Venue Cymru theatre & band stand
Rooms: 16 en suite (2 GF) **S** £40-£50 **D** £80-£100
Notes: Wi-fi under 12yrs

Built in 1861 as a seaside holiday home overlooking Llandudno's promenade for a wealthy Victorian merchant family, Can-Y-Bae continues to provide a comfortable retreat whether your visit is for business or pleasure. With a convenient location just 300 yards from the Venue Cymru theatre and conference centre, the guest house is also a five-minute walk from the town centre. There's a comfortable lounge overlooking the sea, where you can relax and take in the vista of gently curving Llandudno Bay. Can-Y-Bae also has a fully licensed bar, which has a theatrical theme and a cosy and intimate atmosphere. The food served at Can-Y-Bae - both for breakfast and dinner (when advance table reservations are advised) - is all locally sourced. The bedrooms, many of which have sea views, have been recently refurbished to a high standard and come complete with complimentary refreshments, direct-dial telephone, TV with Freeview, hairdryer, trouser press, iron and ironing board and luxury toiletries. The rooms come in a mixture of sizes, most have lift access, and some are available for guests travelling with well-behaved dogs.

Recommended in the area

The Great Orme; Conwy Castle; Ffestiniog Railway

St Hilary Guest House

★★★★ GUEST ACCOMMODATION
Address: 16 Craig-y-Don Pde, The Promenade,
LLANDUDNO, LL30 1BG
Tel: 01492 875551
Fax: 01492 877538
Email: info@sthilaryguesthouse.co.uk
Website: www.sthilaryguesthouse.co.uk
Map ref: 5 SH78
Directions: 0.5m E of town centre. On B5115 seafront road near Venue Cymru
Rooms: 9 en suite (1 fmly) (1 GF) **S** £45-£47
D £65-£85 **Notes:** Wi-fi ⊗ ⚑ under 8yrs
Closed: end Nov-early Feb

This elegant Grade II listed Victorian guest house situated on the seafront has spectacular views of Llandudno's sweeping bay and the Great and Little Orme headlands. The proprietors, Anne-Marie and Howard, do their utmost to provide guests with a comfortable stay in a welcoming and friendly atmosphere. They're continually upgrading the accommodation, so you can expect first-class facilities along with high levels of service and immaculate cleanliness. The tastefully decorated, comfortable bedrooms come with flat-screen digital TV, a very well-stocked hospitality tray including Fairtrade products, top-quality toiletries in the en suite shower room, and free Wi-fi. The sea-facing rooms are even equipped with telescopes or binoculars to help enhance your view of the bay. Breakfasts - cooked exactly to your liking and including a vegetarian option, a good range of teas and a cafetiere of freshly brewed coffee - are served in the lovely breakfast room overlooking the sea. There's also a cosy guest lounge to unwind in, and free on-street parking for guests. Venue Cymru theatre and conference centre is just a five-minute walk along the promenade.

Recommended in the area
Great Orme Country Park; Conwy Castle; Snowdonia

Stratford House

★★★★ GUEST ACCOMMODATION

Address: 8 Craig-y-Don Pde, The Promenade, LLANDUDNO, LL30 1BG
Tel: 01492 877962
Email: stratfordhtl@aol.com
Website: www.thestratfordbandb.com
Map ref: 5 SH78
Directions: A470 rdbt 4th exit on Queens Rd to promenade, on right
Rooms: 9 en suite (2 fmly) (1 GF)
S £45-£55 **D** £55-£70
Notes: Wi-fi ⊗ 🐾 under 8yrs
Closed: Jan

Located right on the seafront with stunning views of sweeping Llandudno bay and the Great and Little Orme headlands, Stratford House makes the perfect base for a holiday or short break in beautiful North Wales. Your hosts Debra and Andrew worked for many years on the QE2 and QM2 before leaving their seafaring life behind, and their considerable experience of looking after cruise customers shows in their warm and welcoming hospitality at Stratford House. The en suite bedrooms are spread between the ground, first and second floors and are all spotlessly clean, non-smoking, and furnished in a traditional and homely style. All come with hospitality tray, LCD television, hairdryer, alarm clock/radio, and a wonderfully comfortable bed - including some four-posters and Victorian beds - made up with crisp white linen. Some rooms have fabulous sea views. Those same views can be enjoyed from the dining room, where a hearty breakfast is served at individual tables. Start with juices, cereals or fruit, followed by a traditional cooked breakfast using top quality local ingredients. Alternatives are offered for vegetarians.

Recommended in the area

Great Orme cable car; Snowdonia National Park; Welsh Mountain Zoo

Plas Rhos

★★★★★ GUEST ACCOMMODATION
Address: Cayley Promenade,
RHOS-ON-SEA, LL28 4EP
Tel: 01492 543698
Fax: 01492 540088
Email: info@plasrhos.co.uk
Website: www.plasrhos.co.uk
Map ref: 5 SH88
Directions: A55 junct 20 onto B5115 for Rhos-on-Sea, right at rdbt onto Whitehall Rd to promenade
Rooms: 7 en suite **S** £50 **D** £70-£100
Notes: Wi-fi ⊗ 🐾 under 12yrs **Parking:** 4
Closed: 21 Dec-Jan

A yearning to live by the sea and indulge their passion for sailing brought Susan and Colin Hazelden to the North Wales coast. Running a hotel in Derbyshire for many years was the ideal preparation for looking after guests at their renovated Victorian home. Built as a gentleman's residence in the late 19th century, Plas Rhos is situated on Cayley Promenade, where it enjoys panoramic views over the bay, beach and coast. Breakfast, a particularly memorable meal, is taken overlooking the pretty patio garden. It consists of cereals, fresh fruit, juices and yoghurt followed by free-range eggs cooked to your liking with Welsh sausage, local back bacon, tomato, mushrooms, beans and fried bread, or your choice of a number of other hot options including kippers or scrambled eggs with smoked salmon. The two sumptuous lounges have spectacular sea views, comfortable chairs and sofas, and interesting memorabilia, while the modest-size bedrooms are individually decorated and have plenty of thoughtful extras. One period room is furnished with a romantic half-tester and antiques, and enjoys those same stunning views. Wi-fi access is available in all rooms.

Recommended in the area

Conwy Castle; Bodnant Garden (NT); Snowdonia National Park

Millennium Stadium, Cardiff

Castle House

★★★★★ BED AND BREAKFAST

Address: Bull Lane (Love Lane), DENBIGH, LL16 3LY
Tel: 01745 816860
Fax: 01745 817214
Email: stay@castlehousebandb.co.uk
Website: www.castlehousebandb.co.uk
Map ref: 5 SJ06
Directions: A55 junct 27 onto A525 to Denbigh. From Vale St take 1st exit at rdbt, pass supermarket, 1st left to T-junct then right. 20yds on left onto unmarked drive
Rooms: 3 en suite **S** £65-£110 **D** £120-£160
Notes: Wi-fi ⊗ **Parking:** 6 **Closed:** 20-30 Dec

Located within Denbigh's medieval town walls, this substantial Grade II listed former gentleman's residence dates back to 1820. As well as enjoying magnificent views across the Clwyd Valley towards the Clwydian range of mountains, designated an Area of Outstanding Natural Beauty, it enjoys prime position within the tranquil grounds of Plas Castell Estate, with two acres of landscaped gardens at guests' disposal, including a croquet lawn and fish pond. Also within the grounds is the 16th-century Leicester's Church, an unfinished cathedral built by the nobleman Robert Dudley. Inside Castle House, with its grand entrance reception hall and feature mirror lending a sense of days gone by, all has been lovingly restored to provide high standards of comfort and facilities. Spacious, individually themed and evocatively named bedrooms are equipped with quality furnishings, a wealth of thoughtful extras and smart, efficient en suite bathrooms with floor lighting and underfloor heating. There is also a romantic lounge and a formal dining room with ornate ceiling plasterwork and log fires in winter, where guests can enjoy delicious breakfasts through to scrumptious afternoon teas and cand elit dinners.

Recommended in the area
Offa's Dyke; Loggerheads Country Park; Snowdonia

Pentre Mawr Country House

★★★★★ GUEST ACCOMMODATION
Address: LLANDYRNOG, LL16 4LA
Tel: 01824 790732
Fax: 01824 790441
Email: info@pentremawrcountryhouse.co.uk
Website: www.pentremawrcountryhouse.co.uk
Map ref: 5 SJ16
Directions: From Denbigh follow Bodfari/Llandyrnog signs. Left at rdbt to Bodfari, 50yds, left into country lane, Pentre Mawr on left
Rooms: 3 en suite 8 annexe en suite (7 GF)
D £130–£190
Notes: Wi-fi 🚫 under 13yrs **Parking:** 14

This property, owned by the same family for 400 years, is a unique destination, bursting with character. Tucked away in an unspoilt corner of North Wales, in an Area of Outstanding Natural Beauty, this former farmhouse is set in nearly 200 acres of meadows, park and woodland. A true Welsh country house, it features well-appointed en suite bedrooms and suites, some with hot tubs and all very spacious and thoughtfully equipped. As well as large drawing rooms, there is also a formal dining room, ideal for family gatherings and special occasions, and a less formal dining area in the conservatory by the saltwater swimming pool in the walled garden. The daily-changing menu includes carefully sourced local meats and cheeses as well as homemade breads and sorbets. Full Welsh breakfasts with Buck's fizz are served in the morning room. Influenced by a love of the outdoors and Africa, owners Bre and Graham have introduced a number of luxurious canvas safari lodges to bring guests closer to nature without compromising on comfort; all are fully heated, have super-king-size beds, oak floors and decks with hot tubs, plus bathrooms with free-standing baths and showers.

Recommended in the area
Snowdonia National Park; Denbigh Castle; Moel Fammau mountain walk

Firgrove Country House B&B

★★★★★ BED AND BREAKFAST

Address: Firgrove, Llanfwrog, RUTHIN, LL15 2LL
Tel: 01824 702677
Fax: 01824 702677
Email: meadway@firgrovecountryhouse.co.uk
Website: www.firgrovecountryhouse.co.uk
Map ref: 5 SJ15
Directions: 0.5m SW of Ruthin. A494 onto B5105, 0.25m past Llanfwrog church on right
Rooms: 2 en suite 1 annexe en suite (1 GF)
S £60-£80 **D** £80-£110
Notes: Wi-fi ⊗ 🐾 **Parking:** 4
Closed: Dec-Jan

This Grade II listed building sits in an award-winning garden and has inspiring views across the Vale of Clwyd to the Clwydian Range, an Area of Outstanding Natural Beauty. The well-proportioned double bedrooms are individually furnished and retain many original features, whilst being equipped with every modern comfort, including smart bathrooms. The two bedrooms in the main house have four-poster beds, while the third guest room is a self-contained ground-floor suite comprising a sitting room with a log-burning stove and a small kitchen. Free Wi-fi is available throughout the house, and should you need any assistance during your stay, you can make use of the bellhop service. Breakfasts at Firgrove are not to be missed, with a wide range of juices, fruits, yoghurts, cereals and continental meats and cheeses to choose from on the buffet table, along with hot dishes cooked to order. Evening meals - taken around the family table with your hosts - are available by prior arrangement. Local produce is used wherever possible and most diets can be catered for. There is plenty of off-road parking.

Recommended in the area
Offa's Dyke Path; Bodnant Garden (NT); Chester

Tan-Yr-Onnen Guest House

★★★★★ GUEST HOUSE
Address: Waen, ST ASAPH, LL17 0DU
Tel: 01745 583821
Fax: 01745 583821
Email: tanyronnenvisit@aol.com
Website: www.northwalesbreaks.co.uk
Map ref: 5 SJ07
Directions: W on A55 junct 28, turn left in 300yds
Rooms: 6 en suite (1 fmly) (4 GF)
S £69-£90 **D** £89-£125
Notes: Wi-fi
Parking: 8

Set in the heart of North Wales, in the verdant Vale of Clwyd, Patrick and Sara Murphy's guest house, Tan-Yr-Onnen, is perfectly located for exploring this beautiful area and nearby Chester. Now awarded the AA's highest B&B rating, quality is the keyword here, with very high standards throughout. The house has been extensively refurbished and the separately accessed bedrooms newly constructed; all are modern and well-equipped. The en suite ground-floor rooms feature king-size beds and some have French doors opening onto the patio, while those on the first floor offer suite accommodation. All provide home comforts such as bathrobes, fluffy towels, comfy beds, flat-screen TVs (with Freeview and DVD players), and tea- and coffee-making facilities, plus little touches to make your stay feel extra special. Free Wi-fi is available. The hearty breakfast buffet will set you up for a day's exploration, with the options including fruit juices, fresh fruit salad, yoghurts, cereals, home-baked bread and a full Welsh breakfast. Adjacent to the dining room is the lounge and large conservatory. Here you can enjoy a cool glass of wine in the evening as you admire the grounds and gardens at the foot of the Clwydian range. Private parking is available.

Recommended in the area
St Asaph; Bodelwyddan Castle; Offa's Dyke Path

Tyddynmawr Farmhouse

★★★★★ FARMHOUSE
Address: Cader Rd, Islawrdref,
DOLGELLAU, LL40 1TL
Tel: 01341 422331
Website: www.wales-guesthouse.co.uk
Map ref: 5 SH71
Directions: From town centre left at top of square, left at garage into Cader Rd for 3m. 1st farm on left after Gwernan Lake
Rooms: 2 en suite (1 GF) **S** £55 **D** £78
Notes: Wi-fi ⊗ ⛔
Parking: 8
Closed: Dec & Jan

Birdwatchers, ramblers, photographers and artists see these spectacular surroundings as a paradise, and the farmhouse accommodation at Tyddynmawr appeals equally to those just happy to sit and look. The house, which dates from the 18th century and is full of lovely oak beams and log fires, is just three miles from the historic market town of Dolgellau in the Snowdonia National Park. Lovingly restored to offer a high standard of accommodation, all rooms are spacious and tastefully decorated with handmade Welsh oak furniture and large, luxurious bathrooms. One room has a balcony, and a ground-floor room benefits from a patio. Olwen Evans has been running Tyddynmawr as a five-star guesthouse since 1986, and continues to pride herself on high standards of customer care, the quality of the food and her warm hospitality - it's no wonder guests return year after year. The magnificent mountain of Cader Idris rises up behind Tyddynmawr and allures guests to explore its beautiful lakes, or perhaps, for the more energetic, a climb to the summit.

Recommended in the area

Walking - Cader Idris, Precipice walk, Mawddach Estuary walk; steam railways; good local food

Crug-Glas Country House

★★★★★ 🏨 🍽 RESTAURANT WITH ROOMS

Address: SCLVA, St David's, SA62 6XX
Tel: 01348 831302
Email: janet@crugglas.plus.com
Website: www.crug-glas.co.uk
Map ref: 1 SM82
Directions: From St David's on towards Fishguard road, 1st left after Carnhedryn, signed
Rooms: 7 en suite (1 fmly) (2 GF)
S £80-£100 **D** £100-£150
Notes: Wi-fi ⊗ 🐾 under 12yrs
Parking: 10
Closed: 24-27 Dec

A stay in this Georgian country house, sitting in the middle of a cereal farm and surrounded by open countryside, offers total peace and tranquillity. There are extensive grounds to relax in and soak up the fresh air, perhaps whilst indulging in a delicious afternoon cream tea. Crug-Glas is situated near the smallest city in Britain, St David's, as well as the pretty fishing villages of Porthgain and Solva and, of course, the breathtakingly beautiful coastal path. In the area there are golf courses and mapped cycle routes, and your hosts will happily arrange personal guided tours of the coastal path and inland walks with packed lunches provided. All the bedrooms at Crug-Glas are individually designed with sumptuous fabrics and wal papers, and the bathrooms are fitted with new powerful showers and deep baths. The award-winning food, served in the dining room, is predominately sourced from the local area, such as crab and lobster from Abercastle Cove and meats and vegetables from Pembrokeshire farms. In the morning a hearty breakfast, including an extensive selection of fresh fruit, traditional cooked dishes, smoked fish, local cheeses and cured meats, will set you up nicely for the day.

Recommended in the area

Abereiddy Beach; Porthgain; St David's

Ramsey House

★★★★★ GUEST HOUSE

Address: Lower Moor, ST DAVID'S,
Haverfordwest, SA62 6RP
Tel: 01437 720321 & 07795 575005
Email: info@ramseyhouse.co.uk
Website: www.ramseyhouse.co.uk
Map ref: 1 SM72
Directions: From Cross Sq in St David's towards Porthclais, house 0.25m on left
Rooms: 6 (5 en suite) (1 pri facs) (3 GF)
S £60-£110 **D** £100-£110
Notes: Wi-fi ⊗ under 16yrs **Parking:** 10
Closed: Nov-13 Feb

Family-run by Suzanne and Shaun Ellison, Ramsey House is just a gentle stroll from the centre of Britain's smallest city, St David's, a place with a rich historical heritage surrounded by beautiful countryside, with the Pembrokeshire coastal path nearby. The Ellisons provide the ideal combination of professional hotel management and the warmth of a friendly guest house with a relaxed atmosphere. They are happy to advise guests on the many activities and places of interest nearby, and there are plenty of books and leaflets too, to help you plan your excursions. All bedrooms have been refurbished in a luxury boutique style; first-floor rooms have views out to sea, over countryside or towards the cathedral, and those on the ground-floor look out over the gardens. Ramsey House has a licensed bar next to the dining room, secure bicycle storage, a wet room, light laundry facilities and ample off-street parking. Shaun is an accomplished chef who champions quality local produce, so you can expect a real flavour of Wales from your meals. Breakfast provides a choice of home-made items including breads and preserves, and a three-course dinner is served in the restaurant. Freshly prepared picnics can also be arranged for your day out.

Recommended in the area

Pembrokeshire islands; St David's Cathedral; Pembrokeshire Coast National Park

The Waterings

★★★★ BED AND BREAKFAST

Address: Anchor Dr, High St, ST DAVID'S, SA62 6QH
Tel: 01437 720876
Email: enquiries@waterings.co.uk
Website: www.waterings.co.uk
Map ref: 1 SM72
Directions: On A487 on E edge of St David's
Rooms: 5 annexe en suite (4 fmly) (5 GF)
S £50-£85 **D** £75-£85
Notes: Wi-fi 🐾 under 5yrs
Parking: 20

The Waterings is set in an acre of beautiful landscaped grounds in a quiet location close to the Pembrokeshire Coast National Park Visitor Centre and only a short walk from St David's 800-year-old cathedral, which is the setting for an annual music festival at the end of May. The magnificent coastline with its abundance of birdlife is also within easy reach. The spacious en suite bedrooms are all on the ground floor and are set around an attractive courtyard. All the bedrooms are equipped with TV and have tea- and coffee-making facilities. The accommodation includes two family rooms with lounge, two double rooms with lounge and a double room with small sitting area. Breakfast, prepared from a good selection of local produce, is served in a smart dining room in the main house. Outside amenities at The Waterings include a picnic area with tables and benches, a barbecue and a croquet lawn. The nearest sandy beach is just a 15-minute walk away; other activities in the area include walking, boat trips to Ramsey Island, an RSPB reserve a mile offshore, sea fishing, whale and dolphin spotting boat trips, canoeing, surfing, rock climbing and abseiling.

Recommended in the area

Ramsey Island boat trips; Pembrokeshire Coast National Park; Whitesands Beach

The Coach House

★★★★★ ≙ GUEST ACCOMMODATION

Address: Orchard St, BRECON, LD3 8AN
Tel: 01874 620043 & 07974 328337
Email: coachhousebrecon@gmail.com
Website: www.coachhousebrecon.com
Map ref: 2 SO02
Directions: From town centre W over bridge onto B4601, Coach House 200yds on right
Rooms: 6 en suite **S** £50-£65 **D** £70-£120
Notes: Wi-fi ⊗ ⚑ under 16yrs
Parking: 6

Coach houses were traditionally warm and welcoming places, and while a warm welcome is assured here in Brecon, this particular example is one of a new breed, offering luxurious townhouse accommodation. The private garden of the Coach House is an oasis of colour, and offers a retreat in which to relax, read a book or take a drink. Hosts Marc and Tony are proud of their local knowledge, and offer advice on the best places to visit, whether by car, on foot or by bicycle. There are also opportunities for sailing or pony-trekking in the area. The strong sense of place evident in the photographs and maps of the Brecon Beacons on the walls, showing some of the most unspoilt countryside in Wales, continues through to the Welsh-speciality breakfasts - try Eggs Brychan, made with scrambled eggs, smoked salmon and laverbread for starters. Much thought has gone into the contemporary design of the light, airy and well-equipped bedrooms, all of which come with flat-screen TVs and DVD players.

Recommended in the area

Brecon Beacons National Park; Dan yr Ogof Caves; Brecon Cathedral

Glangrwyney Court

★★★★★ BED AND BREAKFAST
Address: CRICKHOWELL, NP8 1ES
Tel: 01873 811288
Fax: 01873 810317
Email: info@glancourt.co.uk
Website: www.glancourt.co.uk
Map ref: 2 SO21
Directions: 2m SE of Crickhowell on A40 (near county boundary)
Rooms: 6 en suite 4 annexe en suite (1 fmly) (1 GF)
S £65-£120 **D** £95-£149
Notes: Wi-fi 🐾 under 12yrs
Parking: 12

A privately-owned, Georgian Grade II listed country house, Glangrwyney Court offers delightful luxury accommodation. Forming part of a small country estate on the edge of the beautiful Brecon Beacons and the Black Mountains, it stands in four acres of walled gardens and makes an ideal base for touring this lovely area. The house throughout is tastefully decorated and furnished with period pieces. Guests are encouraged to relax in the cosy sitting room in front of a roaring log fire in the winter months. Glangrwyney Court has been home to the same family for the last 17 years, during which time the main house and the cottages have been sympathetically restored to provide excellent modern comforts. The accommodation comprises eight bedrooms in the main house, one ground-floor room in the garden courtyard, and three cottages which are available on a bed and breakfast basis or for self-catering. All rooms have TV and DVD players, hairdryers, clock radios, quality toiletries, fluffy bath towels and robes, plus tea- and coffee-making facilities.

Recommended in the area
Brecon Beacons National Park; Raglan Castle; Big Pit National Mining Museum of Wales

The Cammarch

★★★★ GUEST ACCOMMODATION
Address: LLANGAMMARCH WELLS, LD4 4BY
Tel: 01591 610802
Email: mail@cammarch.com
Website: www.cammarch.com
Map ref: 2 SN94
Directions: Exit A483 at Garth, signed Llangammarch Wells, opposite T-junct
Rooms: 11 en suite (3 fmly) **S** £59-£69 **D** £79-£89
Notes: Wi-fi
Parking: 16

Kathryn Dangerfield took over The Cammarch in 2008 and has been busy ever since refurbishing and refining it to restore the Victorian building to its original elegance. Built in traditional Welsh stone, The Cammarch is surrounded by stunning countryside and is just a stone's throw from Builth Wells, with the Brecon Beacons National Park nearby and the coast and Aberystwyth just over an hour away. Kathryn offers all guests a warm and friendly welcome in a homely and comfortable environment. The high quality accommodation includes nine double or twin en suite bedrooms on the first two floors, and two excellent family suites with fully fitted kitchen/diner and a separate lounge on the top floor. There's a lovely residents' lounge with comfortable sofas, open fire, games and an honesty bar, while meals are taken in the attractive conservatory restaurant overlooking the garden. All the food is prepared from scratch using as much local produce as possible. The garden is a magical place, especially for children, with the river running around the edge - perfect for a paddle or a spot of fishing. For serious anglers, The Cammarch has fishing rights on the River Irfon.

Recommended in the area

Elan Valley Reservoir and Dams; Rhayader red kite feeding station; Royal Welsh Showground at Builth Wells

Snowdon Mountain Railway

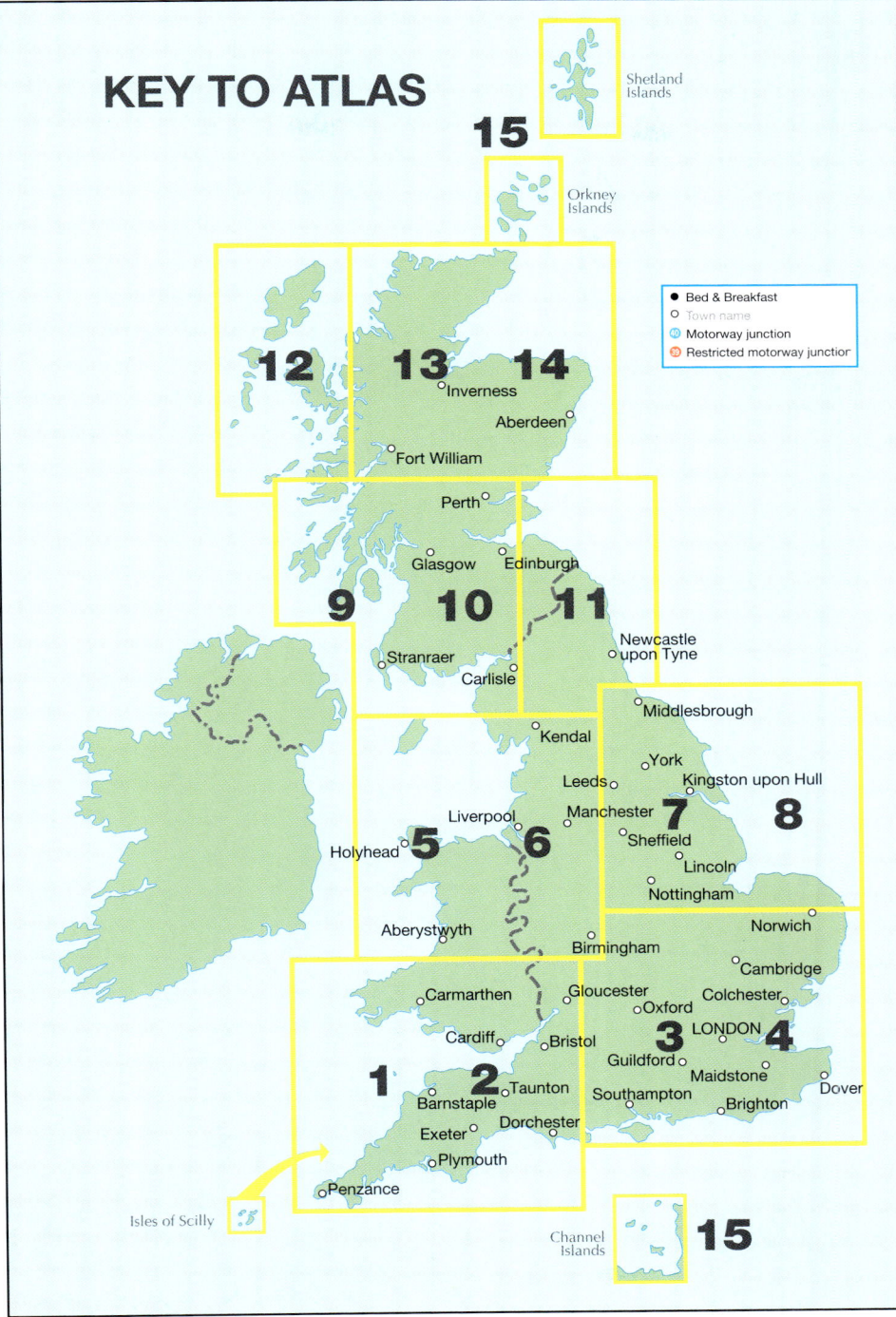

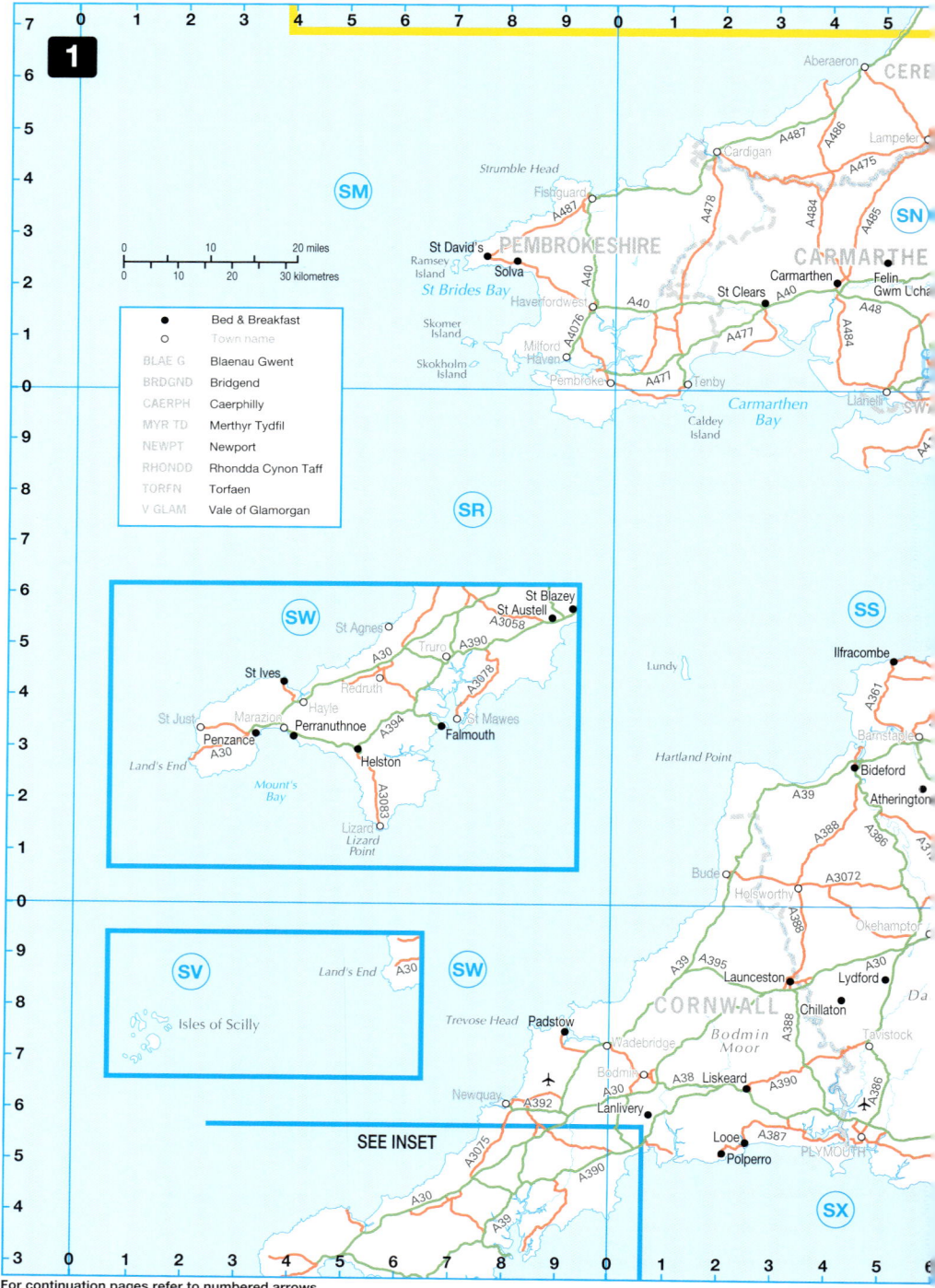

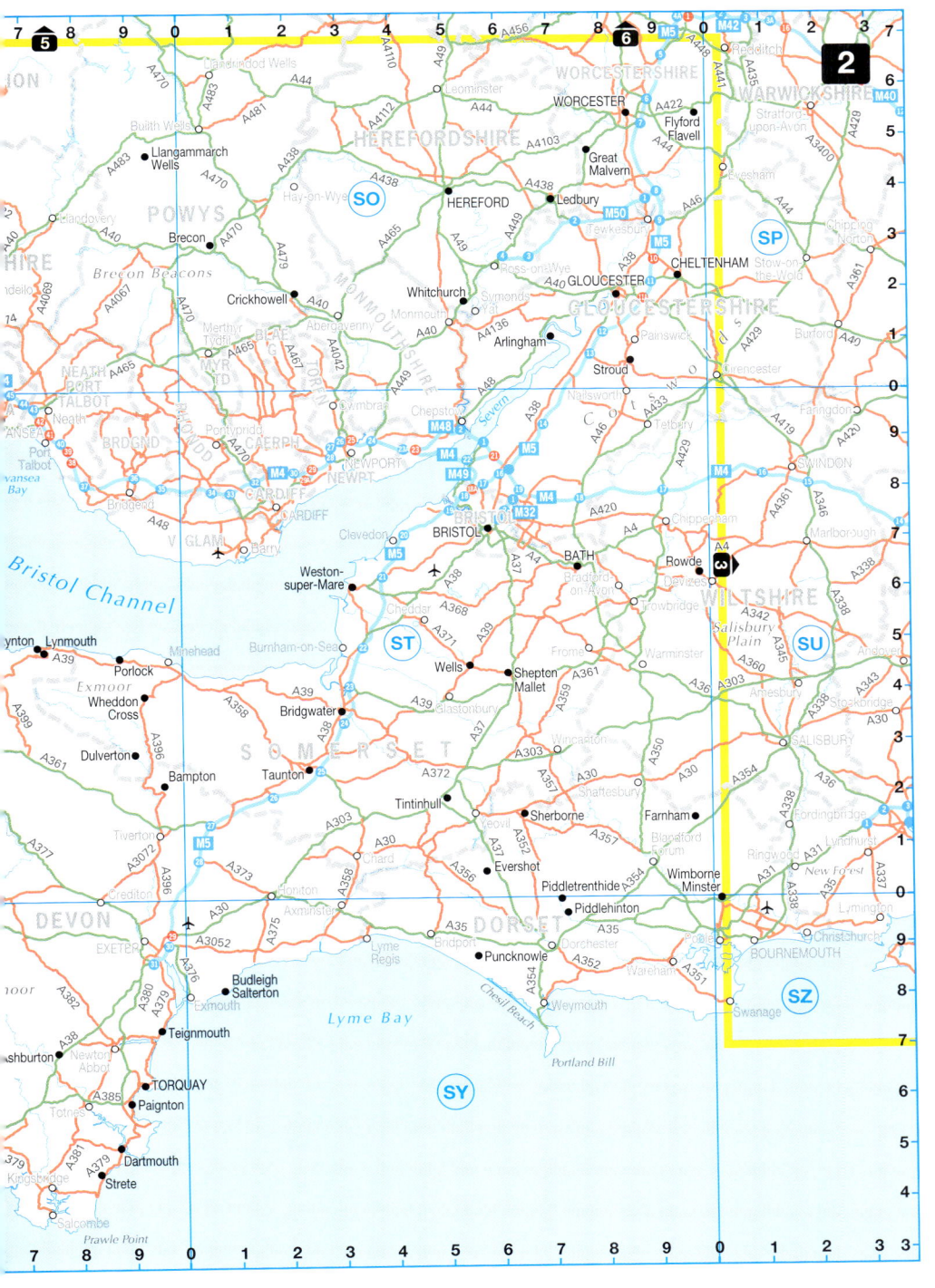

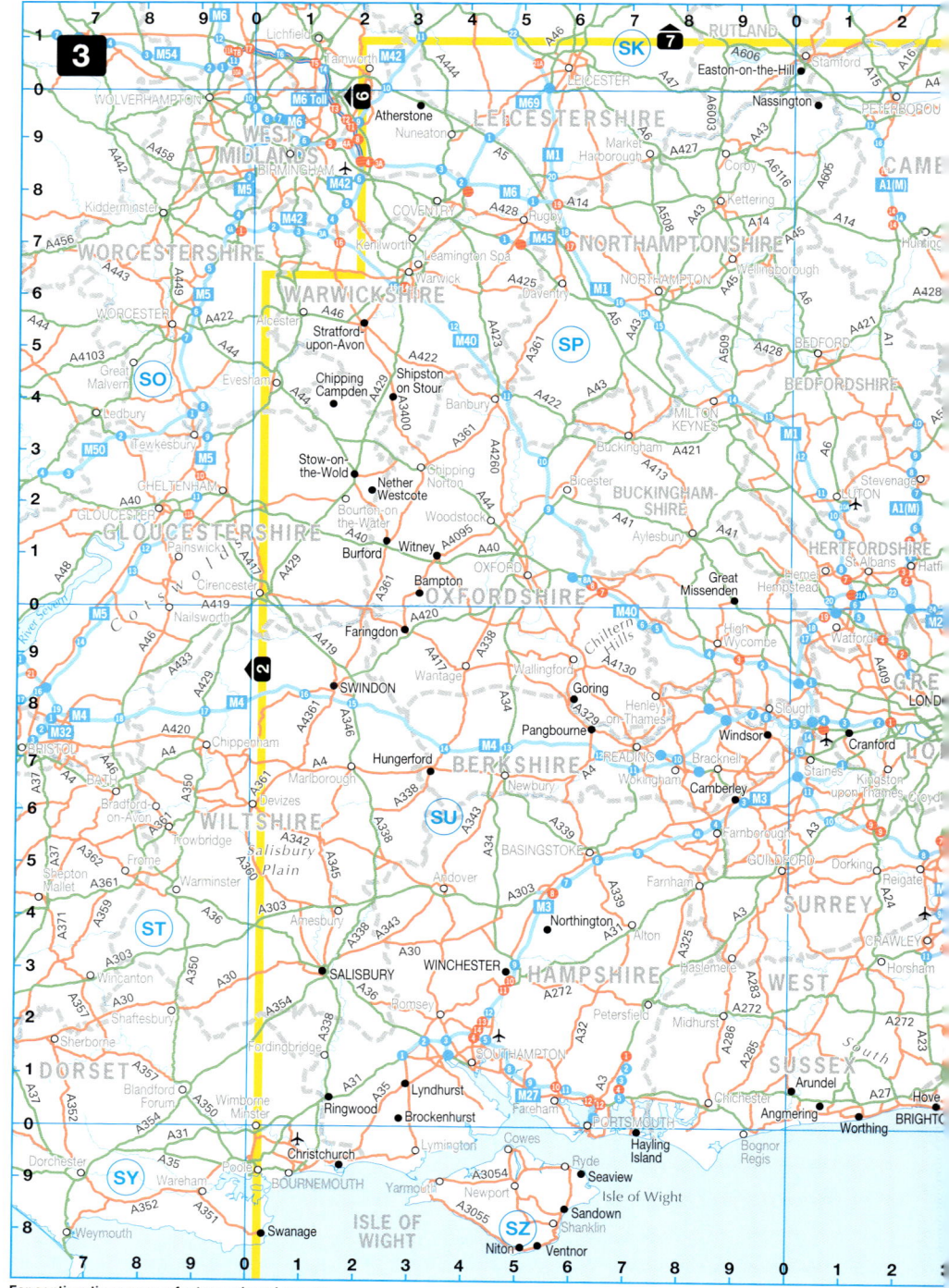

For continuation pages refer to numbered arrows

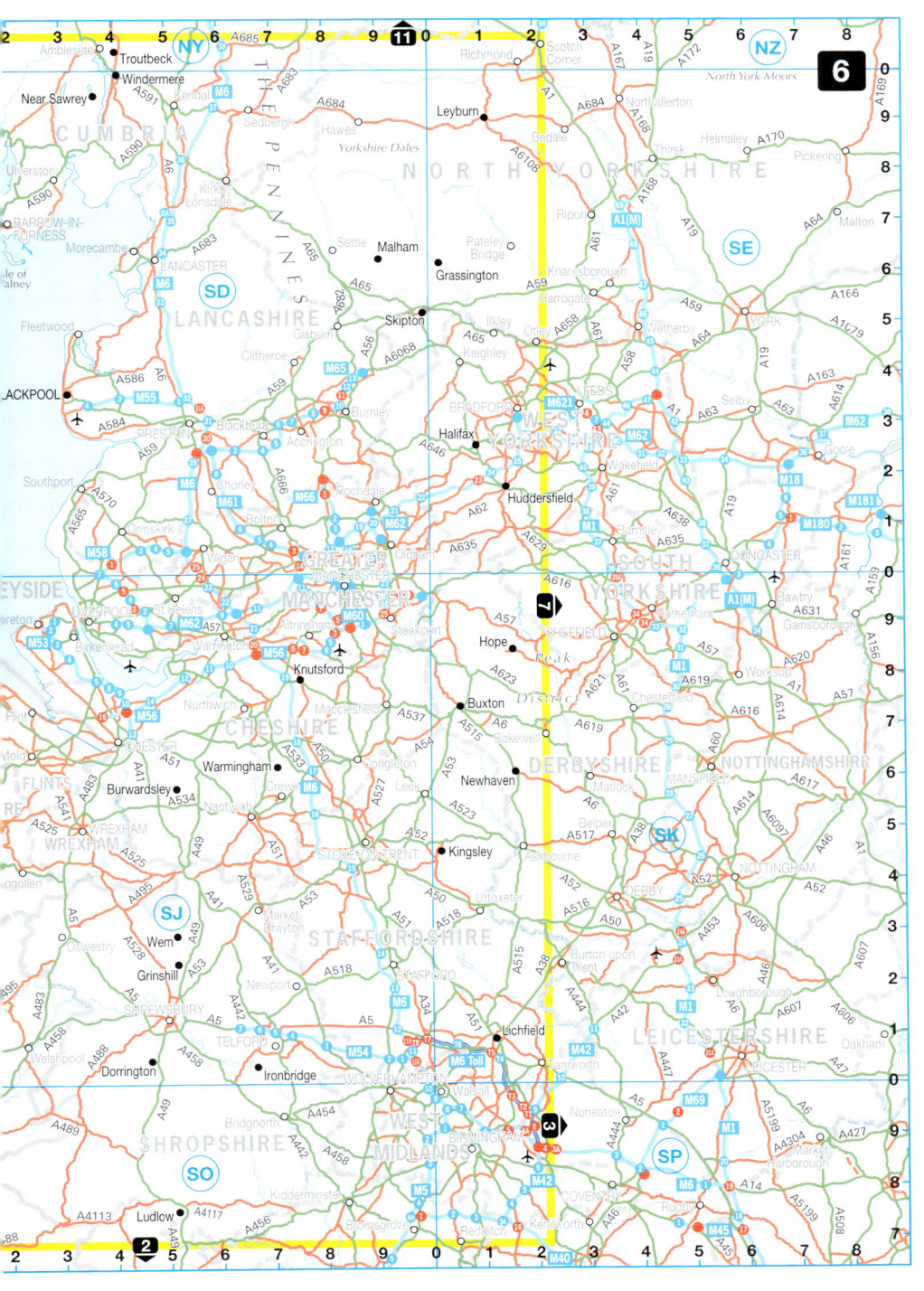

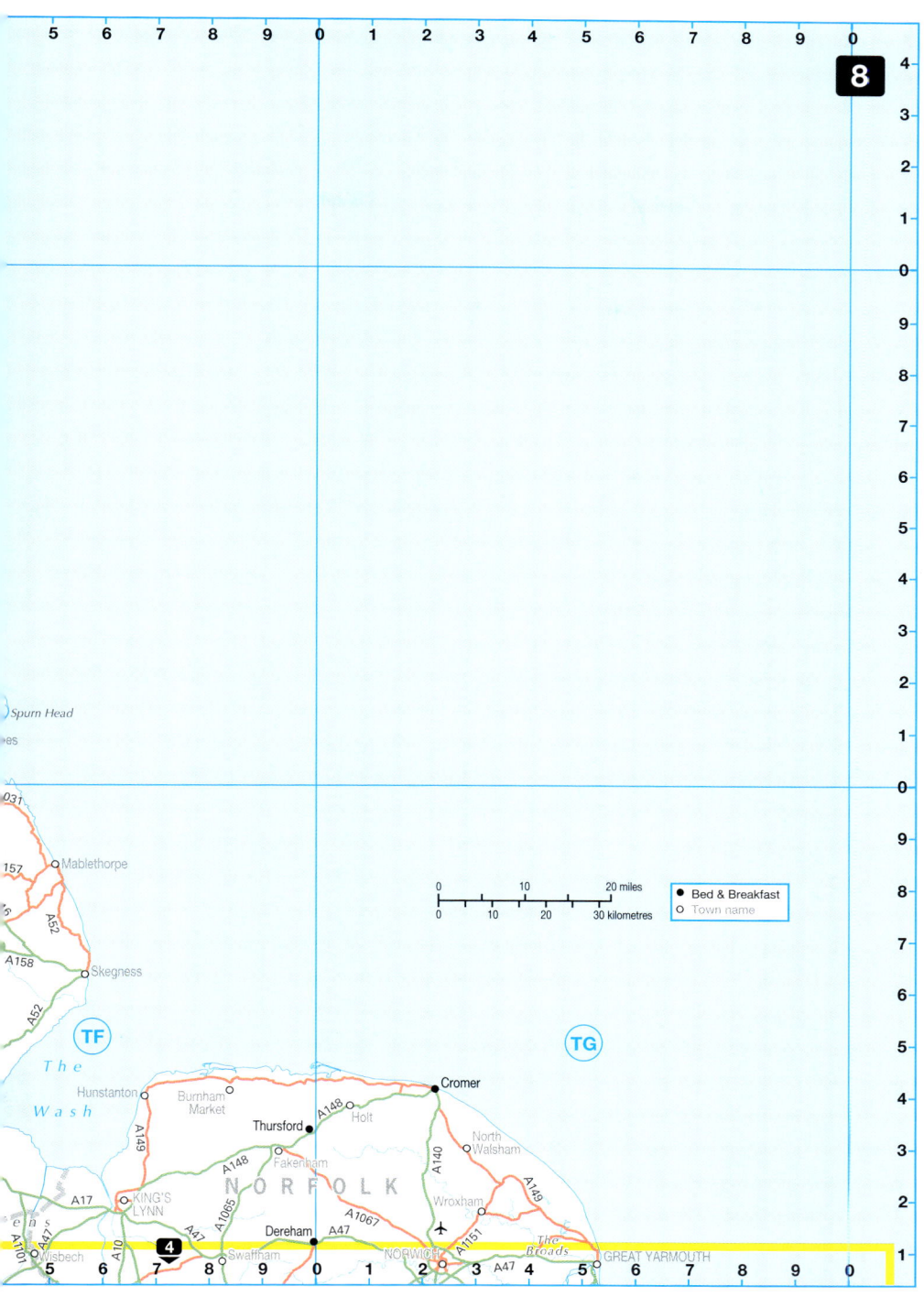

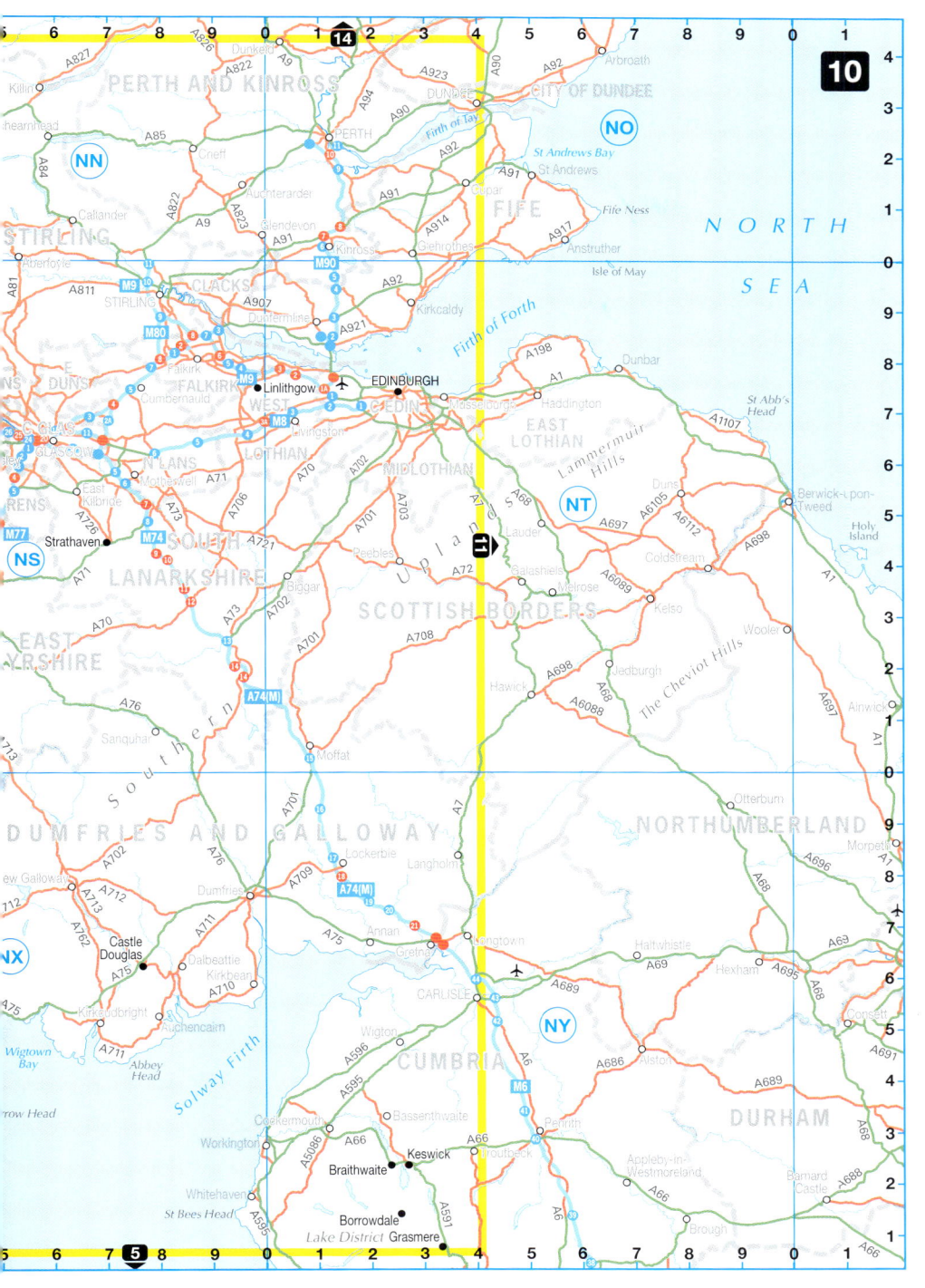

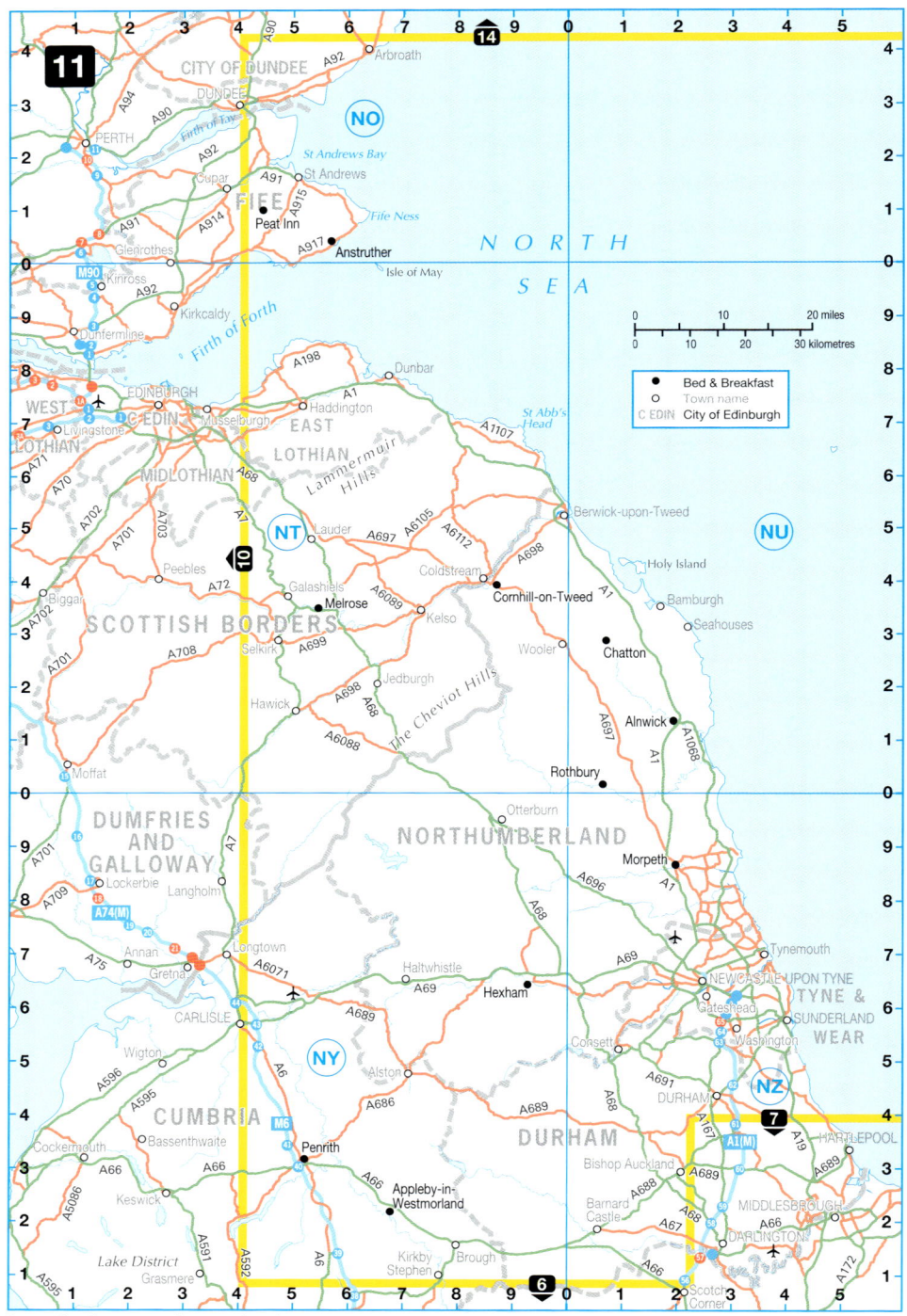

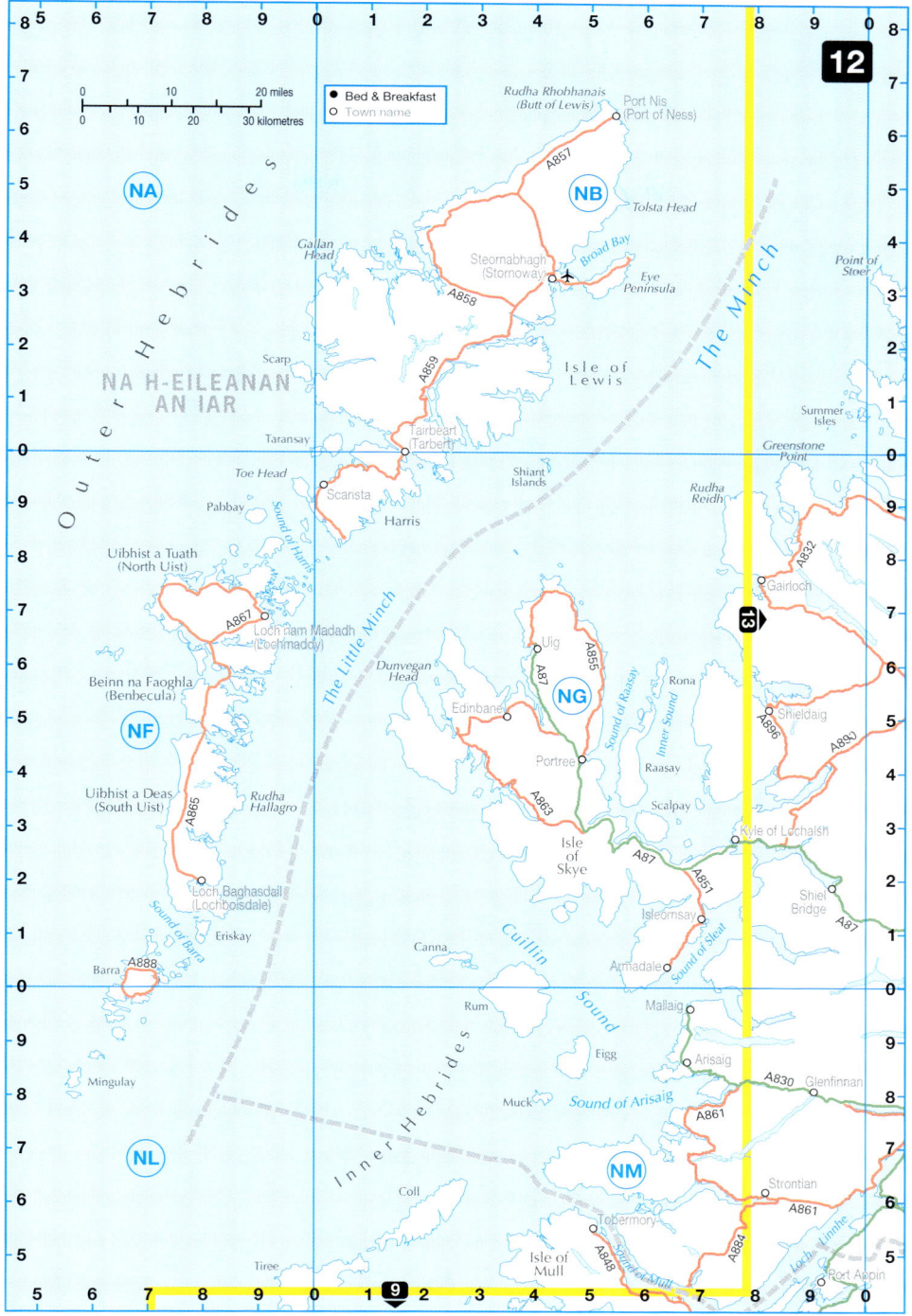

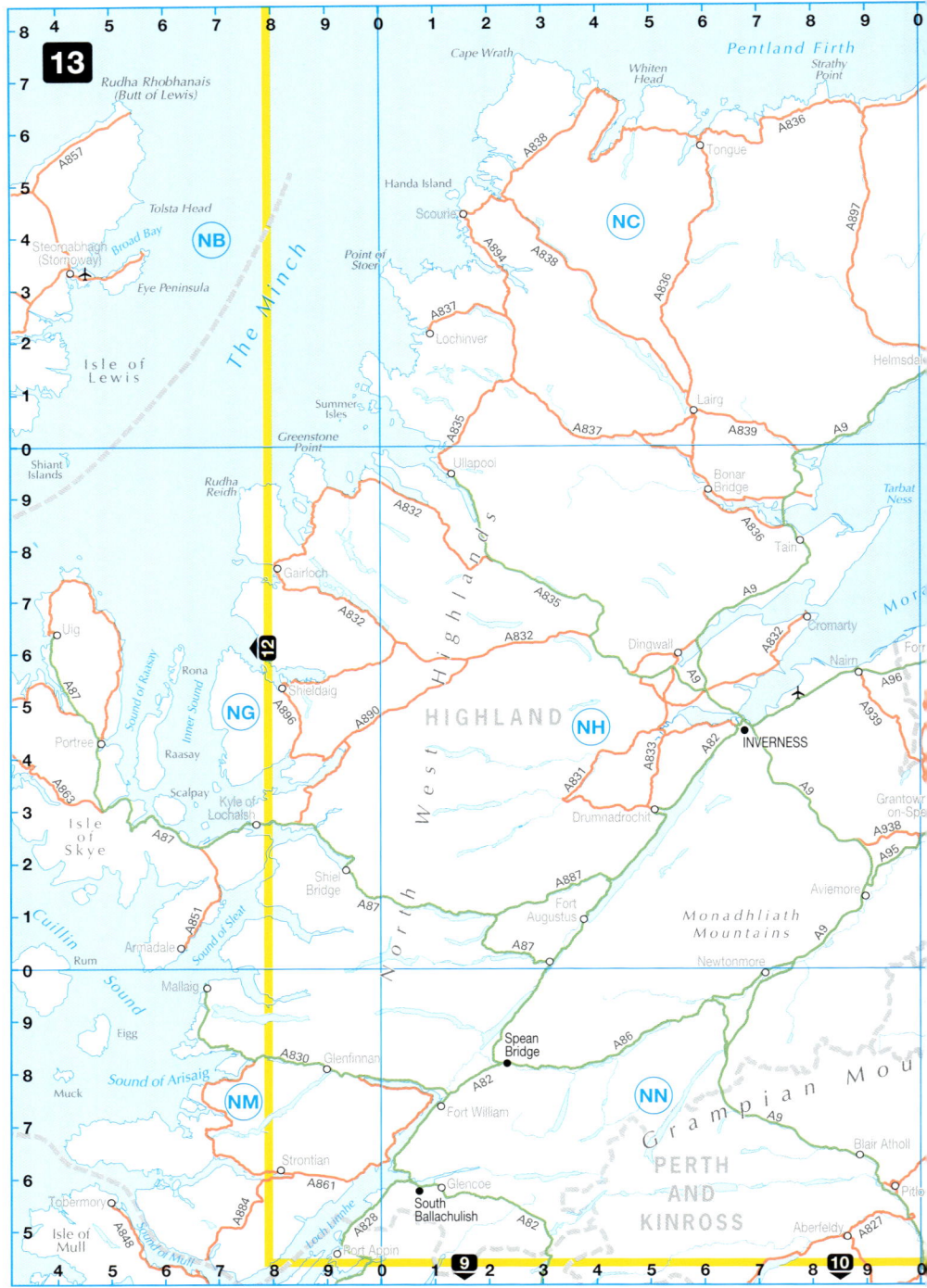

For continuation pages refer to numbered arrows

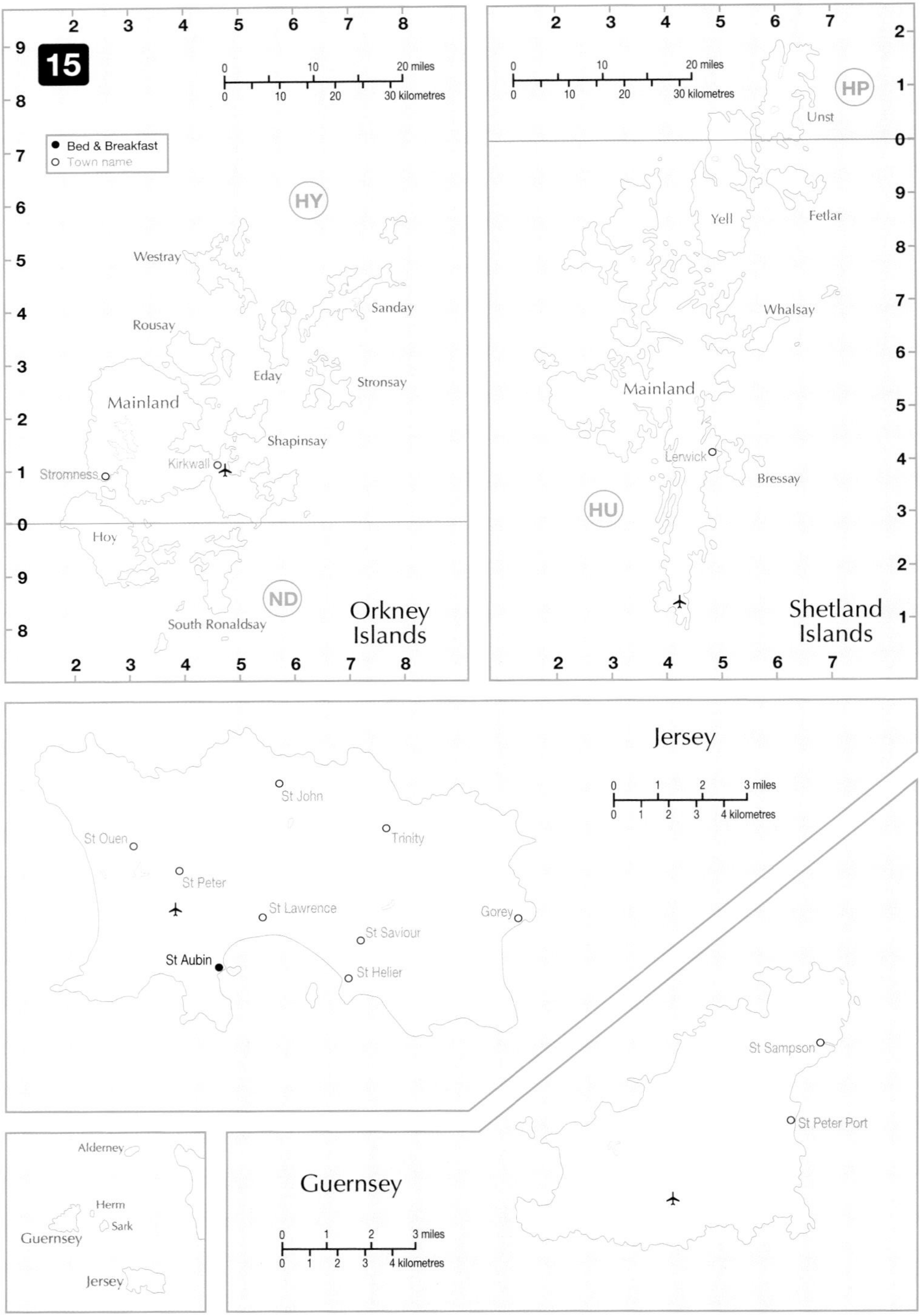

County Map

England
1. Bedfordshire
2. Berkshire
3. Bristol
4. Buckinghamshire
5. Cambridgeshire
6. Greater Manchester
7. Herefordshire
8. Hertfordshire
9. Leicestershire
10. Northamptonshire
11. Nottinghamshire
12. Rutland
13. Staffordshire
14. Warwickshire
15. West Midlands
16. Worcestershire

Scotland
17. City of Glasgow
18. Clackmannanshire
19. East Ayrshire
20. East Dunbartonshire
21. East Renfrewshire
22. Perth & Kinross
23. Renfrewshire
24. South Lanarkshire
25. West Dunbartonshire

Wales
26. Blaenau Gwent
27. Bridgend
28. Caerphilly
29. Denbighshire
30. Flintshire
31. Merthyr Tydfil
32. Monmouthshire
33. Neath Port Talbot
34. Newport
35. Rhondda Cynon Taff
36. Torfaen
37. Vale of Glamorgan
38. Wrexham

Establishment Index

17 Burgate
PICKERING,
NORTH YORKSHIRE 264

23 Mayfield
EDINBURGH,
CITY OF EDINBURGH 283

26 The Crescent
AYR, SOUTH AYRSHIRE 298

A Great Escape Guest House
SWANAGE, DORSET 109

Ab Fab Rooms
SEAFORD, EAST SUSSEX 233

Abbey Lodge
LLANDUDNO, CONWY 311

Acorn Inn, The
EVERSHOT, DORSET 100

Afon View Guest House
BETWS-Y-COED, CONWY 307

Allt Y Golau Farmhouse
FELINGWM UCHAF,
CARMARTHENSHIRE 305

Ambleside
STRATFORD-UPON-AVON,
WARWICKSHIRE 242

Angélique Rooms
DARTMOUTH, DEVON 86

Angmering Manor
ANGMERING,
WEST SUSSEX 236

Applegarth Villa & JR's Restaurant
WINDERMERE, CUMBRIA 65

Ardecca
SWINDON, WILTSHIRE 247

Arden Way Guest House
STRATFORD-UPON-AVON,
WARWICKSHIRE 243

Ascot House
YORK, NORTH YORKSHIRE 269

Ashcroft Farmhouse
LIVINGSTON,
CITY OF EDINBURGH 285

Ashfield House
GRASSINGTON, NORTH YORKSHIRE 257

Aston House
STOW-ON-THE-WOLD,
GLOUCESTERSHIRE 121

Avalon Townhouse
SHERBORNE, DORSET 106

Avondale, The
SEAFORD, EAST SUSSEX 234

Bank Villa
MASHAM,
NORTH YORKSHIRE 261

Barclay House
LOOE, CORNWALL 40

Bark House, The
BAMPTON, DEVON 82

Barn House Seaview B&B
HASTINGS & ST LEONARDS,
EAST SUSSEX 225

Bay View Farm
LOOE, CORNWALL 39

Bear's Paw, The
WARMINGHAM, CHESHIRE 28

Beaumont House
CHELTENHAM,
GLOUCESTERSHIRE 115

Blackmore Farm
BRIDGWATER, SOMERSET 197

Blacksmiths Arms, The
LEWES, EAST SUSSEX 231

Bo'mains Farm
LINLITHGOW,
WEST LOTHIAN 301

Boat House, The
SEAVIEW, ISLE OF WIGHT 139

Bona Vista
BLACKPOOL, LANCASHIRE 152

Boot Inn
FLYFORD FLAVELL,
WORCESTERSHIRE 249

Brandelhow
PENRITH, CUMBRIA 62

Brighton House
BRIGHTON, EAST SUSSEX 219

Broseley House
IRONBRIDGE, SHROPSHIRE 188

Brownlow Arms, The
HOUGH-ON-THE-HILL,
LINCOLNSHIRE 156

Bucklawren Farm
LOOE, CORNWALL 41

Bull at Great Totham, The
GREAT TOTHAM, ESSEX 112

Burford House
BURFORD, OXFORDSHIRE 181

Burton Mount Country House
BEVERLEY, EAST RIDING OF YORKSHIRE 253

Buxton's Victorian Guest House
BUXTON, DERBYSHIRE 73

Callater Lodge Guest House
BRAEMAR,
ABERDEENSHIRE 278

Camilla House
PENZANCE, CORNWALL 44

Cammarch, The
LLANGAMMARCH WELLS,
POWYS 327

Cannards Grave Farmhouse
SHEPTON MALLET,
SOMERSET 201

Can-Y-Bae
LLANDUDNO, CONWY 312

Capple Bank Farm
LEYBURN,
NORTH YORKSHIRE 259

Caro's Bed & Breakfast
DORRINGTON,
SHROPSHIRE 186

Cary Arms, The
TORQUAY, DEVON 96

Castle House
DENBIGH, DENBIGHSHIRE 317

Chantry, The
BURY ST EDMUNDS,
SUFFOLK 210

Chapel House Restaurant With Rooms
ATHERSTONE,
WARWICKSHIRE 240

Chatton Park House
CHATTON,
NORTHUMBERLAND 175

Chevin Green Farm
BELPER, DERBYSHIRE 71

Chislet Court Farm
CANTERBURY, KENT 142

Chowle Farmhouse Bed & Breakfast
FARINGDON, OXFORDSHIRE 182

Church Farm, The
KINGSLEY,
STAFFORDSHIRE 207

Chy-an-Mor
PENZANCE, CORNWALL 45

Clarice House
BURY ST EDMUNDS,
SUFFOLK 211

Cleavers Lyng Country House
HERSTMONCEUX,
EAST SUSSEX 230

Name	Location	Page
Clive Bar & Restaurant with Rooms, The	LUDLOW, SHROPSHIRE	189
Cloudesley, The	HASTINGS & ST LEONARDS, EAST SUSSEX	227
Coach House, The	BRECON, POWYS	325
Coedllys Country House	ST CLEARS, CARMARTHENSHIRE	306
Collingdale Guest House	ILFRACOMBE, DEVON	89
Coppice, The	WINDERMERE, CUMBRIA	67
Corn Croft Guest House	WITNEY, OXFORDSHIRE	184
Corra Lynn	WHITBY, NORTH YORKSHIRE	267
Corriechoille Lodge	SPEAN BRIDGE, HIGHLAND	294
Cotswold House	FALMOUTH, CORNWALL	33
Cottage in the Wood, The	BRAITHWAITE, CUMBRIA	57
Cottage Lodge, The	BROCKENHURST, HAMPSHIRE	124
Cottage, The	HEATHROW AIRPORT, LONDON	158
County Restaurant with Rooms, The	AYCLIFFE VILLAGE, CO DURHAM	31
Craigadam	CASTLE DOUGLAS, DUMFRIES & GALLOWAY	280
Craiglinnhe House	BALLACHULISH, HIGHLAND	288
Crown & Victoria	TINTINHULL, SOMERSET	203
Crown Inn, The	LANLIVERY, CORNWALL	35
Crug-Glas Country House	SOLVA, PEMBROKESHIRE	322
Cwmanog Isaf Farm	BETWS-Y-COED, CONWY	308
Danehurst House	ROYAL TUNBRIDGE WELLS, KENT	150
Dannah Farm Country House	BELPER, DERBYSHIRE	72
Daviot House	AYR, SOUTH AYRSHIRE	299
Dewdrop Inn, The	WORCESTER, WORCESTERSHIRE	250
Dorian House	BATH, SOMERSET	193
Double-Gate Farm	WELLS, SOMERSET	204
Druid House	CHRISTCHURCH, DORSET	98
Edgar's	ST IVES, CORNWALL	53
Edmar Lodge	NORWICH, NORFOLK	164
Ednovean Farm	PERRANUTHNOE, CORNWALL	49
Edwardene, The	KESWICK, CUMBRIA	60
Ees Wyke Country House	NEAR SAWREY, CUMBRIA	61
Elmview	EDINBURGH, CITY OF EDINBURGH	281
Enchanted Manor	NITON, ISLE OF WIGHT	136
Eshott Hall	MORPETH, NORTHUMBERLAND	178
Estbek House	WHITBY, NORTH YORKSHIRE	268
Exeter Arms, The	EASTON-ON-THE-HILL, NORTHAMPTONSHIRE	171
Fairfield House and Gardens	BOWNESS-ON-WINDERMERE, CUMBRIA	66
Farnham Farmhouse	FARNHAM, DORSET	101
Fauhope House	MELROSE, SCOTTISH BORDERS	297
Feathered Nest Inn, The	NETHER WESTCOTE, GLOUCESTERSHIRE	120
Firgrove Country House B&B	RUTHIN, DENBIGHSHIRE	319
Five	BRIGHTON, EAST SUSSEX	220
Gallery, The	LONDON, SW7	159
George & Dragon, The	ROWDE, WILTSHIRE	245
George, The	CAVENDISH, SUFFOLK	212
Ghillies Lodge, The	INVERNESS, HIGHLAND	289
Giffard House	WINCHESTER, HAMPSHIRE	130
Gilmore House	BLAIRGOWRIE, PERTH & KINROSS	296
Glangrwyney Court	CRICKHOWELL, POWYS	326
Glenburnie House	OBAN, ARGYLL & BUTE	279
Gothic House Bed & Breakfast	NORWICH, NORFOLK	165
Greencott	ASHBURTON, DEVON	80
Grosvenor Lodge	CHRISTCHURCH, DORSET	99
Hall Croft	APPLEBY-IN-WESTMORLAND, CUMBRIA	55
Hansard House	BUDLEIGH SALTERTON, DEVON	84
Hatsue Guest House	CAMBERLEY, SURREY	217
Hazel Bank Country House	BORROWDALE, CUMBRIA	56
Heathers, The	YORK, NORTH YORKSHIRE	270
Holly End Bed & Breakfast	SHIPSTON ON STOUR, WARWICKSHIRE	241
Holly Grove	HEATHFIELD, EAST SUSSEX	229
Holly Lodge	THURSFORD, NORFOLK	168
House of Agnes	CANTERBURY, KENT	143
Huddersfield Central Lodge	HUDDERSFIELD, WEST YORKSHIRE	273
Hunter's Moon	ST AUSTELL, CORNWALL	51
Hurdon	LAUNCESTON, CORNWALL	36
Inn at Grinshill, The	GRINSHILL, SHROPSHIRE	187
Kennard, The	BATH, SOMERSET	194
Kew House	EDINBURGH, CITY OF EDINBURGH	282
Kings Arms, The	SHERBORNE, DORSET	107

Lawns, The SANDOWN, ISLE OF WIGHT 137	**Nags Head Inn & Restaurant** GREAT MISSENDEN, BUCKINGHAMSHIRE 25	**Piddle Inn, The** PIDDLETRENTHIDE, DORSET 103
Leconfield, The VENTNOR, ISLE OF WIGHT 140	**Netherstowe House** LICHFIELD, STAFFORDSHIRE 208	**Pines at Eastleigh** BIDEFORD, DEVON 83
Les Bouviers Restaurant with Rooms WIMBORNE MINSTER, DORSET 110	**New Steine** BRIGHTON, EAST SUSSEX 221	**Pines, The** MATLOCK, DERBYSHIRE 77
Longpuddle PIDDLEHINTON, DORSET 102	**No.1 Woodchester Lodge** STROUD, GLOUCESTERSHIRE 122	**Plas Rhos** RHOS-ON-SEA, CONWY 315
Low Skibeden House SKIPTON, NORTH YORKSHIRE 265	**Nonsuch House** DARTMOUTH, DEVON 87	**Portland House Guest House** WHITCHURCH, HEREFORDSHIRE 134
Lower Farm TAUNTON, SOMERSET 202	**North Wheddon Farm** WHEDDON CROSS, SOMERSET 205	**Queen's Head, The** TROUTBECK, CUMBRIA 63
Lypiatt House CHELTENHAM, GLOUCESTERSHIRE 116	**Number Twenty Eight** LUDLOW, SHROPSHIRE 190	**Queens Arms, The** HELSTON, CORNWALL 34
Magna Carta WINDSOR, BERKSHIRE 21	**Offley Bed & Breakfast** PUNCKNOWLE, DORSET 105	**Queens Head Inn, The** NASSINGTON, NORTHAMPTONSHIRE 172
Magnolia House CANTERBURY, KENT 144	**Old House, The** SALISBURY, WILTSHIRE 246	**Ramsey House** ST DAVID'S, PEMBROKESHIRE 323
Manners Arms, The KNIPTON, LEICESTERSHIRE 154	**Old Manse, The** WOOLER, NORTHUMBERLAND 174	**Ravensdale** HAYLING ISLAND, HAMPSHIRE 125
Manor Farm Oast RYE, EAST SUSSEX 232	**Old Mill House, The** PADSTOW, CORNWALL 43	**Red House Farm Bed & Breakfast** TIVETSHALL ST MARGARET, NORFOLK 169
Manse B&B, The EASTBOURNE, EAST SUSSEX 224	**Old Passage Inn, The** ARLINGHAM, GLOUCESTERSHIRE 114	**Redgate Smithy** LISKEARD, CORNWALL 37
Marlborough House BATH, SOMERSET 195	**Old Thorn Barn** NORWICH, NORFOLK 167	**Regency Lansdowne Guest House** BRIGHTON, EAST SUSSEX 222
Maypole Farm B&B CAWOOD, NORTH YORKSHIRE 256	**Orchard Cottage** DEREHAM, NORFOLK 163	**Relish, The** FOLKESTONE, KENT 148
Merritt House B&B PAIGNTON, DEVON 93	**Panorama, The** ST AUBIN, JERSEY 275	**Rissons at Springvale** STRATHAVEN, SOUTH LANARKSHIRE 300
Merzie Meadows MARDEN, KENT 149	**Parkside House** HASTINGS & ST LEONARDS, EAST SUSSEX 228	**River House** MALHAM, NORTH YORKSHIRE 260
Miller of Mansfield, The GORING, OXFORDSHIRE 183	**Peat Inn, The** PEAT INN, FIFE 287	**Rock House** LYNMOUTH, DEVON 91
Moor View House LYDFORD, DEVON 90	**Penarwyn House** ST BLAZEY, CORNWALL 52	**Roseleigh** BUXTON, DERBYSHIRE 75
Moorings WORTHING, WEST SUSSEX 238	**Penmachno Hall** BETWS-Y-COED, CONWY 309	**Royal Bridlington, The** BRIDLINGTON, EAST RIDING OF YORKSHIRE 254
Moortown Lodge RINGWOOD, HAMPSHIRE 129	**Pentre Mawr Country House** LLANDYRNOG, DENBIGHSHIRE 318	**San Domenico House** LONDON, SW3 160
Moss Grove Organic GRASMERE, CUMBRIA 59	**Peth Head Cottage** HEXHAM, NORTHUMBERLAND 176	**Sandpit Farm** SAXMUNDHAM, SUFFOLK 213
Mount Royal PENZANCE, CORNWALL 46	**Pheasant Inn** FALSTONE, NORTHUMBERLAND 177	**Sarnau Mansion** CARMARTHEN, CARMARTHENSHIRE 304
Moyness House INVERNESS, HIGHLAND 290	**Pheasant Inn, The** BURWARDSLEY, CHESHIRE 27	
Munden House SHERBORNE, DORSET 108		

Seagrave Arms CHIPPING CAMPDEN, GLOUCESTERSHIRE 117	**Strete Barton House** STRETE, DEVON 94	**Tyddynmawr Farmhouse** DOLGELLAU, GWYNEDD 321
Shelbourne House HARROGATE, NORTH YORKSHIRE 258	**Summer House, The** PENZANCE, CORNWALL 47	**Underleigh House** HOPE, DERBYSHIRE 76
Shibden Mill HALIFAX, WEST YORKSHIRE 272	**Sutherland House** SOUTHWOLD, SUFFOLK 215	**Upham House Bed & Breakfast** BAMPTON, OXFORDSHIRE 180
Shrublands Farm CROMER, NORFOLK 162	**Swan Inn, The** HUNGERFORD, BERKSHIRE 19	**Victoria Lodge** LYNTON, DEVON 92
Sibton White Horse Inn SIBTON, SUFFOLK 214	**Tan-Yr-Onnen Guest House** ST ASAPH, DENBIGHSHIRE 320	**Wall Hills House** LEDBURY, HEREFORDSHIRE 133
Smithy, The NEWHAVEN, DERBYSHIRE 78	**Tarr Farm Inn** DULVERTON, SOMERSET 198	**Waterings, The** ST DAVID'S, PEMBROKESHIRE 324
Somerville House HEREFORD, HEREFORDSHIRE 132	**Tasburgh House** BATH, SOMERSET 196	**Weir View House** PANGBOURNE, BERKSHIRE 20
Sondes Lodge DEAL, KENT 147	**Temple Lodge** LYNDHURST, HAMPSHIRE 126	**West Down** ATHERINGTON, DEVON 81
Soulton Hall WEM, SHROPSHIRE 191	**Thomas Luny House** TEIGNMOUTH, DEVON 95	**Westfield House** BRISTOL, BRISTOL 23
Southside EDINBURGH, CITY OF EDINBURGH 284	**Tigh Na Leigh Guesthouse** ALYTH, PERTH & KINROSS 295	**Wharf House, The** GLOUCESTER, GLOUCESTERSHIRE 119
Spindrift, The ANSTRUTHER, FIFE 286	**Tor Cottage** CHILLATON, DEVON 85	**Willowsmere, The** WINDERMERE, CUMBRIA 68
Spital Hill THIRSK, NORTH YORKSHIRE 266	**Tovey Lodge** DITCHLING, EAST SUSSEX 223	**Woolpack Inn, The** NORTHINGTON, HAMPSHIRE 128
St Hilary Guest House LLANDUDNO, CONWY 313	**Town House, The** ARUNDEL, WEST SUSSEX 237	**Yorke Lodge** CANTERBURY, KENT 145
Stratford House LLANDUDNO, CONWY 314	**Trafford Bank** INVERNESS, HIGHLAND 291	**Yorkshire Bridge Inn** BAMFORD, DERBYSHIRE 70
	Trehaven Manor LOOE, CORNWALL 42	
	Trenake Manor Farm POLPERRO, CORNWALL 50	
	Tudor Cottage PORLOCK, SOMERSET 200	

Acknowledgments

The Automobile Association would like to thank the following photographers, companies and picture libraries for their assistance in the preparation of this book.

Abbreviations for the picture credits are as follows – (t) top; (b) bottom; (c) centre; (l) left; (r) right; (AA) AA World Travel Library.

4/5 Courtesy Tyddynmawr Farmhouse/Richard Evans; 10 Courtesy The Wharf House; 11 Courtesy Merritt House; 13 Courtesy Netherstowe House; 16/17 AA/Michael Moody; 18 AA/James Tims; 22 AA/James Tims; 24 AA/James Tims; 26 AA/Vic Bates; 29 AA/A J Hopkins; 30 AA/Roger Coulam; 32 AA/Caroline Jones; 38 AA/Adam Burton; 48 AA/Adam Burton; 54 AA/Tom Mackie; 58 AA/Tom Mackie; 64 Neil Barks/Alamy; 69 AA/Tom Mackie; 74 AA/Tom Mackie; 79 AA/Adam Burton; 88 AA/Guy Edwardes; 97 AA/Andrew Newey; 104 AA/Andrew Newey; 111 AA/Neil Setchfield; 113 AA/Hugh Palmer; 118 AA/Hugh Palmer; 123 AA/Andrew Newey; 127 AA/Michael Moody; 131 AA/Caroline Jones; 135 AA/Andrew Newey; 138 AA/Andrew Newey; 141 AA/Neil Setchfield; 146 AA/Laurie Noble; 151 AA/David Clapp; 153 AA/James Tims; 155 AA/James Tims; 157 AA/James Tims; 161 AA/Tom Mackie; 166 AA/Tom Mackie; 170 AA/M Birkitt; 173 AA/Roger Coulam; 179 AA/Caroline Jones; 185 AA/Caroline Jones; 192 AA/James Tims; 199 AA/M Birkitt; 206 AA/Caroline Jones; 209 AA/Tom Mackie; 216 AA/James Tims; 218 AA/John Miller; 226 AA/Derek Noble; 235 AA/John Miller; 239 AA/Caroline Jones; 244 AA/Michael Moody; 248 AA/David Hall; 251 AA/Caroline Jones; 252 AA/David Clapp; 255 AA/Jo Hunt; 262 AA/Jo Hunt; 271 AA/James Tims; 274 AA/Peter Trenchard; 276/277 AA/Karl Blackwell; 292/293 AA/Jonathan Smith; 302/303 AA/George Munday; 310 AA/Chris Warren; 316 AA/Rebecca Duke; 328 AA/Stephen Lewis

Every effort has been made to trace the copyright holders, and we apologise in advance for any unintentional omissions or errors. We would be pleased to apply any corrections in a following edition of this publication.

Location Index

ALYTH, PERTH & KINROSS
Tigh Na Leigh Guesthouse 295

ANGMERING, WEST SUSSEX
Angmering Manor 236

ANSTRUTHER, FIFE
Spindrift, The 286

APPLEBY-IN-WESTMORLAND
Hall Croft 55

ARLINGHAM, GLOUCESTERSHIRE
Old Passage Inn, The 114

ARUNDEL, WEST SUSSEX
Town House, The 237

ASHBURTON, DEVON
Greencott 80

ATHERINGTON, DEVON
West Down 81

ATHERSTONE, WARWICKSHIRE
Chapel House
Restaurant With Rooms 240

AYCLIFFE VILLAGE, CO DURHAM
County Restaurant
with Rooms, The 31

AYR, SOUTH AYRSHIRE
26 The Crescent 298
Daviot House 299

BALLACHULISH, HIGHLAND
Craiglinnhe House 288

BAMFORD, DERBYSHIRE
Yorkshire Bridge Inn 70

BAMPTON, DEVON
Bark House, The 82

BAMPTON, OXFORDSHIRE
Upham House
Bed & Breakfast 180

BATH, SOMERSET
Dorian House 193
Kennard, The 194
Marlborough House 195
Tasburgh House 196

BELPER, DERBYSHIRE
Chevin Green Farm 71
Dannah Farm Country House 72

BETWS-Y-COED, CONWY
Afon View Guest House 307
Cwmanog Isaf Farm 308
Penmachno Hall 309

BEVERLEY, EAST RIDING OF YORKSHIRE
Burton Mount Country House 253

BIDEFORD, DEVON
Pines at Eastleigh 83

BLACKPOOL, LANCASHIRE
Bona Vista 152

BLAIRGOWRIE, PERTH & KINROSS
Gilmore House 296

BORROWDALE, CUMBRIA
Hazel Bank Country House 56

BOWNESS-ON-WINDERMERE, CUMBRIA
Fairfield House and Gardens 66

BRAEMAR, ABERDEENSHIRE
Callater Lodge Guest House 278

BRAITHWAITE, CUMBRIA
Cottage in the Wood, The 57

BRECON, POWYS
Coach House, The 325

BRIDGWATER, SOMERSET
Blackmore Farm 197

BRIDLINGTON, EAST RIDING OF YORKSHIRE
Royal Bridlington, The 254

BRIGHTON, EAST SUSSEX
Brighton House 219
Five 220
New Steine 221
Regency Lansdowne
Guest House 222

BRISTOL, BRISTOL
Westfield House 23

BROCKENHURST, HAMPSHIRE
Cottage Lodge, The 124

BUDLEIGH SALTERTON, DEVON
Hansard House 84

BURFORD, OXFORDSHIRE
Burford House 181

BURWARDSLEY, CHESHIRE
Pheasant Inn, The 27

BURY ST EDMUNDS, SUFFOLK
Chantry, The 210
Clarice House 211

BUXTON, DERBYSHIRE
Buxton's Victorian
Guest House 73
Roseleigh 75

CAMBERLEY, SURREY
Hatsue Guest House 217

CANTERBURY, KENT
Chislet Court Farm 142
House of Agnes 143
Magnolia House 144
Yorke Lodge 145

CARMARTHEN, CARMARTHENSHIRE
Sarnau Mansion 304

CASTLE DOUGLAS, DUMFRIES & GALLOWAY
Craigadam 280

CAVENDISH, SUFFOLK
George, The 212

CAWOOD, NORTH YORKSHIRE
Maypole Farm B&B 256

CHATTON, NORTHUMBERLAND
Chatton Park House 175

CHELTENHAM, GLOUCESTERSHIRE
Beaumont House 115
Lypiatt House 116

CHILLATON, DEVON
Tor Cottage 85

CHIPPING CAMPDEN, GLOUCESTERSHIRE
Seagrave Arms 117

CHRISTCHURCH, DORSET
Druid House 98
Grosvenor Lodge 99

CRICKHOWELL, POWYS
Glangrwyney Court 326

CROMER, NORFOLK
Shrublands Farm 162

DARTMOUTH, DEVON
Angélique Rooms 86
Nonsuch House 87

DEAL, KENT
Sondes Lodge 147

DENBIGH, DENBIGHSHIRE
Castle House 317

DEREHAM, NORFOLK
Orchard Cottage 163

DITCHLING, EAST SUSSEX
Tovey Lodge 223

DOLGELLAU, GWYNEDD
Tyddynmawr Farmhouse 321

DORRINGTON, SHROPSHIRE
Caro's Bed & Breakfast 186

DULVERTON, SOMERSET
Tarr Farm Inn 198

EASTBOURNE, EAST SUSSEX
Manse B&B, The 224

EASTON-ON-THE-HILL, NORTHAMPTONSHIRE
Exeter Arms, The 171

EDINBURGH, CITY OF EDINBURGH
23 Mayfield 283
Elmview 281
Kew House 282
Southside 284

EVERSHOT, DORSET
Acorn Inn, The 100

FALMOUTH, CORNWALL
Cotswold House 33

FALSTONE, NORTHUMBERLAND
Pheasant Inn 177

FARINGDON, OXFORDSHIRE
Chowle Farmhouse Bed &
Breakfast 182

FARNHAM, DORSET
Farnham Farmhouse 101

FELINGWM UCHAF, CARMARTHENSHIRE
Allt Y Golau Farmhouse 305

FLYFORD FLAVELL, WORCESTERSHIRE
Boot Inn 249

FOLKESTONE, KENT
Relish, The 148

GLOUCESTER, GLOUCESTERSHIRE
Wharf House, The 119

GORING, OXFORDSHIRE
Miller of Mansfield, The 183

GRASMERE, CUMBRIA
Moss Grove Organic 59

GRASSINGTON, NORTH YORKSHIRE
Ashfield House 257

GREAT MISSENDEN, BUCKINGHAMSHIRE
Nags Head Inn & Restaurant 25

GREAT TOTHAM, ESSEX
Bull at Great Totham, The 112

GRINSHILL, SHROPSHIRE
Inn at Grinshill, The 187

HALIFAX, WEST YORKSHIRE
Shibden Mill 272

HARROGATE, NORTH YORKSHIRE
Shelbourne House 258

HASTINGS & ST LEONARDS, EAST SUSSEX
Barn House Seaview B&B 225
Cloudesley, The 227
Parkside House 228

HAYLING ISLAND, HAMPSHIRE
Ravensdale 125

HEATHFIELD, EAST SUSSEX
Holly Grove 229

HEATHROW AIRPORT, LONDON
Cottage, The 158

HELSTON, CORNWALL
Queens Arms, The 34

HEREFORD, HEREFORDSHIRE
Somerville House 132

HERSTMONCEUX, EAST SUSSEX
Cleavers Lyng Country House 230

HEXHAM, NORTHUMBERLAND
Peth Head Cottage 176

HOPE, DERBYSHIRE
Underleigh House 76

HOUGH-ON-THE-HILL, LINCOLNSHIRE
Brownlow Arms, The 156

HUDDERSFIELD, WEST YORKSHIRE
Huddersfield Central Lodge 273

HUNGERFORD, BERKSHIRE
Swan Inn, The 19

ILFRACOMBE, DEVON
Collingdale Guest House 89

INVERNESS, HIGHLAND
Ghillies Lodge, The 289
Moyness House 290
Trafford Bank 291

IRONBRIDGE, SHROPSHIRE
Broseley House 188

KESWICK, CUMBRIA
Edwardene, The 60

KINGSLEY, STAFFORDSHIRE
Church Farm, The 207

KNIPTON, LEICESTERSHIRE
Manners Arms, The 154

LANLIVERY, CORNWALL
Crown Inn, The 35

LAUNCESTON, CORNWALL
Hurdon 36

LEDBURY, HEREFORDSHIRE
Wall Hills House 133

LEWES, EAST SUSSEX
Blacksmiths Arms, The 231

LEYBURN, NORTH YORKSHIRE
Capple Bank Farm 259

LICHFIELD, STAFFORDSHIRE
Netherstowe House 208

LINLITHGOW, WEST LOTHIAN
Bo'mains Farm 301

LISKEARD, CORNWALL
Redgate Smithy 37

LIVINGSTON, CITY OF EDINBURGH
Ashcroft Farmhouse 285

LLANDUDNO, CONWY
Abbey Lodge 311
Can-Y-Bae 312
St Hilary Guest House 313
Stratford House 314

LLANDYRNOG, DENBIGHSHIRE
Pentre Mawr Country House 318

LLANGAMMARCH WELLS, POWYS
Cammarch, The 327

LONDON, SW3
San Domenico House 160

LONDON, SW7
Gallery, The 159

LOOE, CORNWALL
Barclay House 40
Bay View Farm 39
Bucklawren Farm 41
Trehaven Manor 42

LUDLOW, SHROPSHIRE
Clive Bar & Restaurant with Rooms, The 189
Number Twenty Eight 190

LYDFORD, DEVON
Moor View House 90

LYNDHURST, HAMPSHIRE
Temple Lodge 126

LYNMOUTH, DEVON
Rock House 91

LYNTON, DEVON
Victoria Lodge 92

MALHAM, NORTH YORKSHIRE
River House 260

MARDEN, KENT
Merzie Meadows 149

MASHAM, NORTH YORKSHIRE
Bank Villa 261

MATLOCK, DERBYSHIRE
Pines, The 77

MELROSE, SCOTTISH BORDERS
Fauhope House 297

MORPETH, NORTHUMBERLAND
Eshott Hall 178

NASSINGTON, NORTHAMPTONSHIRE
Queens Head Inn, The 172

NEAR SAWREY, CUMBRIA
Ees Wyke Country House 61

NETHER WESTCOTE, GLOUCESTERSHIRE
Feathered Nest Inn, The 120

NEWHAVEN, DERBYSHIRE
Smithy, The 78

NITON, ISLE OF WIGHT
Enchanted Manor 136

NORTHINGTON, HAMPSHIRE
Woolpack Inn, The 128

NORWICH, NORFOLK
Edmar Lodge 164
Gothic House Bed & Breakfast 165
Old Thorn Barn 167

OBAN, ARGYLL & BUTE
Glenburnie House 279

PADSTOW, CORNWALL
Old Mill House, The 43

PAIGNTON, DEVON
Merritt House B&B 93

351

PANGBOURNE, BERKSHIRE
Weir View House　20
PEAT INN, FIFE
Peat Inn, The　287
PENRITH, CUMBRIA
Brandelhow　62
PENZANCE, CORNWALL
Camilla House　44
Chy-an-Mor　45
Mount Royal　46
Summer House, The　47
PERRANUTHNOE, CORNWALL
Ednovean Farm　49
PICKERING, NORTH YORKSHIRE
17 Burgate　264
PIDDLEHINTON, DORSET
Longpuddle　102
PIDDLETRENTHIDE, DORSET
Piddle Inn, The　103
POLPERRO, CORNWALL
Trenake Manor Farm　50
PORLOCK, SOMERSET
Tudor Cottage　200
PUNCKNOWLE, DORSET
Offley Bed & Breakfast　105
RHOS-ON-SEA, CONWY
Plas Rhos　315
RINGWOOD, HAMPSHIRE
Moortown Lodge　129
ROWDE, WILTSHIRE
George & Dragon, The　245
ROYAL TUNBRIDGE WELLS, KENT
Danehurst House　150
RUTHIN, DENBIGHSHIRE
Firgrove Country House B&B　319
RYE, EAST SUSSEX
Manor Farm Oast　232
ST ASAPH, DENBIGHSHIRE
Tan-Yr-Onnen Guest House　320
ST AUBIN, JERSEY
Panorama, The　275
ST AUSTELL, CORNWALL
Hunter's Moon　51
ST BLAZEY, CORNWALL
Penarwyn House　52
ST CLEARS, CARMARTHENSHIRE
Coedllys Country House　306
ST DAVID'S, PEMBROKESHIRE
Ramsey House　323
Waterings, The　324
ST IVES, CORNWALL
Edgar's　53

SALISBURY, WILTSHIRE
Old House, The　246
SANDOWN, ISLE OF WIGHT
Lawns, The　137
SAXMUNDHAM, SUFFOLK
Sandpit Farm　213
SEAFORD, EAST SUSSEX
Ab Fab Rooms　233
Avondale, The　234
SEAVIEW, ISLE OF WIGHT
Boat House, The　139
SHEPTON MALLET, SOMERSET
Cannards Grave Farmhouse　201
SHERBORNE, DORSET
Avalon Townhouse　106
Kings Arms, The　107
Munden House　108
SHIPSTON ON STOUR, WARWICKSHIRE
Holly End Bed & Breakfast　241
SIBTON, SUFFOLK
Sibton White Horse Inn　214
SKIPTON, NORTH YORKSHIRE
Low Skibeden House　265
SOLVA, PEMBROKESHIRE
Crug-Glas Country House　322
SOUTHWOLD, SUFFOLK
Sutherland House　215
SPEAN BRIDGE, HIGHLAND
Corriechoille Lodge　294
STOW-ON-THE-WOLD, GLOUCESTERSHIRE
Aston House　121
STRATFORD-UPON-AVON, WARWICKSHIRE
Ambleside　242
Arden Way Guest House　243
STRATHAVEN, SOUTH LANARKSHIRE
Rissons at Springvale　300
STRETE, DEVON
Strete Barton House　94
STROUD, GLOUCESTERSHIRE
No.1 Woodchester Lodge　122
SWANAGE, DORSET
A Great Escape Guest House　109
SWINDON, WILTSHIRE
Ardecca　247
TAUNTON, SOMERSET
Lower Farm　202
TEIGNMOUTH, DEVON
Thomas Luny House　95
THIRSK, NORTH YORKSHIRE
Spital Hill　266

THURSFORD, NORFOLK
Holly Lodge　168
TINTINHULL, SOMERSET
Crown & Victoria　203
TIVETSHALL ST MARGARET, NORFOLK
Red House Farm B&B　169
TORQUAY, DEVON
Cary Arms, The　96
TROUTBECK, CUMBRIA
Queen's Head, The　63
VENTNOR, ISLE OF WIGHT
Leconfield, The　140
WARMINGHAM, CHESHIRE
Bear's Paw, The　28
WELLS, SOMERSET
Double-Gate Farm　204
WEM, SHROPSHIRE
Soulton Hall　191
WHEDDON CROSS, SOMERSET
North Wheddon Farm　205
WHITBY, NORTH YORKSHIRE
Corra Lynn　267
Estbek House　268
WHITCHURCH, HEREFORDSHIRE
Portland House Guest House　134
WIMBORNE MINSTER, DORSET
Les Bouviers Restaurant with Rooms　110
WINCHESTER, HAMPSHIRE
Giffard House　130
WINDERMERE, CUMBRIA
Applegarth Villa & JR's Restaurant　65
Coppice, The　67
Willowsmere, The　68
WINDSOR, BERKSHIRE
Magna Carta　21
WITNEY, OXFORDSHIRE
Corn Croft Guest House　184
WOOLER, NORTHUMBERLAND
Old Manse, The　174
WORCESTER, WORCESTERSHIRE
Dewdrop Inn, The　250
WORTHING, WEST SUSSEX
Moorings　238
YORK, NORTH YORKSHIRE
Ascot House　269
Heathers, The　270